Pasta, AI & Quantum Lasagna

Italian Cooking Taught Me Everything About Machine Learning and Life

Dr. John Giordani

SenAnSys Publishing

ISBN: 979-8-218-94623-4

DEDICATION

To my wife.

And, to my friends and family, the ones who have endured my experimental cooking, my long-winded rants about neural networks, and my obsession with pasta and caffeine metaphors.

This book is for you, because without your friendship, curiosity, and laughter, none of this would be al dente.

Mangia bene, code responsibly.

CONTENTS

1	The Secret Ingredient: Curiosity	Pg 1
2	Al Dente and Algorithms	Pg 12
3	The Recipe for Success: Data Preparation	Pg 23
4	A Dash of Creativity: Building Neural Networks	Pg 33
5	The Boiling Point: Training Models	Pg 44
6	Tasting as You Go: Validation Techniques	Pg 55
7	Layering Flavors: Ensemble Methods	Pg 65
8	Finding the Right Pairing: Feature Selection	Pg 76
9	Cooking Under Pressure: Tuning Hyperparameters	Pg 86
10	The Art of Presentation: Visualization Techniques	Pg 97
11	Leftovers: Continuous Learning in AI	Pg 107
12	Cooking for Everyone: Ethical AI	Pg 118
13	Kitchen Confidential: AI in the Workplace	Pg 129
14	The 7 Cooking Principles: Fundamental AI Concepts	Pg 140
15	The Family Table: Collaborating Across Disciplines	Pg 150
16	Simplicity is Key: Avoiding Overcomplication	Pg 161
17	Lost in Translation: Overcoming AI Misconceptions	Pg 172
18	The Taste Test: Evaluating AI Models	Pg 182
19	The Quantum Factor: The Future of AI and Beyond	Pg 191
20	Pasta, AI, and Life: The Final Serving	Pg 200

ACKNOWLEDGMENTS

Writing a second book is a lot like making a second batch of homemade pasta, you're more confident, the movements come a bit easier, but you still find flour on the ceiling and sauce in places it doesn't belong. This project, much like the first, has been a journey of curiosity, experimentation, and a fair amount of creative mess.

Once again, I found myself leaning on both old friends and new tools. Generative AI, which served as a thoughtful companion during my first book, returned to the kitchen with me, this time as an even more seasoned sous-chef. It helped me mix metaphors, clarify complex concepts, and clean up the occasional word salad. But, as before, it was never the chef. That role remained firmly mine, driven by a distinctly human blend of passion, perspective, and pasta-fueled perseverance.

The ideas in this book are rooted in lived experience, drawn from moments shared with friends, reflections at the stovetop, and countless late-night thoughts sparked by cold leftovers and warm data sets. Every insight, joke, and analogy came from a place of genuine wonder about life, learning, and the absurdly beautiful overlap between lasagna and algorithms.

To my friends: thank you for coming back for a second helping. Your encouragement, humor, and tolerance for culinary metaphors have made this journey not only possible but joyful. And to my readers, both new and returning, I'm honored to have your attention in a world overflowing with noise. I hope these pages feed your mind and your spirit, maybe even your appetite.

Once again, we've proved that human creativity, when paired thoughtfully with modern tools, can create something deliciously original.

Let's keep cooking.

Chapter 1

The Secret Ingredient: Curiosity

The Role of Curiosity in Cooking and Machine Learning

Curiosity is the secret sauce that makes both cooking and machine learning utterly delectable. Just as a pinch of basil can elevate a bland marinara to culinary stardom, a healthy spoonful of curiosity can spice up your journey in the ever-evolving domain of AI. Each recipe starts with a curious chef standing in front of a fridge, wondering, "What on earth can I create with these random leftovers?" Each machine learning model begins with inquisitive minds asking, "What patterns can be unearthed from this mountain of data?" In both realms, curiosity is the engine that drives innovation and transformation, pushing us to explore the depths of our ingredients and the complexities of algorithms alike.

Cooking is one massive experiment in flavor. I mean, what could possibly go wrong when a food scientist decides that adding peanut butter to a traditional spaghetti carbonara would create a fusion masterpiece? This idea may or may not warrant a spot on a cooking show, but it exemplifies the core of curiosity. We toss ingredients together with improvisation; sometimes you get a gastronomic delight, other times, an abstract art project that has gone wrong.

Similarly, in machine learning, if we never asked the hard questions or chased the odd hypotheses, we'd still be stuck with linear regressions. Boring! We'd never have the genius of neural networks or the AI wizardry that now curates cat videos on demand.

In both cooking and machine learning, curiosity leads us down paths we might never have traversed if we were stuck following a recipe or a predetermined outcome. Talented chefs often toss aside the recipe books in favor of their imagination. Successful data scientists do the same; they stray from standardized models, nudging boundaries like someone trying to shove the last slice of pizza into their mouth during a family gathering. Both fields require us to look beyond the conventional, to taste and discover. It's the curiosity that prompts chefs to ask: "What if I use saffron instead of turmeric?" or "Can I make lasagna using only gluten-free ingredients and a dash of desperation?" It's the same spirit that drives breakthroughs in machine learning, with questions like, "What if we teach a robot to write poetry?" floating around like pasta noodles in boiling water, waiting to discover their purpose in life.

Curiosity isn't just the catalyst for experimentation; it's also what saves us when things go wrong. Anyone who's ever burned a soufflé or grilled chicken until it resembled a charcoal briquette knows the psychological struggle of culinary failure. The same holds true in algorithms, where feedforward neural networks can go sideways faster than a runaway ravioli. Rather than drown in a pool of culinary despair (or algorithmic catastrophe), curiosity can rescue us. Curiosity begs us to ask why the soufflé sank instead of soaring like a victorious balloon: Was it the egg whites? The oven temperature? Was it someone's evil plot ruining my dinner party? Similarly, in machine learning, setbacks often uncover insights. Understanding a model's failure brings us closer to delicious accuracy. So next time your spaghetti turns out as a sticky glob of regret, embrace it! Pencil in your notes,

"Keep well away from the smoke detector next time. Acquit the smoke alarm of arson charges!"

Curiosity breeds resilience, which is essential in both the kitchen and the data lab. Those glossy cooking shows may make it look effortless when Gordon Ramsay tosses a perfect omelet in two seconds flat, but behind every smooth turn of the spatula is a lifetime of burnt eggs and persistent curiosity. In coding, the best minds relentlessly pursue the "what if" obstacles, whether an overcooked meatball or a faulty data input, shouldn't crush our spirits but stoke the flames of relentless curiosity, enticing us to keep experimenting, tasting, and tinkering.

At the end of the day, curiosity serves as the bridge between cooking and machine learning. It turns both mundane tasks into exciting quests. So, the next time you whip up a dish or parse a dataset, sprinkle in some curiosity and let the magic happen. You might end up creating a five-star meal, or at least a great story about the Great Burrito Lasagna Incident of 2026. Either way, you're making progress in both culinary mastery and machine learning, one curious question at a time. And isn't that what life, and dinner parties, are all about?

Finding Inspiration in the Kitchen and Beyond

Inspiration often strikes when we least expect it. For me, it's usually while standing in front of an open fridge at 7 p.m., armed with nothing but a stubborn will, a half-empty jar of marinara, and the remnants of last week's grocery shopping. A sudden wave of brilliance sweeps over me: "What if I took these wilting vegetables, a block of questionable cheese, and that emergency stash of penne, and created culinary art worthy of a Michelin star?" Of course, the reality is often closer to a five-alarm disaster than a five-star meal, but the beauty lies in the exhilarating chaos of inspiration.

Much like cooking, the world of machine learning often leads us on exploratory journeys filled with twists, turns, and unexpected results. Inspiration is our trusty compass as we navigate the tangled web of algorithms and datasets. After all, when it comes to data analysis, each number and variable has its own story. Imagine each dataset as a half-used bag of flour left over from a baking adventure gone wrong. With a dash of creativity, you can whip up something entirely new, transforming what was once a forgotten nuisance into a delightful surprise, like cookies or perhaps the next great data model.

One of the most extraordinary aspects of the kitchen is its ability to inspire beyond food. Just a whiff of garlic sizzling can spark ideas that have nothing to do with cooking. The way an ingredient transforms under heat can mirror innovation in machine learning. In the same way that a simple tomato can become a nuanced sauce, allowing the flavors to marry and deepen, ideas simmer in the back of our minds as we tinker with code and explore the magic hidden within data. Suddenly, you realize you've adopted the problem-solving approach of a master chef! "How can I combine these disparate tactics to create something unique?" That question deserves a place of honor in the halls of creative genius, right next to "How much cheese is too much cheese?" (Hint: the answer is always "more").

And let's not ignore the role of culture in inspiring our culinary endeavors. Anyone who claims to be immune to the influence of travel hasn't truly tasted their way through life. For me, each culinary adventure is a crash course in different ways of thinking. From the sultry spices of a Moroccan tagine to the soul-warming embrace of a steaming bowl of ramen, every dish tickles my imagination, leading me to the realization that inspiration can come from anywhere, even the random food truck parked outside a bookstore! Picture me, a tweed-coated academic, munching fusion tacos while contemplating a new feature to add to an existing AI model. Truly, nothing screams "intellectual" quite like a taco stuffed with unpredictable flavor combinations.

Even in machine learning, the principles of inspiration closely mirror those in the kitchen. We glean insights from unconventional places: the latest TikTok trend, memes that occasionally make us giggle, or even our dog's judgmental stare as he evaluates our culinary skills. It's this eclectic gathering of ideas that can help us craft innovative models. That urge to blend the seemingly unrelated, like a dash of Cheetos in mac 'n' cheese (which I assure you is an undiscovered classic), leads to unexpected breakthroughs in both kitchen and code. Who would think an elementary understanding of quantum mechanics might arise during a late-night brainstorming session layered with garlic bread and a belief that “anything is possible”?

Many people find inspiration through design, art, or nature. But let's not forget one crucial player, the fine art of failure. Every time a soufflé collapses or an AI model throws a tantrum, the seed of creativity is planted. Each epic culinary catastrophe, like boiling the spaghetti into a gooey mass, sparks ideas or the resolve to try again. It's akin to a toddler picking himself up after tumbling, gaining the courage to walk. Failures in both kitchens and data labs only serve as fuel for relentless pursuit, igniting a flame that lights the path to discovery.

In the end, it's clear: inspiration doesn't follow the rules. It struts into the room uninvited, often demanding that you unleash your creative Spirit. It may show up as you rename leftover food concoctions or when you identify patterns among datasets that lead to the next big breakthrough. Whether inspired by vibrant culinary experiences, chance encounters, or an unexpected flop, let yourself be swept away by the currents of creativity. So next time you find yourself rummaging through the pantry or dissecting the latest machine learning problem, take a moment to appreciate the magical dance of inspiration in your life. It's messy, unpredictable, and often downright absurd, but that's precisely what makes it delicious!

Curiosity-Driven Experimentation: Recipes and Algorithms

When it comes to cooking, the phrase “let's experiment” often sends shivers down the spine of anyone who just finished scrubbing a kitchen grater of stubborn cheese remnants. Yet, curiosity-driven experimentation in the kitchen can yield glorious and sometimes baffling results, much like a toddler's finger-painting, sometimes abstract, and other times, a colorful masterpiece. As a Technology Risk Manager turned aspiring chef (with an unusually healthy respect for disposable takeout containers), I've learned that the same principles apply when diving into the realm of algorithms.

Imagine standing in your kitchen, a parade of ingredients sprawled before you. You`ve got a cabbage that seems to have taken on a personality of its own, some questionable-looking curry powder, and your dog contemplating whether it, too, might enjoy a life of culinary adventure. With curiosity as your guide, the culinary stones begin to line up. This is where the magic happens: the concoction of a deeply unorthodox cabbage-curry stew that will either make you the star of the neighborhood potluck or a pariah begging for forgiveness. In the world of machine learning, this phase closely resembles the initial experimentation with various algorithms, where we toss different models together and wait with bated breath to see what emerges, a grand dinner party or a failed attempt at edible art.

At its core, both cooking and algorithm creation thrive on fearless experimentation. What is a recipe, if not a data-driven hypothesis that tests our taste buds? I like to think of my kitchen as a bustling laboratory, where flavors collide in ways that are sometimes delicious and other times, um, inexplicably tragic. The same concept holds when creating models: we start with data as our ingredients, seasoning them with algorithms in the hope of uncovering insights that yield delightful results. Every tweak in the recipe, be it a dash of salt or a perplexing mix linear and non-linear models, takes us one step closer to culinary (and analytical) brilliance or utter disaster.

Curiosity drives us to push boundaries, and quite often, leads to astonishing discoveries. You might be surprised to learn that the best way to grill asparagus might involve throwing a handful of cheese into a blender and pairing it with an obscure algorithm rather than cooking it dry on the grill. Curiosity prompted me to try this wild idea during one Sunday dinner, and behold! A cheese-covered asparagus casserole was born! Enter: people's eyebrows lifting in disbelief as I casually mention the algorithmic apocalypse, the data modeling equivalent of last-minute kitchen miracles. Inspired by its bubbling glory, I realized we often learn the most from failures and delightful surprises rather than adhering strictly to the recipe book's guidelines.

Let's not forget the role of improvisation. When you're knee-deep in experimentation, there comes a moment when you're presenting dishes that have gone off the rails. Maybe your spaghetti sauce has turned into a viscous soup instead of a robust blend of flavors. Well, instead of panicking, embrace it. Adjustments, boosting the heat, adding some mystery spices, or even conducting a taste test involving a neighbor's cat, might lead to the sensational hybrid we never knew we needed. In the world of machine learning, this improvisational spirit shines through as well; it's the adaptability to tweak parameters, refine our data scrub, or suddenly realize that our model was misinterpreting an entire dataset like an untrained sous-chef struggling to chop vegetables.

The art of curiosity-driven experimentation blooms in the intersection between freedom and skill. When you develop a solid foundation, be it classic French cooking techniques or the basic principles of linear regression, your creative powers expand. Knowing how and why things work gives you the confidence to experiment boldly. Many chefs shout, "throw caution to the wind," before unleashing their untested dishes on family and friends, and it's equally exhilarating in data science when you look at your bewildering stacks of numbers and confidently say, "Let's run a recursive regression on this!"

Thinking of it, there's always a magical aspect of discovery, finding the misfit ingredient or unexpected parameter that transforms an "okay" dish or model into an "amazing" one. Think of it as the beautiful clash of flavors where pineapple, in all its controversial glory, finds itself crowned the unexpected hero of a pizza. Will it taste good? Will the neighbors cringe? In the machine learning world, we're daring enough to dive into unfaithful features, pairing those that offer surprising benefits against all conventional wisdom.

The dance of curiosity-driven experimentation in cooking and algorithms teaches us how to embrace the unpredictable. Whether it's whipping up a surprisingly delectable roasted cabbage surprise or AI achieving learning outcomes from bizarre input data, what remains constant is that curiosity, seasoning, and a dash of irreverence can lead to creations worthy of both applause and laughs. So, the next time you whip out your whisk or line up your datasets, remember to approach it enthusiastically. The delicious concoctions, or sometimes ridiculous fails, await as you embark on yet another cooking adventure or experiment with your machine learning algorithms. After all, who knows? Your next culinary odyssey might spark a crazy trend; we may very well become the wonder chefs of the data age!

Asking the Right Questions: A Chef's and Data Scientist's Approach

When I first stumbled upon the correlation between cooking and data science, it hit me harder than an unexpected wave of flour from a poorly zipped bag. Both require us to ask questions, lots of them! The best chefs aren't just swaying rhythmically with a whisk; they're probing the nuances of flavor combinations, experimenting with textures, and the time it takes to transform a humble egg into an exquisite soufflé (if they're lucky, that is). And in the same breath, data scientists are brimming with questions, analyzing variables, and practically drooling over data sets as they contemplate, "What patterns might emerge and how can they possibly break my brain today?"

Let's start with what we "chefs" call "the initial premise." In cooking terms, it's the question of what dish you want to create. Are we diving into a comforting lasagna, or are we riffing on a classic French ratatouille? Asking the right questions in life, not just cooking, sets the entire tone. A successful chef must understand the essence of their offerings: What flavor profiles will resonate with guests? What unfortunate outcomes might stem from an egregious overuse of garlic (yes, there's such a thing, I say, but some may disagree)? Surprisingly, the same logic applies to data science. Rather than being stuck with "What algorithm do I use to solve this problem?" we need to ask deeper questions, questions that lead us to exploratory paths of interest.

Curiosity guides the culinary mind to propel itself into uncharted territory. I recall a time when I decided to challenge myself with a pastry that looked deceptively simple: a classic Sicilian cannoli. As I ferociously whipped that ricotta filling, I inevitably began to wonder: "What makes a filling truly stand out? Is it the perfect balance of sweetness? The zest of citrus? Or should I dare to add a sprinkle of cinnamon as my Zia insisted?" The questions quickly transformed the experience into an opportunity to explore flavors. Similarly, in data science, we find ourselves asking, "What new features can add clarity to my model? What data is extraneous, and how might I omit it to let the key elements shine?" Precisely interrogating our subject allows us to iterate upon our culinary or analytical experiments effectively.

Now, the art of asking questions doesn't stop at inception; it also plays a crucial role in refining the process. You may find yourself elbow-deep in tomato sauce and are suddenly struck by the thought: "Is this sauce giving my diners that necessary umami punch? Could it lose dominance to the pasta?" This moment of reflection is essential, and, dare I say, it's where the magic happens. Continuous reflection ensures flavors evolve, much as we revisit our algorithms based on feedback and model performance. In machine learning, the key question becomes, "What version of this model will give me the most accurate results?" Every taste test brings us closer to a final product, one that is brimming with flavor or an algorithm polished to perform at its peak.

On the other hand, let's not forget that we sometimes need to interrogate our process for potential pitfalls. Picture that all-too-familiar moment when the beautifully structured soufflé becomes a sad pancake of defeat. You may find yourself questioning your baking technique: "Did I overmix the batter? Did I dare to open the oven door before it was set? Or worse, was I using expired baking soda?!" In data science, similarly crucial questions arise: "Did I collect biased data? Did I overlook relevant features?" Each of these inquiries allows us to learn, adapt, and avoid future catastrophes. I daresay that a failed soufflé can inspire future triumphs, just as flawed algorithms prompt us to reconsider our methodology.

There's a fancy term called "iterative questioning," which could easily replace the phrase "having dinner with family." Each follow-up question opens the door to new possibilities, just like how I sometimes wonder whether I should replace the parsley garnish with truffle oil and watch my dinner host lift an eyebrow in astonishment. In data analysis, iterative questioning can lead to better feature engineering or hyperparameter fine-tuning. Instead of sticking rigidly to our initial feature selection, we must continuously ask ourselves and be willing to adapt: What else can we bring to the plate, or in this case, the data set, that might deliver richer insights?

It would be remiss of me not to mention the vital role emotional intelligence plays in asking the right questions, whether over dinner or during a corporate presentation. The ability to sense the mood in a room is critical! For instance, a friend may not appreciate the sudden influx of tripe a la Romana on a dinner menu, just as a data analyst might discover the stakeholders are dreading intricate statistical representations. Emotional intelligence allows us to navigate these discussions with grace, ensuring a fruitful culinary feast or an impressive data presentation that resonates with every audience member.

At the end of the day, whether you're cooking a divine meal or tackling the complexities of data, asking the right questions is your leading ingredient for success. Cook with heart and a dash of creativity while you explore life's appetizing choices and your data's delectable mysteries. So, the next time you find yourself perplexed in the kitchen or scratching your head over an algorithm, ask a question, don't hold back! What's the worst that can happen? You may just find a delightful surprise that serves up a feast for the senses or uncovers nuggets of data gold you never expected. After all, life, just like a good risotto, is richer when you keep stirring!

Cultivating a Curious Mindset: Tips for Lifelong Learning

Cultivating a curious mindset is like making a perfect risotto; it requires patience, a touch of technique, and a willingness to embrace the possibility that something might go terribly wrong before it all comes together beautifully. As I've barreled my way through kitchens, classrooms, and boardrooms alike, I've discovered that curiosity is the catalyst that transforms passive learning into vibrant exploration. So grab your apron and maybe a glass of wine because we're about to embark on a flavorful journey toward lifelong learning!

First and foremost, let's embrace the power of questioning. If there's one thing I've learned throughout my attempts at cooking, it's that asking questions is the key to discovery. Take a moment to consider the last time you roasted vegetables. Did you stop at "What temperature should I bake them at? "or investigate deeper into unusual inquiries like, "How would they taste if I slathered them in peanut butter?" (Warning: results may vary drastically, and not in a good way). The willingness to ask curious questions opens new dimensions of understanding, much like exploring the prima materia of a dish. Being question-happy fuels conversations, ignites creativity, and strengthens connections between seemingly unrelated ideas.

Experiencing the beauty of curiosity in action can also happen when we submerge ourselves in a variety of interests. Much like experimenting with a spice rack full of unusual flavors, exposing your mind to diverse subjects helps you build a robust knowledge base. I've found that dabbling in topics such as philosophy, astrophysics, or even folding laundry (it's surprisingly calming!) can inspire connections in unexpected areas. Often, insights from one activity can reveal fascinating parallels in another, such as discovering the optimal balance of salt in both a seafood dish and a predictive model. Mix up your intellectual recipes, don't stick to the same old pasta and marinara when you can have spaghetti with a side of quantum physics!

Another essential tip for nurturing a curious mindset is to adopt the spirit of playfulness. Recall your childhood when experimentation was an everyday affair. Who hasn't made a mud pie, convinced it would turn into a five-star dessert? This element of whimsy should never fade, even amid the seriousness of adulthood and the corporate world, a place where risottos at lunch serve more as a haunting reminder of something that went wrong rather than a celebration of creativity. So, lean into the absurd! Put on a chef's hat when presenting a new idea during a meeting. Share the most ludicrous food combination you've ever tasted, invoking laughter and opening up dialogues. By creating a playful atmosphere, you invite others to unleash their boundless curiosity, transforming even the most ordinary day into a grand culinary event.

Let's not forget about the staggering power of failure. Much like burning a batch of cookies sends us spiraling down the path of culinary embarrassment, failures in learning can often feel like a doom-filled downpour. But what if we shifted our perspective? Instead of wallowing in regret, we need to view our mishaps as valuable lessons -lessons that seasoned chefs quietly chuckle about while acknowledging their extensive collection of failed soufflés. By reframing failure as an opportunity for growth rather than a setback, we can transform our mindset. Tripped-up attempts provide a goldmine of insight: each ill-fated dish or flawed algorithm brings us a step closer to success, making us further equipped for our next culinary or data-driven adventure.

Additionally, surrounding ourselves with curious minds is crucial. Just as a pinch of paprika can elevate an entire meal, hanging out with inquisitive people can lift our own curiosity to new heights. Engage with those who challenge traditional thought - be it your neighbor with peculiar hobbies or that enigmatic friend who insists that conspiracy theories about spaghetti monsters are worth a serious discussion. Leaning into diverse perspectives can challenge your cognition, driving you to ask questions you never thought to consider. Plus, this interaction is often accompanied by interesting food for thought - literally speaking, as lively discussions tend to happen over good meals! Nothing like a round of burritos to ignite a debate about the cultural significance of hot sauce!

Finally, don't forget to document your journey through culinary or intellectual escapades. Journaling lets you track your growth, highlight your intriguing discoveries, and identify areas you'd like to explore further. These tangents can evolve into unique recipes -whether that's literal food or a theoretical concoction- leading you toward new insights. Plus, years down the line, you can look back and laugh at those cringe-worthy attempts at culinary stardom that turned out to be more "Taco Tuesday Gone Wrong" than French Bistro. Your documentation will serve as a delightful reference point for your experiences, helping you reflect, adapt, and blossom as both a chef and a lifelong learner.

In conclusion, cultivating a curious mindset is a flavorful journey peppered with whimsical explorations, a sprinkling of failures, and a dash of playfulness. Questions not only transform our understanding but also lead us to richer conversations, ignite creativity, and ultimately open our minds to a world full of possibilities. So, whether you're dicing onions or deciphering data, keep that curiosity simmering. Take risks, make mistakes, and enjoy the quest for knowledge, because life -like a beautiful plate of pasta- is ultimately about embracing those delicious moments and nurturing the adventurous spirit within each of us! Who knows? Your next culinary innovation or fresh data discovery might just be a curious question away. Sprinkle generously and voilà! The world is your kitchen; feast upon it!

Chapter 2

Al Dente And Algorithms

The Importance of Balance in Cooking and Machine Learning

Balance! The ever-elusive quality in both cooking and machine learning that can mean the difference between a brilliant dish (or a reasonable AI model) and a culinary catastrophe (or a predictive disaster). Think of it this way: a chef attempting to create the ultimate spaghetti carbonara who throws in a whole jar of salt is not simply over-seasoning; they are performing culinary sabotage! Similarly, a data scientist who throws a handful of features into a machine learning model without consideration for their relevance may very well be doing the analytical equivalent of creating an unpalatable pasta disaster.

One of the first lessons I learned from both my Italian roots and my deep dive into AI is the importance of balance. The culinary arts, much like the world of algorithms, require precision. When you're whipping up a Bolognese that could make even the toughest customer sigh in pleasure, achieving the right balance of flavors is essential. Too much acidity, and your sauce resembles a failed chemistry experiment! Too little, and you might be serving what can only be described as a flavorless paste. Similarly, in machine learning, we'd need the perfect balance of features to prevent models from being biased or overfitting to the noise rather than the signal, which, let's be honest, can make anyone want to throw their hands up in sheer frustration.

Now, let's talk about wine. How could we not? As an Italian, I could sit here and ramble on about the weight of Chianti versus the refreshing notes of a Pinot Grigio. Still, balancing wine pairings with food is a crucial aspect of both dining and data preparation! You wouldn't want a light, fruity wine overwhelming a rich, meaty lasagna, nor would you want your data sets intertwined so ferociously that they split like an overcooked quiche. Every feature in your dataset has a role to play, just as every wine at a dinner party must complement the meal. After all, featuring a Zinfandel alongside artichoke hearts makes about as much sense as including irrelevant features in your feature set, utter chaos!

Speaking of chaos, let's touch on the balance that occurs during the cooking process itself. You might think the process is straightforward, right? Throw some ingredients in a pot, heat it, and boom, culinary triumph! But no! Just like tuning the parameters of your machine learning model, cooking requires mindful adjustments based on observation. Red sauce simmering too rapidly? Lower the flame! Model accuracy plateauing? Let's reevaluate those features! This is where intuition kicks in. Just as a chef needs to listen to the bubbling of their sauce (and perhaps even its whispers of "add more garlic!"), a data scientist must pay attention to their model's performance metrics. If your AI model is screaming for improvement like a toddler denied dessert, you may realize it's time to backtrack, analyze the data, and make the necessary adjustments for sweet success.

And oh, the beauty of iteration! In the kitchen, sometimes you have to taste and adjust, add a dash of this, a pinch of that, until you strike that perfect balance. The same applies in machine learning. Training a model is never a simple "set it and forget it" kind of activity. Much like perfecting an al dente pasta (a key life skill!), it's about timing and relentless experimentation. You'll need to evaluate your model's performance and make iterative modifications, a sort of dance between data and individual judgment, much like swirling your pasta with just the right amount of sauce. And if something goes awry (like that one overzealous chef who gobbled down all the alcohol before the flambe), you course-correct and keep moving forward.

Balance is the anchor amidst the whirlwinds of flavor and data. Just as you master each ingredient to create a harmonious dish, understand your data and features to forge an effective machine learning model. Whether you're stirring a pot of marinara on the stove or tuning hyperparameters in Python, the principles are remarkably similar. So let's take these lessons from the kitchen into the world of algorithms, and remember: maintain balance, taste as you go, and never, ever skip the garlic!

Precision in Culinary Measurements and Algorithmic Tuning

Precision! The holy grail of both culinary arts and machine learning. Imagine, if you will, that I decide to whip up my nonna's famous lasagna. I gather all the ingredients: pasta sheets, ricotta cheese, mozzarella, and ground beef (not to mention tomatoes, herbs, and spices). Now, what if instead of following the recipe exactly, I toss in ingredients haphazardly, like an AI model randomly sampling feature inputs without a plan? I risk creating a lasagna that's essentially a disorganized pile of goo. So here it is: in the world of cooking, as in the world of algorithms, precision in measurements is not just essential; it's the difference between culinary bliss and a slapdash disaster.

When we step into the kitchen, the weight of our ingredients matters immensely. A cup of flour here, a teaspoon of salt there, a perfect soufflé hangs in the balance. If I mistakenly add two cups of salt instead of a teaspoon, I won't just ruin a dish; I'll create something that could tarnish the proud Italian name for generations. In the same way, too much or too little of a hyperparameter in our algorithm can disengage the whole model, choking it like an overcooked spaghetti strand. So, my friends, consider this a public service announcement; Never underestimate the power of precision! It can save you from the culinary emergency department.

Now, let's briefly discuss the age-old battle of the measuring devices. Cups, tablespoons, ounces, the chaos can drive a novice cook to despair! Meanwhile, over in the world of AI, we have algorithmic tuning that resembles a juicy pizzeria with a confusing menu. Do we measure the learning rate in tiny increments? What about the batch size? A scattered approach serves only to create abominations, like pretending to follow a recipe while secretly trying to perform culinary alchemy. Whether in the kitchen or in code, knowing the exact measurements transforms your dish and model from a half-hearted attempt into a resounding success that would make your grandmother proud.

Here's where it gets really interesting. Imagine finding out that a pinch of paprika turns a mediocre pasta into a flavor explosion, or that a well-tuned neural network can outperform competitors. With cooking, it's all about that "aha!" moment when you taste and realize you got it right. The key discernment lies in observing the subtlety of flavors, just as we notice the sweet spot in algorithm performance metrics. And let's not forget the importance of calibration. If I were to dump spices into a pot aimlessly, I'm bound to miss that sweet burst of flavor that my taste buds crave. Similarly, if I do not tune my algorithm to pick the best hyperparameters, I risk being trapped in the purgatory of mediocre predictions.

The beauty lies not only in following the recipe with strict parameters but also in adapting and modifying based on the results. Perhaps you add a bit more garlic because, let's face it, garlic is never wrong. In machine learning, we continually assess and re-evaluate our models, making fine adjustments until we reach optimal performance. This iterative process of tasting and adjusting translates beautifully to tuning our algorithms, where we aim to minimize loss functions with the finesse of a maestro orchestrating a grand symphony of flavors.

But beware! Just as cooking requires a certain finesse to avoid ruining the meal, algorithmic tuning has its own share of pitfalls. Overzealous application of adjustments can lead to overfitting, much like sprinkling too many garnishes on a stunning dish. You may think, "I'll just add more complexity, and it will be better!" But, trust me, an outlandishly decorated dish or a convoluted model does not necessarily lead to good outcomes. Know when to show restraint; it's the artistry of the simple and sublime that captivates the hearts and taste buds.

The precision in culinary measurements and algorithmic tuning is akin to the balance of flavors in a well-executed dish. It is an experience that demands both respect and creative intuition. As we chop, mix, and sauté, we must parallel this approach in our work with data and models. Donate yourself to the power of precise measurements, whether in the kitchen or code, and relish the harmony of each dish and each algorithm you create. Remember, culinary success and machine learning mastery are not just about numbers; they are a celebration of intuition, patience, and the delightful dance of skillful execution. Thus, with a dash of humor and a sprinkling of precision, we shall conquer both pasta and AI!

Finding the Sweet Spot: Trade-offs in Cooking and AI

The sweet spot! That glorious realm where flavors harmonize and models excel, a wondrous intersection of culinary artistry and the technical mastery of machine learning. Finding this sweet spot can be akin to attempting to balance a plate of spaghetti while riding a bicycle; doable, but fraught with peril. In both domains, navigating trade-offs is not just an art; it's practically a rite of passage that separates casual cooks from culinary virtuosos and hobbyist data scientists from seasoned AI professionals. So sit back, grab a bowl of warm pasta (because carbs are essential for brainpower), and let's explore the delicate dance of trade-offs that define our endeavors in both the kitchen and the digital realm.

Let's start with the humble decision of ingredient substitutions. Imagine you're halfway through preparing a classic risotto, only to realize you've run out of Arborio rice! Do you panic and grab the nearest long-grain rice in desperation, thus risking your reputation as a risotto aficionado? Or do you find a way to adapt, knowing what you're giving up in creaminess while simultaneously embracing it as an opportunity for innovation? In cooking, trade-offs involve making choices that influence texture, flavor, and overall satisfaction, much as tweaking model parameters can significantly affect an algorithm's performance. Achieving that creamy texture? Not a simple feat! It requires careful observation and adjustment of the broth level, just as fine-tuning the number of hidden layers in a neural network requires precision and insight.

Let's not forget the cardinal sin of undercooking pasta. Ah, the dreaded al dente, an Italian culinary principle that means "to the tooth," a delightful texture that embodies perfection. However, if you overshoot your timing while chatting away with your guests, you might end up serving them a plate of gooey, mushy chaos! This is the classic trade-off between the perfect cooking time and the pleasure of multitasking. Similarly, in AI, we face the dilemma of speed versus accuracy; we might choose to streamline the algorithm for quicker results at the expense of precision. The dreaded scenario? Deploying a model that spits out erroneous predictions because we were rushing like a chef attempting to plate herb-crusted salmon at the speed of light. Just like waiting for pasta to boil gracefully, we must respect the rhythm of our models to allow them to mature and learn.

Then, we come to ingredient proportions, one of the most tangible trade-offs in the kitchen. Consider the delicate balance of sweet and savory that lifts a classic marinara into something extraordinary! Here, one must ask: how much garlic is too much garlic? For an AI model, this is akin to evaluating how many features it should incorporate before it becomes an overzealous attempt at complexity. Sure, piling on ingredients might sound like a good idea in theory, but unless you're aiming for a hidden-camera cooking show disaster, you'll want to select your inputs with care! Like the trials of feature selection, we must curate our data thoughtfully to avoid the pitfalls of high dimensionality; a model that is complex for the sake of being complex is usually about as popular as an anchovy on pizza. Nobody wants to take a bite of contradictions.

Now, let's address the matter of flavor profiles, think spices! When I cook, I often wonder whether the subtlety of the nuances will be lost in translation if I add just a bit more heat. Will my guests erupt in culinary joy, or will they sneeze through the meal like a cartoon character caught in a fireball explosion? Similarly, the trade-off between a simple, comprehensible model and a more complex one that might yield slightly better performance often challenges our decision-making in machine learning. Just as we carefully tread the line between experimentation and chaos in cooking, AI practitioners grapple with the balance between model interpretability and predictive power. As you drown your "experimental dish" in cayenne pepper, I urge you: Consider the implications!

Lastly, let's touch upon the timing of flavors and model adjustments, yet another facet of this delicate trade-off waltz. Some culinary creations benefit from slow development; think of a rich ragu that simmers for hours, coaxing flavors into a tantalizing unison. In AI, we often need to practice the art of patience as well; rushing to deploy a model before it's fully trained can lead to disappointments of unmet expectations. A chef knows to respect the integrity of flavors as they meld, just as we must respect the necessity of time and iteration in refining an algorithm. It's all about waiting for that sweet revelation of flavors or output, a transition that might require finesse but pays off with delightful rewards.

Finding the sweet spot in cooking and AI is a continuous journey rife with trade-offs. Each decision leads to flavors dancing in delightful tandem or algorithms making glorious predictions. Whether you're sauteing onions or fine-tuning hyperparameters, embrace each trade-off through trial and error. After all, great cuisine and groundbreaking AI are marked not by flawless execution, but by your willingness to explore, adapt, and, the best part, taste along the way. So arm yourself with patience and creativity, and find that sweet spot! Or, you know, just cover everything in cheese. It works for pasta, and it might just work for your models too!

Intuition vs. Formula: The Right Approach for Recipes and Models

Intuition versus formula: the ultimate culinary and computational showdown! It's the classic battle between the free-spirited cook who adds a pinch of this and a dash of that based on gut feeling, and the meticulous chef who adheres to the recipe like a mathematician clinging to the Pythagorean theorem. In the kitchen, it's the difference between a whimsical creation that reminds you of your nonna's home-cooked meals and an overly complicated soufflé that collapsed under the weight of its own expectations. When it comes to machine learning, we encounter the same dramatic rivalry, relying on instinct versus rigidly following a formula. So grab your apron and digital notepad; we're diving into the blend of taste and tech.

Let's begin with the kitchen and the allure of culinary intuition. Picture yourself standing in front of a countertop littered with ingredients; there's olive oil, garlic, and tomatoes, and that intriguing lump of blue cheese you've been saving. The question arises: Should you follow a recipe that instructs you to create a classic marinara, or do you listen to your gut and venture into uncharted territory? Ah, the sweet siren song of creativity! In the end, it could lead you to culinary ecstasy or to the dark clutches of culinary regret. Those who eschew recipes often have tales of spontaneous zesty delights, disposable recipes that don't know a thing about weighing their ingredients, let alone how long to stew them. Sound familiar? Yes, it's the same energy that fuels countless creative endeavors in both cooking and AI.

However, let's not discard the tried-and-true recipe! It serves as a reliable starting point, like a safety net for a tightrope walker. In the kitchen, a recipe provides proportions and timings that guide you into the realm of gastronomic glory. It's the sacred text that assures you that, yes, a teaspoon of salt is vital for every 500 grams of dough. Without that formula, your homemade bread might resemble an unholy brick, one that could be mistaken for a doorstop! The same can be said in machine learning, where models grounded in structured algorithms often provide a baseline performance that allows us to expand from a solid foundation. Having the formula allows us to take calculated risks, knowing we have something to fall back on.

Now, my dear chefs and data enthusiasts, let's ponder the irony of unorthodox creation. In the culinary world, intuition often leads to magical combinations, perhaps a hint of crushed chili flakes in your tiramisù, marveling at how sweet and spicy harmonize like a duet between Julia Child and a jazz saxophonist. Similarly, in AI, there's this wondrous phenomenon known as "feature engineering"; a euphoric blend of creativity and analytical thinking, where you create features inspired by gut feelings, hoping they will become the secret sauce that powers your model. Too often, this approach can transform standard algorithms into dazzling successes, but tread lightly! You might find yourself lost in a jungle of variables, painting yourself into a corner that even Houdini would struggle to escape.

What we need, dear readers, is balance! That's right, we need neither flamboyant intuition that spends unwarranted time on an artistic exploration of flavors nor rigid formulas that can turn us into robots at the stove; sometimes, blending the two results in pure culinary magic. Imagine crafting a dish that starts with a classic gnocchi recipe as your framework, letting your instinct guide you toward a flavorful addition of sage and walnuts, fusing the rules with the uniqueness of you! In the machine learning realm, it's about iterative refinement: stepping back to evaluate when to rely on established theories and when to let your creativity flourish.

But let's not disregard the reality that intuition can lead to disaster. We've all been there, right? Those moments when confidence overrides common sense, and you think to yourself, "How can I do this without following rules?" Armed with enormous conviction, you try to whip up a dish inspired by a late-night cooking show only to find yourself staring at what resembles a plate of regrets. The algorithmic equivalent? A model that becomes overfitted to noise instead of being trained on genuine data patterns. Both lead to outcomes no one wants to claim at the dinner table or, for that matter, at the stakeholder meeting.

At the end of the day, the guiding mantra should be: trust your palate and your data judiciously. Embrace the balance between intuition and formula; like a well-tuned piano, when harmonized, both can create magnificent symphonies of flavor and insight. So as you saute your vegetables or fit your model parameters, remember, sometimes it's alright to let loose and improvise. Other times, following the tried-and-true will keep you from veering into murky waters. Find that sweet harmony, and you just might create something transcendent, be it dish or algorithm! Life's too short to serve bland pasta or oversimplified models; embrace the flavorful adventures where intuition meets formula!

The Finale: Achieving the Perfect Al Dente Outcome

The pursuit of al dente! That glorious texture that transforms ordinary pasta into an extraordinary culinary experience, bridging the gap between simply "eating" and "savoring." As the Italian saying goes, "In cucina, non ci sono segreti" (In the kitchen, there are no secrets), as long as you know the importance of achieving that perfect al dente outcome. So, let us embark together on this exploration of the balancing act that is cooking pasta and the valuable life lessons it uncovers, because achieving al dente isn't just about noodles; it's about existence itself!

You see, the term "al dente" translates as "to the tooth", a delightful phrase that encapsulates the essential texture you want when biting into your pasta. It's that magical moment of resilience, when the pasta fights back just a tad against your teeth, resulting in a satisfying experience that says, "I'm not just a blocking agent for marinara; I'm a culinary hero!" This quest for the perfect bite mirrors our own daily lives. We often seek to avoid the mushiness of complacency, swirling instead in the dynamic waters of aspiration, challenges, and growth. After all, nobody wants to live life like an overcooked noodle, limp and flavorless!

When it comes to cooking pasta, timing is everything. The secret to attaining that perfectly cooked al dente is the ability to gauge the delicate balance between boiling your water and the precise moment you pull the pasta from the pot. No one wants to be the cook pondering a life-altering decision over the bubbling chaos, thinking, "Is this the right moment?" Panicked, you might go from "I've got this!" to "Why did I ever attempt homemade pasta?" To avoid such turmoil, one must embrace the arc of patience and practice (and perhaps invest in a good kitchen timer). It's about finding that zen spot, both in cooking and life, where we tune out the noise and apt efficiently to what matters.

However, here's where the plot thickens, cooking pasta isn't just about standing over boiling water like a hopeful oracle of texture! For a truly gratifying al dente, you need to consider the quality of your pasta, the water hardness, the brand, the temperature, oh, the complexities at play! It's like trying to nail down the parameters of a machine learning model. If your inputs are subpar, your outcomes are going to be tragically uninspiring. You don't want to present your guests with a bowl of soggy carbs masquerading as a culinary triumph. In the same sense, if you feed your AI model mediocre or imbalanced data, the results will be a humorless facsimile of the insights you were aiming for, like modeling a masterpiece, only to produce a cartoon caricature of Picasso!

And let's talk about the concept of "testing." A wise chef knows that the only way to guarantee pasta reaches that esteemed al dente state is to conduct taste tests, a ritual where culinary pride may soar or plummet! Strain a few noodles, taste, and adjust if necessary, an exhilarating mix of passion and computation. The same holds true in machine learning, where we're constantly iterating and validating our models, checking results to ensure accuracy. Just as you wouldn't serve pasta before ensuring optimal texture, you should never release a model without checking its performance metrics. The risk of disappointment is too great, and trust me, no one wants to be that person sipping on their overcooked spaghetti soup while their friends indulge in expertly crafted dishes!

But one must also remember the inevitable setbacks that come with this pursuit, much like an occasional clump of gooey pasta when we abandon protocol. Overcooked pasta can rear its ugly head at any moment and ruin the confidence of even the best of chefs. Similarly, in the world of AI, it only takes one rogue parameter adjustment or data anomaly to throw everything into chaos. The trick lies in knowing how to recover gracefully. Instead of spiraling into despair, turn it into a moment of levity. After all, the kitchen is where we learn resilience! Gather your ingredients and try it again, when perhaps all eyes are not on you, blissfully whispering themes of camaraderie and support rather than judgment.

Finally, once you've achieved that succulent al dente pasta, it's time for the proverbial celebration, a plate that doesn't just sit there but dances across the table, celebrating all the elements of taste! You've done it! And as you pair it with a glorious homemade sauce, one that encapsulates all those glorious late-night experiments in your kitchen, you realize that life, like culinary mastery, is an evolving adventure, where triumph is interspersed with failures and growth.

In conclusion, achieving the perfect al dente outcome is more than just mastering the art of pasta; it's a reflective journey that reveals the importance of timing, quality, testing, and the ability to rise from setbacks. Much like the world of AI, it mirrors our quest for knowledge, precision, and success, with a hint of humor, of course. So, as you close this chapter, remember that whether in the kitchen or navigating the complexities of life, all it takes is a little patience, determination, and an occasional taste test along the way. Now grab that fork, dive into a plate of glorious al dente pasta, and let the journey begin! Buon appetito!

Chapter 3

The Recipe for Success: Data Preparation

The Importance of Data Quality

When it comes to cooking, we all know that the secret to a fantastic dish lies not just in the chef's skill but also in the quality of the ingredients. You wouldn't want to prepare a sumptuous pasta dish with tomatoes that are more questionable than a used car salesman's smile, would you? Much like how a ripe, juicy tomato can elevate a simple marinara to culinary heights, the quality of your data can make or break your machine learning models, turning them from breadsticks to bangers. In this world, bad data is the equivalent of expired milk - it might look fine on the outside, but one whiff, and you know your dreams of a creamy carbonara are doomed.

Data quality is about integrity, accuracy, and reliability, essentially the holy trinity of ingredients necessary to whip up AI systems that actually work and don't resemble something your cat might leave as a surprise gift. Poor data quality results in models that are more confused than a chameleon in a bag of Skittles. These models could lead to outcomes that make you question whether you've accidentally invented a sophisticated pizza-flavored shoe instead of a recommender system for your favorite pizzerias. Trust me; no one wants to find themselves in such a pickle, especially when the only shoes that should taste like pizza are, well, slices of pizza!

You might be wondering, "But John, what constitutes data quality? Is it a flavor profile I can enhance with some olive oil?" Let me break it down: data quality encompasses dimensions like accuracy, completeness, consistency, timeliness, and uniqueness. Think of it as the five basic food groups for your data. Accuracy relates to how correctly your data reflects reality; if the numbers are inaccurate, it's like trying to make a marinara sauce with dried herbs from the '90s, not great. Completeness refers to whether your dataset has all the necessary ingredients; without a full pantry, you can't create a full-flavored dish or a robust model.

Let's not forget about consistency, which ensures that your data doesn't play tricks on you like a magician at a wedding. Imagine pouring a nice glass of Chianti and discovering it's actually apple juice, cue the disappointment! Timeliness is equally paramount. Imagine trying to put together a beautiful summer dish with winter produce; it just won't taste right. In machine learning, outdated data can lead to predictions that are about as useful as a fork in a soup convention. Lastly, uniqueness helps us avoid duplicates; after all, you want to create one perfect recipe, not end up with three versions of overcooked lasagna layered into a single pan.

But how do we ensure data quality? Welcome to the world of data cleaning, where the magic happens! This is the part where we transform that questionable, clumpy mess of information into beautiful, clean datasets ready to serve up to our models. It'll involve identifying and eliminating unnecessary duplicates (like a bad guest who keeps coming back), correcting inconsistencies (say goodbye to input values that are half-true), and making sure we fill in the gaps instead of just pretending they don't exist. Just like whipping up a well-balanced Bolognese, it takes time and patience to perfect, but once you do, the results are utterly rewarding!

The best part about maintaining data quality is that it's a continuous affair, an ongoing relationship reminiscent of nurturing a sourdough starter. You can't just toss some flour and water together, walk away for a year, and hope for the best. No, you have to tend to it regularly, adjusting ingredients when necessary, adding a pinch of salt (or a dash of validation) to ensure it remains fresh, relevant, and delightful. Different batches will require different care and attention. Still, with practice and consistency, you'll have a mouthwatering dataset that will serve you well when it's time to churn out models that people genuinely want to use.

So, remember, when you're dreaming up your next AI model, think of the importance of data quality as the anchor in your stormy seas of endless spreadsheets, messy databases, and untamed data sets. Treat it like the most stringent Italian nonna keeping an eye on you in the kitchen. Follow her rules closely, and you'll be rewarded with a model that performs as well as a perfectly cooked ravioli, one that doesn't burst open upon the first bite but stands proud, holding within it the richness of your data's finest qualities. In the world of AI, it's the difference between transforming your culinary dreams into a nightmare or serving up that delectable lasagna you've always wanted to share with your family. Now that, my friends, is the taste of success!

Cleaning and Preprocessing Techniques

The moment has come: the dreaded yet necessary ritual of cleaning and preprocessing data. Just like how I wouldn't dare start making a ragu sauce without first cleansing my workspace of last week's leftover pizza (and you should see the state of my kitchen after a good cooking binge!), we must first tidy up our datasets before we can whip up any machine learning magic. So roll up your sleeves, put on your metaphorical apron, and let's dive into this mess, admittedly, a mess that's not nearly as deliciously cheesy as my beloved lasagna but vital nonetheless!

First things first, think of data cleaning as a simplified version of organizing your kitchen. You wouldn't want to rummage through a cluttered fridge filled with ketchup packets from the 90s (or was it the 80s? Time flies). Similarly, we need to examine our data for missing values, outliers, or inconsistent entries. You wouldn't want a rogue data point ruining your beautiful recipe, like finding out that one tomato you thought was fresh has a delightful hint of mold. Scan through your dataset like a hound sniffing out a bad ingredient; if it doesn't belong, it's time to polish it off!

Next up, let's tackle those missing values. Whether they're blank fields or awkwardly absent entries, missing values can leave your dataset feeling incomplete, like showing up to a dinner party without your favorite dish. The question arises: What do we do with these pesky little problems? Well, we have choices! You could simply throw out the entire row, akin to tossing out the whole batch of linguine because one noodle happened to break. A tad extreme, don't you think? Or, you can fill in the gaps using techniques such as mean or median imputation, much like substituting one ingredient for another when you realize you mistakenly grabbed jalapenos instead of bell peppers. Adjustments can be made without losing the essence of the dish, although I must admit that mixing up those peppers could yield a rather"spicy" surprise.

Once you've tamed those missing values, it's time to confront the outliers, those strange data points that stand out like a lone anchovy on a veggie pizza. We see you, glorious but unsolicited anchovy, lurking among the bell peppers and olives! While some outliers might yield interesting insights, others may be the result of errors or simply reflect a data entry mistake, like the time I thought "3" in my recipe meant "30" (pro tip: don't put in 3 cups of salt). We have to decide whether to keep, transform, or remove these misfits so they don't skew our model results. In machine learning, even the outliers deserve a second glance; with the right analysis, they might add a special flavor to your dish you never expected!

Moving forward, it's vital to standardize and normalize our data so that all features are comparable, think of it like making sure all the ingredients in your pasta are seasoned to perfection. If one feature is measured in grams and another in teaspoons, you might be left with a culinary catastrophe. Conversion is your friend! But beware of excessive normalization; we don't want to end up with a sterile meal lacking flavor. A touch of careful thought about how you scale your data can make all the difference, and trust me, we want our models to be seasoned just right, not bland and boring.

And just when you thought we were done, here comes the wonderful world of feature extraction and selection! This is akin to deciding what makes the cut in your pasta primavera. Which vegetables add life? Which flavor profiles will make your mouth dance? Similarly, we need to figure out which features truly improve our model's performance and which are just extra fluff, like that one cousin who always overstays his welcome at family dinners. If your model can be trained effectively without "Cousin Fluff," then it's time to bid adieu.

Now, let's not forget about transforming categorical variables into numerical ones, akin to converting grandma's handwritten recipes into a digital cookbook. We need to encode these glorious categories into a format our models can understand! This includes using techniques like one-hot encoding to ensure no cherished ingredient is left behind in translation. After all, wouldn't it be tragic if "Pasta" turned into "Carbohydrates" because our model was confused? The result would be an unappetizing representation of what's actually a culinary masterpiece.

Cleaning and preprocessing data is similar to preparing the perfect meal; it's an essential step that lays the groundwork for your success. From tidying up those inconsistencies to embracing the goodness of encoding categorical variables, every detail matters. When done right, this phase transforms your data from a chaotic kitchen to a Michelin-star experience. And just like in cooking, it's all about indulging in the joy of creating something wonderful, because when your data is clean and well-prepared, the results will be as delightful as a freshly baked ziti straight from the oven!

Understanding Different Data Types

The glorious world of data types, where everything makes sense, and yet nothing makes sense all at once. It's almost like trying to differentiate between the myriad of pasta shapes on a rainy afternoon; we have tubes, spirals, sheets, and I'm left wondering if I'm attempting to create a feast or a modern art installation! Understanding the different data types in machine learning is crucial, much like deciphering a recipe written in Italian. So grab your measuring cups, and let's unravel this delightful conundrum together.

At the very heart of data are two main categories: qualitative (or categorical) data and quantitative data. Categorical data, my dear culinary enthusiasts, are akin to the delectable toppings of a pizza. You've got your pepperoni, olives, mushrooms, and of course, the controversial pineapple, each distinct and flavorful in its own right. However, don't let their uniqueness fool you; categorical data doesn't follow any specific mathematical operations. You can't add pepperoni slices to olive slices and expect to create something like a "pepperoni-olive fusion." That would be chaos! Similarly, when handling categorical variables in your machine learning models, you must treat them like gracious dinner guests, each with their preference but none of them able to play the piano.

Now, on to the main course: quantitative data! This type of data is where the fun really begins. Quantitative variables represent measurable entities, just like the amount of pasta you need for a family of four. You can slice and dice it, add it, and multiply it until your heart is content (but perhaps don't take it to the lengths of converting it into a mathematical equation for rocket size, that's a bit too far, even for me). There are two flavors within quantitative data: discrete and continuous. Discrete variables are like the number of meatballs you can fit on your plate, countable and finite. In contrast, continuous variables are like the height of that tower of spaghetti, which could stretch infinitely toward the sky if someone didn't intervene, oh, the tragedy! These allow for an infinite number of values within a range, much like my thoughts on how many servings of tiramisu are "just right."

As you sink your teeth into data types, you'll soon notice the importance of realizing how to manage these delicious morsels. Imagine trying to apply regression analysis to categorical data, much like trying to toss a firm gnocchi into a blender (come on, don't do it!). You'll end up with a messy, unappetizing shake that looks like a culinary crime scene. Instead, we can convert those categories to numerical values using techniques such as one-hot or label encoding. This process allows our models to grasp the subtlety of categorical variables while preserving their unique flavor profiles, much like creating a meticulously organized pantry ready to inspire the most complex of dishes.

But wait, there's more to this pasta of data types! Have you ever crossed paths with the enigmatic notion of ordinal data? Ordinal data is the delightful third wheel in this culinary relationship. Think of it as seasoning; some ingredients add more flavor than others, but they still belong to the same category. For instance, in a chef's rating system, we might rank a dish as "poor," "fair," "good," and "excellent." Even though they're words, they hold an adorable hierarchy, much like the way my grandmother places her favored dishes on the dining table based on their level of deliciousness. So remember, ordinal data carries an inherent order, but you can't do complex arithmetic with it because, well, one person's "good" isn't equal to another's "excellent."

Next up, let's venture into the delicious world of timestamp data, though not quite as tasty as a slice of panna cotta, it's crucial in its own right. Timestamps let us track changes over time, creating a rich history akin to that of your family recipes, handed down like a sacred scroll bearing the secrets of your culinary lineage. This data type helps algorithms understand patterns, seasonality, and trends, whether we're examining restaurant visits over the week or looking at trend lines that show how much more coffee is consumed when attempting a new recipe!

Finally, we should not overlook the ever-important "mixed data types", the chaotic pasta salad of your datasets. Sometimes we end up with ingredients that don't quite belong together, much like al dente pasta overlapping with a rigid vegetable. Here, we're often dealing with datasets that include both categorical and numerical variables. For instance, imagine a restaurant dataset filled with ratings and types of cuisine. This delightful mishmash might keep your model on its toes!

Understanding the different types of data is much like mastering the flavors in Italian cooking. Knowing when to use each type and how to blend them together will ultimately make the difference between a dish that sings and one that falls flat. As we navigate this landscape, remember that each data type is as vital to our culinary and machine learning exploits as deciding whether to serve garlic bread with that lasagna. Embrace the differences, mix the data beautifully, and serve up a dish that will have everyone begging for seconds! Mangia!

Feature Engineering: The Secret Sauce

Feature engineering, the secret sauce of the machine learning kitchen! If data cleaning is about kicking out the riff-raff and organizing the pantry, feature engineering is where you whip up that delicious lift that transforms a mediocre dish into a Michelin-star masterpiece. It's the bay leaf that elevates your tomato sauce, the perfect blend of spices that takes your chicken cacciatore to divine levels. And much like a dash of salt can enhance flavor, the right features can radically enhance the predictive power of your models. So grab your chef's hat; we're diving into the art (and science) of crafting those glorious features that will have your algorithms singing!

First, let's define what we mean by features. In the world of machine learning, features are the attributes that serve as input variables, essentially the ingredients of our dish. They are the building blocks the model uses for predictions, like how pasta shapes and sauces come together to create an unforgettable meal. Now, the reality is that you might start with a pan full of raw, unrefined ingredients, some good, some not-so-good, and it's your job to channel your inner culinary genius to transform them into something brilliant. Who knew data scientists were, in a way, the culinary artists of the digital world?

The magic of feature engineering lies primarily in creativity and understanding, which is a fancy way of saying we need to think outside the box and sprinkle in some innovation. Let's say we're working with a dataset of restaurant reviews. We may have various raw features, such as star ratings, review text, number of reviews, and more. But just like you wouldn't dump uncooked pasta into boiling sauce to serve, raw features may not have the right flavor yet. Here's where you come in! You could create a new feature that captures the sentiment of the reviews, using that text data to create an 'overall sentiment score.' Now you've taken a bland, unseasoned feature and transformed it into something spicy and intriguing! Your model can now understand not just numbers but the emotional soul behind those reviews, talk about a flavor evolution!

Another classic example involves timestamp features, pretty much like organizing all your cooking timers to maximize efficiency. You might receive timestamp data for orders made over the weekend or during holidays.

Great information, but the raw time alone is about as useful as a rubber spoon in a kitchen fire. Here, feature engineering can rescue the day by extracting useful elements like day of the week, month, or time of day. Maybe Friday evenings yield the highest sales, which helps us predict when to promote that special "Buy One, Get One Free" ravioli deal! Think of it like figuring out the best time to serve your family their favorite meal; you want to maximize their delight!

But wait, there's more! You can also strive for interaction features, creating new combinations by multiplying or adding existing features. For example, if you're analyzing restaurant prices, you might find that average order value multiplied by average star rating allows you to uncover high-yield hidden gems in the restaurant scene. You're effectively combining different food elements to create a dish bursting with flavor, transforming simple data into something truly gourmet. It's pure alchemy whether you're learning about flavor pairings or incrementing your AI project's success!

Let's not leave out aggregating features; this method is like slow cooking, taking your time to let flavors meld together beautifully. You can use existing features to calculate averages, totals, and other summary statistics over time. For instance, you might derive a feature that computes average dish prices over a specified time frame or total sales during peak hours, allowing your model to predict future performance. This can be a game-changer, akin to realizing that the secret to your grandma's sauce lies in letting it simmer for hours, letting each ingredient meld into a fabulous blend of deliciousness.

Now, remember that not all features need to be created from scratch. Sometimes, they're already out there, hiding in the dataset like forgotten treasures beneath a mountain of flour. It's essential to practice feature selection, having the innate ability to recognize which features are the creme de la creme and which are just plain duds. Just as you wouldn't put spaghetti sauce on a dessert plate, we don't want unnecessary, noisy features to disorder our predictions. It's all about serving your model the best ingredients possible!

In conclusion, feature engineering is the secret sauce that turns your machine learning projects from average to extraordinary! By combining creativity, intuition, and a sprinkle of analytical thinking, we can unlock the potential lying dormant within those raw ingredients. As you explore flavors, keep in mind that the cooking metaphor isn't just about food; it's about the art of combining distinct elements to create a cohesive, delightful feast. So, let's cook up some fantastic features and watch our models shine like the brightest stars in the culinary cosmos! Bon appetit to your data-driven endeavors!

Iterative Improvement: A Continuous Process

Welcome to the lovely world of iterative improvement, where the mantra is ''perfect is a journey, not a destination." If you were expecting an instant recipe for success, I hate to break it to you, but there's no magic pasta shape that guarantees a Michelin star overnight. In the culinary realm, mastery takes time and finesse, and the same is true for creating effective machine learning models. Think of iterative improvement as that wonderful cycle of trial and error, much like perfecting your grandma's secret pizza dough recipe. You knead, you stretch, and sometimes you poke it in all the wrong places, but eventually, you find that perfectly chewy texture!

Much like a budding chef experimenting in a home kitchen, you'll find that trial and error lead to better results. Each time you run your model, it's as if you're tasting a new dish and deciding whether it needs a little more kick or a bit less salt. Perhaps you gather your squad (or let's face it, your very confused and slightly disgruntled family) to try the latest version of your creation, only to hear one of them pip up about the lack of flavor, leading you to realize that maybe switching from dry herbs to fresh basil is the game-changer you didn't know you needed. That's machine learning in a nutshell: adjusting, retesting, and sprinkling in new features until you strike flavor perfection!

Now, one of the beauties of this iterative cycle is that it embraces feedback as a prized ingredient. Instead of knocking heads over stubborn tomatoes, bring in constructive feedback like a blockbuster pizza critic. Fret not; this is not the place for a "too much pineapple" debate! Gather insights as you deploy your model to real-world scenarios. Pay attention to how your users interact with your creation. Are they delighted or left in bewilderment? Are they sipping on wine while praising your culinary accomplishments or questioning their existence? Learning from those interactions will inform your next tabletop revisions and enhance the overall experience. Just remember, every feedback serves as a precious ingredient for your next round; without it, you're just a chef aimlessly tossing ingredients into the pot!

As you journey down this delightful path of enhancement, let's emphasize the role of data in your iterative endeavors. You see, gathering more data can be like finding that secret stash of truffle oil hidden in the pantry. Your model thrives on fresh input just as your culinary masterpieces flourish with top-notch ingredients. By continually updating your dataset and refining your features, you empower the model to adapt and evolve. As the food critic says, "This dish really brings out the taste of the ingredients," while simultaneously, your model thrives on the nuances added by fresh, high-quality data. And every iteration is an opportunity to "season" it further, like adjusting for the trends of spaghetti carbonara; it simply gets better with time!

In this iterative dance, employ the principle of "fail fast, learn fast." It might seem counterintuitive to embrace failures, but in the kitchen, every soggy soufflé provides invaluable lessons for next time. Dismiss that cringe-worthy data run as a wrong order on the menu, learn from what went wrong, adjust, and prepare for a robust comeback! A failed model can unveil insights that no success ever could. It's like experimenting with a new pasta dish a la your last dinner disaster, leading to something new and fabulous! Perhaps you discover that your audience prefers something bolder, less traditional.

Of course, keep in mind that improvements shouldn't happen in one grand swoop. That's like trying to boil an entire pot of spaghetti in one go, impractical, right? Instead, focus on smaller increments of change. Incremental adjustments allow you to pinpoint what works and what doesn't without overwhelming your artistic palette. Plus, it's way easier to track progress when you're not trying to keep tabs on everything, all while avoiding the "sauce explosion" caused by clashing flavors.

Lastly, iterative improvement is not a one-time affair; it is an ongoing process. Great dishes constantly evolve, and similarly, you must view your model as a living entity, one that remains susceptible to change and refinement, ml ops! When new trends emerge or when patrons' tastes shift, bring your model back to the table for another round of exciting exploration. An effective machine learning solution is never quite ''done''; perfection is more of an elusive muse, much like that perfect meal that somehow ends up being the best you've ever eaten.

Embrace iterative improvement with open arms, much like accepting a mountain of pasta on your plate. It's all about continuous learning and growing, tasting, adapting, and trying again. Celebrate each experience, whether it's a culinary delight or a moment where things go hilariously awry, because that's where the true magic happens. Journey onward with your spaghetti strings of knowledge, and remember that every iterative loop leads you closer to delectable insights. So, roll up those sleeves, sharpen that knife, and let's get cooking! Buon lavoro!

Chapter 4

A Dash of Creativity: Building Neural Networks

The Essence of Creativity in Cooking and AI

The sweet aroma of creativity, one of life's most delectable spices, whether found bubbling away in a pot of marinara or dancing through lines of code in a neural network! When I think of creativity, my mind flashes to my Nonna, who would whip up a fantastic spaghetti carbonara from nothing but spaghetti, eggs, pancetta, and unshakeable confidence. Just as she believed that each dish could, and should, tell a story, creativity in both cooking and artificial intelligence is not just about following a set of instructions; it's about infusing a little bit of yourself into the process.

In the kitchen, creativity begins with the fundamental ingredients. You might have a can of tomatoes, a head of garlic, and an old bag of dried pasta that survived an apocalypse. But it's not just the ingredients; it's how you combine and transform them that creates culinary magic. It begins with a daring leap of the imagination: perhaps you toss in that odd leftover pepper or contemplate whether the basil from last month can still impart some charm. This adventurous spirit is echoed in AI, where innovation arises from the playful tweaking of parameters or algorithms outside traditional bounds. Neural networks evolve not merely by crunching numbers but by daring to take a step into the unknown, just like my Nonna might've done when she decided to add a touch of nutmeg to her meatballs. What was she thinking?!

Imagine a neural network as an ambitious chef standing before an endless stove of potential. The chef can draw on established recipes but isn't shackled by them; this is where the real artistry comes into play. They need to assess their pantry, understand their audience, and maybe understand that nobody in the room truly likes olives, no matter how much they think they could be implemented. The beauty of AI, similarly, lies in these networks' ability to learn from both their successes and their many, many spectacular failures, like my disastrous attempt at homemade gnocchi that ended up resembling lead weights rather than pillow-soft pasta. It's in those moments of trial and error that creativity flourishes, fueled by curiosity and the recognition that perfection is an illusion.

Moreover, there's a delightful tension in both domains between structure and freedom. In cooking, we must adhere to a basic recipe, at least if we want our guests to eat what we've prepared, but within that structure lies the freedom to innovate and season to taste. This is what makes a dish uniquely yours, and similarly, a well-structured model can create a pathway for innovation. Just as I might strategically sprinkle ridiculous amounts of cheese on a lasagna, because cow-friendly Italian cooking mandates a cheesy abundance, AJ thrives on augmenting base architectures with layers of creativity that might just surprise you.

One cannot overlook the leading talents guiding our culinary and tech ventures. Master chefs like Massimo Bottura have turned the culinary scene upside down, infusing their creations with a zest for the unexpected. Likewise, maverick AI researchers are pushing the envelope, concocting advanced algorithms that mimic the whimsical spark of human creativity. Much like how Bottura might turn an unused lasagna sheet into a crunchy dessert, AI experts also find imaginative solutions to problems, breathing life into mundane tasks through inventive machine learning applications. And let's be honest, both food and AI innovation often involve an element of luck. Remember my last attempt at combining frying and quantum mechanics? Spoiler alert: the kitchen didn't survive.

As we revel in this creative milieu, we must think about the future. Imagine the day when AI doesn't just assist us in our culinary endeavors but becomes a partner in the creative process. Picture your cooking assistant suggesting the boldest of flavor fusions or gently nudging you away from using microwaved spaghetti (a travesty to any Italian's ears). An AI that learns your flavors, preferences, and aversions, developing and evolving more delicious recipes than your average cookbook, now that's a collaboration you'd want at your dinner table.

So there it is, the essence of creativity, permeating both cooking and AI, dancing together like a perfectly twirled forkful of spaghetti. As I toss my next batch of fresh fettuccine into boiling water, I can't help but smile. In both the kitchen and the coding world, creativity breathes life into the mundane, transforms the ordinary, and reminds us that we're all just chefs in our own right. Whether you're making a risotto or training a neural network, remember: throw in a little creativity and a dash of humor, and you might just cook up something spectacular!

Drawing Parallels: The Ingredients of Neural Networks

Neural networks! The mystical spaghetti of the AI world, where synapses and algorithms twirl together like the perfect forkful of pappardelle. To the untrained eye, a neural network may seem as complex and intimidating as deciphering a handwritten Italian menu in a dimly lit trattoria. But fear not, dear reader, because I'm here to unveil the culinary goodness behind the layers of neurons, a recipe much more straightforward than my inability to make a soufflé rise. Think of it as an Italian feast of bytes and data!

To begin, let's establish the fundamental ingredients of our neural network that resemble a well-structured lasagna. First off, we have the neurons, our equivalent of those delightful layers of pasta. Each neuron is like a perfectly cooked lasagna sheet, holding everything together but still capable of bending and wobbling under pressure. It receives inputs and, through the magic of activation functions, decides how to pass along that culinary essence. Picture a neuron weighing its options: will it take in the fresh tomatoes of data, or opt for the aged parmesan of past experience? Decisions, my friends, are made by neurons, fueling the entire process while embracing a diet of input data and feedback like it was on a comforting Italian holiday.

Next, we have the weights, and no. I'm not talking about that weight your Aunt Maria always uses to convince you to eat more at family gatherings. In a neural network, weights determine how much importance to give to specific inputs, much like how I'd prioritize garlic over, let's say, raisins when making a sauce. If a neuron is our pasta, the weights are the rich, flavorful sauces perfecting the dish. Each layer of our neural network adjusts these weights as it learns from data. So, if you were to mistakenly add too much salt to your risotto, you'd likely lower the weight of the salt in the next batch. Similarly, a neural network learns that some input flavors are simply not a winning combination.

Speaking of layers, we can't forget about those sweet hidden layers. Imagine layers of melting cheese nestled between sheets of lasagna, a hidden treasure of gooey goodness waiting to get discovered. Each hidden layer processes inputs and transforms them into increasingly abstract representations. In human cooking, this would be akin to chopping, simmering, and blending various elements together until you achieve the exquisite result of a rich, velvety sauce. In the neural network kitchen, hidden layers elevate, abstract, and enhance the inputs as they cascade through this culinary adventure toward some heavenly output, voila!

As we continue our gastronomic exploration into neural networks, let's not overlook the bias, which you may remember as that pesky friend who always insists on choosing dinner, much to your chagrin. In the realm of neural networks, bias helps the program learn and fine-tune information in tandem with the weights, ensuring that the output doesn't get too lost in translation. Think of bias as the seasoning in your dish, a little pinch of salt here, a dash of pepper there, intended to adjust and refine the overall outcome. It entertains the palate and keeps the tastebuds guessing, just like a neural network needs that touch of bias to enhance its predictions.

Now, for the grand finale, we must discuss the "activation function." Ah, yes! That delightful gatekeeper of creativity! The activation function is the one that says, "Yay or nay!" to whether a neuron should fire or not, essentially answering whether your food should make it to the table or end up in the wastebasket of shame. It's akin to the chef tasting the sauce before serving. If that tomato marinara isn't twinkling with flavor, the activation function quickly says, "Not yet!" and encourages you to stir in more spices and let it simmer longer until it achieves perfection.

In summation, just like every delicious Italian dish requires carefully chosen ingredients combined with a splash of creativity, a neural network comes alive through its interdependent parts: neurons, weights, layers, bias, and activation functions. There you have it! The intricacies of neural networks explained through the beloved language of Italian cooking. So, as you dig into your next neural network, or, dare I say, attempt to tackle your next lasagna recipe, remember: boiling down complexities into accessible ingredients can yield wildly successful culinary and computational creations. And if not, well, there's always pizza delivery, both your neural network and stomach will thank you later!

The Role of Experimentation: Trial and Error in Recipes and Models

Experimentation! The glorious journey where culinary dreams collide with reality, much like the time I decided to turn my humble kitchen into a mad scientist's laboratory. You know, the kind where you toss everything into the pot and hope for the best while sporting goggles, an apron, and perhaps a questionable number of wine glasses. Experimentation is the lifeblood not only of cooking but also of machine learning, where trial and error lead us through a delightful mess that eventually resembles dinner, and in the case of AI, a functioning model.

Imagine this: you stand in your kitchen, staring at a collection of ingredients as mismatched as a pair of socks I wore during an AI conference (don't ask). Just like the best chefs, you know that no great dish ever came from simply following the recipe word for word. You've got to play around with it! Maybe add an extra clove of garlic or replace the standard basil with that basil-infused chocolate you oddly purchased last year because it looked cool (spoiler alert: it doesn't work). That's the essence of experimentation, daring to bend the rules, make mistakes, and discover magical flavor combinations.

In the realm of machine learning, experimentation has an equally vital role. Picture it as tossing various ingredients into a bowl of training data and delicately mixing them up in the hopes they turn into something scrumptious. Just like you can't put raw onions and ice cream in a blender without potential disaster, machine learning models require a significant amount of trial and error to figure out which features work best. Ever tried whisking together zucchini, dog food, and nutmeg? I have, and let's just say that the dog thanks me for sparing it that culinary experiment! Similarly, AI developers must navigate through the "what-not-to-do-soup" as they test and refine their models.

One might say that failure is a fundamental ingredient in learning how to cook, much like adding salt to a pot of boiling water rather than a cake batter (good luck with that!). Each failure teaches us something essential, whether it's recognizing that introducing raw bacon in a carbonara might lead to unintended chewy surprises or that categorizing images of cats and dogs can go dreadfully wrong if you don't clean your training data first. Every time I've had a culinary flop. I've made a note, mental or physical, on what to avoid next time. The chefs who create the best dishes are the ones who've burnt the chicken, mixed strawberries into meatballs, and colored their pasta pink through experimentation.

Sometimes, the most miraculous dishes arise from mistakes, like when I accidentally created a pasta salad that turned out to be a hearty, unintentionally gourmet feast instead of last night's leftovers fated for boring sandwiches. And that's the beauty of trial and error: unearthing those happy accidents that can lead to delightful surprises. Similarly, in machine learning, unexpected outcomes often provide the most insight. When a model misclassifies data, it's akin to my discovery that adding cinnamon to a savory dish can yield a surprisingly delicious twist. Instead of discarding the failed model, data scientists analyze the missteps, tweak parameters, and retrain until they derive the creme de la creme of algorithms.

Not to mention the unpredictable nature of taste! Just when you think you've created the perfect dish, someone at your table has a wild distaste for cilantro or a deep-seated fear of textures. Sounds familiar? That's akin to how various model tuning techniques lead researchers to true neural network highs or lows after an extensive mix of approaches. One tiny change can send the whole thing spiraling into oblivion faster than my bread dough does when it explodes in the oven from too much yeast. But each time we tweak our models, experiment, and fail forward, we steadily inch closer to success.

Ultimately, whether I'm fluttering about with my spatula or galloping through datasets, the same principle reigns supreme: embrace the chaos of experimentation. In cooking, it's about having the guts to mix unconventional ingredients and trusting your instincts to lead you to culinary heights. In AI, it's about recognizing the inherent complexity and unpredictability while exploring territories you never dreamed could yield precious insights. After all, the same spirit of trial and error that saves you from kitchen catastrophe while whipping up a risotto can lead to the breakthrough that advances AI into our hearts and minds. So let us don our aprons and safety goggles, and dive into the delicious chaos of both cooking and AI, creating something delectable along the way, or at the very least, an experience to learn from and laugh at together!

Balancing Structure and Freedom: Recipes vs. Algorithms

The eternal dance of structure and freedom, an intricate ballet akin to twirling spaghetti on a fork while avoiding the inevitable splash of marinara on your white shirt. In both cooking and artificial intelligence, this balance is crucial. Much like a well-crafted Italian dish demands both a solid recipe and a splash of creativity, machine learning algorithms need a robust framework while allowing for experimentation and improvisation. Think of it as navigating the chaotic universe of pasta shapes, where some insist that only bowtie pasta is fit for a particular dish, while others will boldly proclaim the merits of farfalle in a gourmet salad!

Let's begin with structure! In cooking, recipes offer the foundational support every chef needs. They are the reliable grandmas of the culinary world: always there to guide you, sharing their wisdom with precise measurements of flour, eggs, and perhaps a pinch of love, because let's face it, love is always a major ingredient. For instance, when whipping up a stunning risotto, you can't just toss the ingredients in and hope for the best; you must adhere to a process of toasting the rice, gradually adding broth, and patiently stirring until the creaminess unfolds. Similarly, algorithms have a structure, defined by mathematical principles and frameworks that enable them to learn from data. A neural network's architecture, its layers and nodes, is like a well-organized kitchen, filled with the right instruments ensuring smooth operations.

However, let's not kid ourselves; structure can be limiting! Just as a scrumptious fettuccine dish may benefit from an unexpected splash of white wine or that rogue sprinkle of cumin defining your marinara, sometimes exploring the uncharted territories of food brings serendipitous results. In the same way, algorithms thrive on flexibility. You might devise a perfect script under structured conditions, but balk at the thought of letting those rules bind your creativity. The beauty of machine learning lies in experimentation, parameter tuning, and model reconfiguration as you go. It's essential to be ready to throw away the recipe, and possibly the measuring cups, when inspiration strikes and the muse beckons. When I once decided to add a rogue dash of chili flakes to my grandmother's secret marinara sauce, it felt liberating. The result? Euphoria or half-pain, half-delight, depending on my guest's tolerance for heat!

To further illustrate the delicate balance between structure and freedom, consider the famed soufflé. It requires a careful set of instructions that dictate temperature, mixing, and timing. But as everyone knows, one misplaced flip of the wrist, and you end up with a pancake rather than a puff, a tough lesson on why too much structure can stifle the creative spirit. This experience directly correlates to how algorithms can deliver catastrophic results if they become too rigid. In AI, blindly sticking to a set structure can leave you overlooking key features, leaving the entire dish bland and uninspired. Thus, successful chefs and engineers alike must constantly tap into that essence of adaptability, knowing when to step outside the rigid protocols.

Of course, there's also the delightful contradiction of cultural recipes that evolve over time, much like AI models. When I scroll through toppings on my grandma's pizza recipe or witness gallant Italians remixing classic Neapolitan with your typical Californian flair, it's clear: culinary traditions bend and shift alongside the seasons and personal preferences. Likewise, machine learning is a living, breathing entity; it needs to evolve, accommodate new data, and respond to the ever-changing world. That spontaneity and flexibility must go hand in hand with the foundational structures that ground them.

In this venture, the structure provides a safety net, while freedom invites a delightful kind of chaos. Much like the artful smear of olive oil atop a colorful Caprese salad, experimentation infuses algorithms with life, character, and flavor. Imagine drawing parallels like a chef documentarian narrating their way through chaotic kitchens while balancing a delightful tiramisu and an innovative new recipe for machine learning!

So, as we navigate through the spaghetti of life, both in the kitchen and as we mold algorithms, let's embrace the balance of structure and freedom. This culinary adventure helps us understand the fine line between a well-executed recipe and the inspirational whimsy of flavors that daringly collide. You become the gourmet chef, or in the case of AI, the artist creating something beautiful and meaningful by managing those tantalizing intricacies. After all, whether your dish or your model brings joy or is just a one-time wonder, there's always the next meal or iteration to perfect! And guess what? You won't have to worry about gaining weight with knowledge; that's the beauty of wisdom: it's calorie-free!

The Future of Creativity: AI as a Collaborative Chef

The future is upon us, and it's sizzling! In a world where our culinary aspirations converge with the mind-boggling capabilities of artificial intelligence, we stand on the precipice of a culinary revolution, poised to welcome AI as our next collaborative chef. Yes, folks. I'm talking about a future where the sous-chef is a smart algorithm, listening intently as you ponder whether to add sage or rosemary to the roast chicken. Imagine the possibilities! Now, you might be rolling your eyes, thinking, "Is this the dystopia where AI decides our dinner?" Fear not! Instead, envision a scenario that's more delightful than an Italian grandmother handing you her pasta recipe.

Imagine stepping into your kitchen where an AI-powered device, let's call it ChefBot 3000, patiently awaits your culinary whims, equipped with a library of recipes and a personalized understanding of your taste preferences. It analyzes your past meals, dietary restrictions, and even mood (because let's face it, some days you simply need to drown your sorrows in a bowl of mac and cheese). This AI chef has the potential to revolutionize home cooking by collaborating with you, ensuring your complex palates are considered, all while offering suggestions that can up your culinary game by several notches. Goodbye, bland meals! Hello, gastronomic delight!

Alongside this exciting future comes the ability to use machine-learning-driven algorithms to create entirely new recipes from combinations of foods you've never thought of. Amidst the aroma of olive oil and spices, imagine tossing random ingredients onto the counter: leftover pine nuts, a rogue tomato, and maybe a mystery herb from that bizarre market you visited last summer. ChefBot 3000 observes this visually chaotic yet inspiring scene and, with a few precise algorithms, proposes an innovative dish that could very well be the next Pinterest sensation. "Tomato-Pine Nut Fusion Salad with a Hint of Mystery Herb," anyone?

Now, let's not forget the research behind this brilliance. AI's capability to simulate and predict tastes draws from a treasure trove of existing culinary data, not unlike how a seasoned chef extracts knowledge from years spent honing their craft. By analyzing food composition, historical data, and flavor pairings, AI brings a scientific approach to creativity. In a way, it acts as an ever-enthusiastic junior chef, suggesting ingredient combos that you, armed with only a faint recollection of flavors, might've overlooked, a soggy pizza crust no more!

But what if you yearn for that human element, the love, the laughter, the occasional anarchy that a kitchen like mine thrives on? Fret not, because AI is not here to replace the soul of human cooking; it's here to complement it! After all, if you think your grandmother's secret sauce recipe cannot be improved upon, you should rethink your position. ChefBot 3000 is your enthusiastic sous-chef, capable of amplifying creativity while allowing your whims to take the wheel. Just as talented chefs remain rooted in tradition while dauntlessly exploring the new, AI can enrich our culinary adventures by providing surprising suggestions, like infusing strawberry basil into your fresh summer dishes!

There's also the critical aspect of inclusivity, a vital ingredient for any future chef. AI can democratize great cooking by making gourmet recipes more accessible to all. Have dietary restrictions? ChefBot 3000 understands and can adapt recipes to accommodate food allergies and health issues, ensuring that no one is left behind. It brings people together through food, creating tailored culinary experiences that span cultures, preferences, and needs, all while showcasing how collaborative creativity can break boundaries. Food becomes the bridge that connects people and allows them to share their heritage, with AI acting as a trusty guide!

As we gaze into the future of collaborative culinary innovation, let's embrace the joy of working with AI, which breaks down the barriers to complexity. It allows us to blend the artistry of cooking with the analytical

prowess of machine learning. Together, we can savor delightful meals that tantalize our taste buds while exploring dish recommendations that vibrate with zingy excitement and unexpected surprises.

So here's to the future, folks! Raise your forks, tap your screens, or simply nod in agreement. A spectacular partnership lies ahead as AI joins the ranks of chefs and home cooks alike, a partnership destined to redefine how we create and enjoy food. Who knows, maybe one day we'll be ordering dinner from a Michelin-starred restaurant across dimensions, relying solely on our AI collaborators to recreate a version of heaven that resides among the cosmos. Until then, embracing the quirks, spices, and splashes of sauce is the key to a future filled with culinary joy! Buon Appetito to all, both human and AI!

Chapter 5

The Boiling Point: Training Models

The Heat of Training Algorithms: Finding the Right Temperature

Training machine learning algorithms is much like cooking pasta; there's a delicate balance involved, and a little too much heat can lead to a disastrous outcome. You want that sweet spot where the algorithm can learn and adapt without succumbing to the dreaded overcooked state. Picture this: you plop your pasta into boiling water, but instead of waiting for the perfect al dente bite, you walk away for just a minute too long. When you return, you find a mushy tangle of noodles that would make any Italian grandmother weep. In the realm of machine learning, the same principle applies. Too much heat, whether it's in the form of training iterations or the power of your model, can lead your algorithm to spoil its learning potential.

Finding the right ''temperature'' for training algorithms can be a tricky endeavor. Too little heat and you wouldn't even achieve a mediocre sauce; too much heat and you risk burning your neural net to cinders. It's not unlike cooking risotto, where constant stirring is required, except in this case, you're stirring parameters rather than arborio rice grains. The goal here is to identify the optimal learning rate, a parameter that governs how quickly your model adjusts its weights. Finding that right temperature means knowing when to crank up the heat to speed things along and when to dial it back to let the flavors, or, in this case, the data, marinate in their complexity.

Now, this is where the ''goldilocks" concept comes into play, not too hot, not too cold, but just right. If your learning rate is set too high, your model might overshoot the optimal solution, akin to that hapless chef who thinks a flambe is the solution for every dish (Spoiler alert: it's not!). On the opposite end, a learning rate that's too low can result in a model that takes an eternity to converge, dragging its virtual feet like a guest at an Italian family dinner who just can't say no to another plate of pasta. Patience is indeed a virtue, but in the world of algorithms, we want progress, not a never-ending sauce simmering on the stove.

This concept also involves the temperature of your training environment, namely, your data. If you throw in a batch of data that's as inconsistent as a poorly made lasagna, you're bound to get unsavory results. Just like a bay leaf won't redeem a poorly prepared sauce, neither will shiny new algorithmic features save a model fed with garbage in, garbage out. Train your model on clean, high-quality, and diverse datasets, and you'll not only adjust the heat but also elevate the dish's overall flavor profile.

As you crank the temperature, you'll need to adopt a keen sense of observation. You wouldn't just let your pasta boil away without a glance, no, that would be heresy! Similarly, while your algorithm is training, you should be monitoring its performance. Look at the evaluation metrics as you would to assess the consistency of your sauce. If it's nowhere near the desired thickness, adjustments may be necessary, such as tweaking hyperparameters or modifying the training dataset. This is where you get to be a chef and a scientist all at once, sizzling and bubbling under the learning curve of experimentation.

Before you serve up your model, it's vital to consider how things are put together. Each algorithm has its own nuances and particulars, meaning you'll need to understand the cooking times for each. Some models, like decision trees, might prefer a slow roast, while others, like neural networks, could benefit from a blast of high heat. Mastering the idiosyncrasies of your algorithmic dishes will lead to a well-rounded menu of results, one that's palatable to both engineers and non-expert enthusiasts, you know, like the uncle who knows just enough about cooking to weigh in on every family meal but wouldn't dare touch the pots himself.

In this culinary journey through machine learning, finding the right temperature isn't just about what you throw into the pot; it's about nurturing the entire process. Keep an eye on the noodles, snatch them from the boiling abyss before destruction lurks, and revel in the beauty of a well-cooked algorithm. After all, whether it's your lasagna or your neural net, perfection is often a matter of timing, observation, and just the right amount of heat. Remember: confidence in the kitchen and in machine learning helps lead to delicious outcomes, one bubbling pot at a time.

Iteration: Why Stirring is Key

When it comes to cooking, iterations are practically as essential as olive oil in Italian cuisine. Just like you wouldn't toss spaghetti into boiling water without stirring it occasionally, unless you're trying to audition for a horror movie where pasta becomes an unspeakable menace, neither should you allow your machine learning models to train without a little attention. Iteration is the act of revisiting your work, making adjustments, and refining each iteration until you reach a delicious final product. In machine learning, it's the sacred practice that transforms a raw algorithm into a Michelin-star-worthy piece of technological art.

Let's begin with an analogy from my childhood in Italy, where culinary trial-and-error was part of the deal; after all, nobody gets spaghetti carbonara right the first time, particularly if they forget to substitute bacon for guanciale. One of the first things I learned in the family kitchen was that once you toss those ingredients into the pot, you've got to stir. Otherwise, you might end up with half your pasta clinging to the pot like a particularly

needy ex. In ML (that's short for machine learning, not to be confused with the infamous 'MLA', the only thing less appetizing than a cold pasta is an unwelcome debate), this stirring takes form through iterative training processes. It keeps the models from becoming stuck in meaningless local minima, much like your pasta being stuck in a pot of despair rather than an al dente paradise.

Iterations are as much about the process of trial and error as they are about adjustments. After programming the initial model, it's time to sit back, taste the results, and if it's left wanting, try again! Just as a chef conducts a quality check after every stirring, machine learning engineers must monitor model performance metrics to tune their algorithms. Is it a tad too salty? Not flexible enough? Perhaps a sprinkle of hyperparameter tuning is in order to ensure that nothing gets overcooked. This consistent revisiting is what allows a model to learn, adjust, and adapt like a skilled amateur chef rapidly becoming a master.

Take, for instance, adjusting the learning rate, a fundamental hyperparameter that determines how quickly our model learns. Too fast, and it's like trying to saute fresh garlic; one moment too long, and you've got a smoking disaster on your hands. Too slow, and your model is like a doughy pizza crust that simply refuses to rise. What's crucial here is iterative experimentation: repeatedly testing and adjusting the learning rate, monitoring how well it performs, and refining as necessary. After all, unlike the long-gone days of cooking with an ancient recipe handed down through generations, this is the digital age! There's room for mistakes, and iteration allows us to embrace those errors as teaching moments rather than culinary catastrophes.

Now, let's not forget the importance of the tasting process in our iteration journey. Every good chef knows the golden rule: you've got to taste your food as you cook. It's an art form akin to the validation techniques applied in machine learning. When we evaluate our models, we're essentially tasting what we've cooked up, and if it's bland? Well, back to the spice cupboard! Iteration gives us the freedom to enhance sweetness, balance tanginess, and add those secret, magical ingredients that bring a dish, or a data process, to life. Think of cross-validation as)^our taste testers, making sure that what you serve up is worthy of repeating at every family gathering.

While it can feel tedious at times, much like repeatedly whisking a troublesome soufflé, iterative processes ultimately build depth and flavor in your models, much like how a good sauce is built layer by layer. Each loop through the training process allows a model to emerge with newfound insight, spotting patterns previously hidden like a secret stash of dessert at the back of the fridge. We collect knowledge along the way, and eventually, we find our dish bubbling with success.

Finally, just like in cooking, iteration is about finding joy in the process. We're not just churning out patterns and predictions; we're engaging in an ongoing culinary art form that will continue evolving. Each iteration is a reflection of our commitment to improvement and exploration. Cooking was never just about the plate on the table, it was also about the experiences around it. And similarly, machine learning should be about the excitement of discovery, the satisfaction of problem-solving, and an inevitable pinch of laughter along the way.

So, the next time you're faced with a perplexing model that refuses to budge, remember to add a little more iteration into the mix. Stir it up, taste frequently, and be prepared to adjust based on feedback. It's all part of the delicious dance between AI and pasta, an intricate recipe that takes time, finesse, and continual improvement to get just right. Bon appetit, or as we say in my family, "Mangi bene e provi di nuovo!" (Eat well and try again!) out there in the world of machine learning!

Overcoming the Burn: Addressing Bias and Variance

Let's face it, when it comes to cooking up a delectable dish or whipping up a machine learning model, no one wants to serve burnt offerings at the dinner table. Yet, here we find ourselves grappling with two notorious culprits that can char our culinary creations and our AI efforts alike: bias and variance. In the grand kitchen of machine learning, these two adversaries are like the warped tablecloths that threaten to make every temperamental plate wobble precariously. Fear not! I'm here to guide you through the charring flames of modeling errors, so you can relish the sweet taste of success.

Bias, as a concept, is akin to that overly simplistic recipe that promises a perfect lasagna but ends up being about as satisfying as a cup of lukewarm water. Bias refers to an error due to overly simplistic assumptions in the learning algorithm. Picture a chef who thinks boiling pasta is enough to make it delicious, but forgets to pair it with a rich marinara sauce. In the realm of machine learning, a model with high bias oversimplifies the dataset, misses essential patterns, and ultimately leaves you with a dish that lacks depth. It's like trying to eat cardboard and calling it pizza, hoping for a gourmet experience. The first rule in this battle against bias is to ensure that your model complexity is appropriately matched to the data you're working with. If your model is as rigid as a '90s sitcom, it's time to add some sitcom-worthy twists to the plot.

On the other side of the spectrum lies variance, which is equally troublesome, almost theatrical in its delicious chaos. This is the notorious drama queen of our kitchen chaos, overfitting to the data noise rather than focusing on the main ingredients. Variance is the uninvited guest who, instead of complementing your elegant four-course meal, insists on taking center stage and throwing a wild party with every errant data point. Remember when I mentioned that too much heat can ruin that beautifully al dente pasta? Well, too many takeout orders may leave you wondering how you ever thought that frozen pizza was a suitable dinner. Variance means your model is too complex, taking every little noise and rattling it into an opera performance of predictions that nearly rivals the chaos of your Aunt Maria's family gatherings.

So how do we overcome these culinary catastrophes? Much like balancing a delightful dish, we must strive for that sweet spot between bias and variance, an exquisite tightrope walk made all the more enjoyable with a hearty glass of Chianti in hand. In machine learning, this is known as the bias-variance tradeoff, where we aim to minimize both simultaneously. Ironically, achieving this balance can sometimes feel like trying to pull off an intricate dance while seeking precisely how much cheese to sprinkle on that baked ziti. Too much cheese? You risk losing the essential flavor. Too little cheese? Why even bother?

Using techniques like cross-validation can serve as your trusty taste testers, ensuring you get the right blend of bias and variance. Imagine lining up your data sets like you would for a beautiful antipasto platter; you want to sample each delightful section without overwhelming your palate with any one flavor. Cross-validation lets you train your model on different subsets of your data, ensuring it develops a deeper understanding from multiple angles without compromising its integrity. It's essentially the family recipe, improved over decades, allowing you to glean the best secrets from every iteration while avoiding burnt edges.

Moreover, simplify your models where possible. Just like a pasta dish adorned with one too many pretentious ingredients can distract from the essential flavors, overly complicated algorithms are often more harm than help. An overly intricate model can create interpretations that convolute rather than clarify, leaving your stakeholders confused and wondering if they accidentally entered a modern art gallery instead of the data kitchen. Keeping things simple and concise while ensuring the key flavors remain prominent is the way to go.

And of course, let's talk about data preprocessing, the unsung hero of this mischievous kitchen escapade. Cleaning and preparing your data before it hits the stove is crucial; you wouldn't saute vegetables before washing off the dirt, would you? Filtering irrelevant features is getting rid of burnt ends, and scaling your features ensures that all your ingredients come together blissfully. In this crazy culinary world of algorithms, we must be diligent in addressing the underlying issues that can lead to bias or variance.

In the end, overcoming bias and variance requires persistence and a touch of adventurous spirit. It's a delightful balancing act, one that may not always land you a Michelin star, but good pasta and AI could very well lead to a satisfying evening! So the next time you're simmering a bowl of machine learning, remember to stir those biases and variances just right.

Avoid the burns, maintain balance, taste often, and, most importantly, don't forget to enjoy the delicious nature of both learning models and well-cooked spaghetti! Buon appetito!

Taste Testing: Evaluating Training Progress

Taste testing, a practice sacred in the culinary arts and equally essential when it comes to evaluating training progress in machine learning. If you've ever spent a tranquil afternoon in a bustling Italian kitchen, you know that the heart and soul of any great dish lies in the moments you stop to take stock of what you've created. You don't just throw a roast in the oven and walk away with your hands behind your back. No way! You've got to be brave, right? Be curious! You need to taste, adjust, and, when necessary, toss that half-baked turkey out the window before anyone sees it, metaphorically speaking, of course.

In machine learning, we have our version of this taste-testing ritual, where every iteration gives us a chance to gauge the flavor of our algorithms and ensure they're on the right track. When training a model, the evaluation process is akin to sampling a pot of simmering sauce as it cooks. Each stir opens up specific flavors, and it's your job, as both chef and critic, to discern what's missing or what needs that delightful extra pinch of salt. The first thing to understand is that taste testing is a regular affair, not just a one-time event. Just like with a good bolognese, flavor develops over time, and so will your model's performance. But unlike their slow-cooked counterparts, our algorithms require much more immediate feedback to avoid sulking in the kitchen corner.

So, what are the ways we can evaluate our algorithm's ''taste"? The first step is to establish performance metrics, which act like your judging panel of culinary connoisseurs. Numbers don't lie (unlike that aunt who claims her meatballs are "secret family recipes"). Metrics like accuracy, precision, recall, and Fi score are the tasting spoons we use to gauge how well our model is performing. It's essential to understand that while high accuracy sounds impressive, like that gnocchi that melts in your mouth, it might not always be the best indicator of a model's effectiveness. The true flavor of a dish lies in the balance, and that should apply to our model's performance across various aspects. You wouldn't just toss flour into boiling water and call it a pasta dish, right? You'd want to elevate it, to create a symphony of tastes!

Next comes the challenge of validation samples, those illustrious moments where you test your model against new data, allowing it to truly shine or fall flat on its face. It's about gathering honest feedback from those taste testers who haven't been given a heads-up about what to expect. Ideally, this follows the train-validation-test split methodology, where a portion of the data helps your model learn, and the other portion serves as the ultimate taste test. Did it hold up? Did your food critic identify any undercooked bits, or worse, ingredients that were painfully stale? If your model is overfitting, it might perform like a chef who only knows how to make one dish spectacularly but can't adapt when it's time to mix things up.

But don't stop there! No chef worth their salt serves a dish without letting a few other souls taste it first. Enter your cross-validation techniques. It's like getting your extended family together for a family-style dinner where everyone has a right to weigh in. With techniques like k-fold cross-validation, you partition your ingredients into k sets and cook the same recipe iteratively to see which variation yields the tastiest results. A little practice goes a long way; you'll begin to know what combinations work best, like figuring out which herbs complement that classic marinara.

Now let's dive into error analysis, or as I like to call it, the moment where we put down the spaghetti fork and ask, "What the heck went wrong here?" Just as a good chef dissects why their soufflé collapsed, it's vital to investigate the misclassified samples your model churned out. This is your chance to restore harmony and identify patterns in errors, whether it's a data imbalance that results in undercooked spices or straight-up confusion, like mistaking sugar for salt in the pantry. By dissecting these failures, we can make adjustments that bring the overall flavor profile back in line with our expectations.

In this world of machine learning, it's easy to fall into the trap of believing that each of our models is a culinary masterpiece destined for Michelin stardom merely because we've trained it well. However, continual monitoring and evaluation are key. As the pasta cooks, keep an eye on the progress, taste it, and let that keyboard become your utensil of choice. The dish is never truly complete until you've gone through this iterative cycle of cooking, testing, seasoning, and figuring out what works and which garnishes to leave behind.

Ultimately, tasting processes are what give AI its human touch, guiding us toward delectable outcomes inviting enough to share publicly. So grab your metaphorical Chef's hat, and embrace the joy of evaluating those algorithms. Remember, just like in cooking, there are always flavors to discover, insights to uncover, and adjustments to be made, because the beauty of machine learning, my friends, is much like the beauty of a perfect pot of risotto: it's all about the journey, seasoning, and, most importantly, tasting as you go! Buon appetito, fellow data chefs!

Serving Up Success: Evaluating Model Outcomes

The moment we've all been waiting for, serving up success! Evaluating model outcomes is like the sensational crescendo in an opera, when the chef finally unveils the much-anticipated dish and the diners sit in suspense, forks poised for a culinary experience sure to be memorable. Just as the first bite of lasagna should transport you to a sun-drenched Italian vineyard, your machine learning model's outcomes must not only meet expectations but also enhance and astonish. The secret? A robust evaluation process that wraps around the final product like a well-timed embrace of flavors.

First things first, when it comes to evaluating model outcomes, it's essential to have clear metrics that define success. And, dear readers, I cannot stress this enough: setting the bar at a reasonable height is key. You wouldn't embark on a family road trip expecting to land in Venice by midday just because you filled the tank with gas! Similarly, evaluating your model should

involve realistic expectations based on the performance measures at your disposal. From accuracy to F1 scores to evaluate how well a classification model performs on a dataset, from precision to recall, each metric is like a seasoning in your final dish; when appropriately aligned, they come together to bring the best flavors to life.

Now, let's talk about the comparison between your model and the benchmarks, your "gold standard" for determining whether you're still stuck in the land of mediocrity or heading for gourmet acclaim. It's about finding your culinary inspiration, whether it be that one heavenly recipe passed down through generations or a few well-curated examples from peer-reviewed articles. Benchmarking against your competitors' outcomes is pivotal; are you delivering delightful surprises, or just standing there like a wilted basil leaf? Having that point of reference is crucial, as it gives you the information you need to appreciate your hard work or identify just how far you still have to go.

Confusion matrices! Oh, don't get me started on these delectable tools, akin to an exquisitely arranged charcuterie board where every savory ingredient has its rightful place, and each section reveals its secrets. A confusion matrix visualizes your model's performance, highlighting true positives, false positives, true negatives, and false negatives. It's the perfect opportunity to dissect where your model excels and where it might as well have been trying to bake a soufflé in a windstorm. If you see too many false negatives, it's a polite way of saying that your model is missing the mark. With a hearty laugh, you realize it's time to adjust the cooking temperatures and clarify your recipe.

But don't rest on your laurels! Once you've evaluated the model using these metrics, the real fun begins, interpretation! What do the outputs say about your algorithm? It's the moment you put on your best chef's hat, squint at the data, and unleash your inner food critic. Much like tasting a dish, interpreting model outcomes requires a blend of scientific rigor and gut feelings. This is where you can confidently proclaim: "Aha! This aspect works well, while that one could use a little more zest, perhaps a hint of chili flakes!" A good evaluator knows when it's time to whisk in additional ingredients or make adjustments to enhance flavor, and the same should apply when enhancing model predictions.

This evaluation process doesn't simply end with one round of taste testing. Just as a chef learns from every dinner service, you must remain vigilant in monitoring your model's performance over time. Keeping an eye on how your algorithm adapts to new data, just as you would when checking whether that beloved family recipe still holds up against modern dining expectations, ensures you're serving up relevance and accuracy to satisfy the ever-changing palate of users.

Lastly, let's not dismiss the role of collaboration, a critical ingredient in the great kitchen of machine learning! Solicit feedback from your team, treating it as a family gathering where everyone brings their favorite dish to share at the table. Engaging with the stakeholders, be they colleagues, users, or the mystical data elves who twiddle numbers in the ether, will provide you with a range of perspectives that can help refine your recipe. Acknowledge the many voices as they season your final model; you may gain insights that completely transform your understanding of what needs to be done.

Ultimately, serving up success is more than just clicking 'run' on your algorithm and reveling in the results that pop up like freshly baked garlic knots. It's about infusing your work with evaluation, interpretation, and ongoing improvement. Celebrate those juicy, satisfying predictions, and don't hesitate to sprinkle in a little humility as you identify the areas for future growth. Transformation is a conscious decision for both the culinary master and the data scientist, so dive straight into this appetizing world and savor each moment. Bon appetit on this thrilling journey of serving up that machine-learning success, one delightful model outcome at a time!

Chapter 6

Tasting as You Go: Validation Techniques

The Importance of Continuous Feedback

When it comes to cooking, every chef knows that feedback is as essential as salt; too little can leave your dish bland, while too much can lead to a sodium catastrophe. It's the same in the world of machine learning; continuous feedback is like that trusty spoon you keep on hand to taste your sauce. You wouldn't dream of serving up a half-baked dish without sampling it first, right? Similarly, in AI, if you don't evaluate and adjust based on ongoing feedback, you might end up with a model that's about as useful as a fork in a soup kitchen.

Let's take a moment to visualize this. Imagine you're making lasagna, the piece de resistance of Italian meals (and by 'Italian meals' I mean anything not involving pineapple on pizza). You've layered noodles, sauce, cheese, and perhaps a questionable amount of love. But before you pop this masterpiece into the oven, you take a moment, yes, I said *a moment*, to taste the sauce. Why? Because every good dish demands that crucial taste test along the way, a ritual as sacred among cooks as finding the end of the pasta roll is to the Heimlich Maneuver.

In machine learning, the process is no different. You train your model, running algorithms and feeding it data, but without continuous feedback, it's like trying to serve lasagna while it's still in the freezer. You need to know what's working and what's heading south faster than a soufflé in a thunderstorm. This iterative process requires you to taste your AI's output, be it predictions, classifications, or whatever culinary analogy you choose, to ensure it meets expectations. If your model isn't performing well, do you really want to serve it up at the table? I didn't think so.

Now, imagine you run a pizzeria and are experimenting with a new type of crust. After the first batch, you invite everyone from your grandmother to the guy selling fresh basil on the corner to get their two cents. "Does it have that perfect crunch? Is it thin enough? What do you mean it tastes like cardboard?" These are vital pieces of information! In AI, user feedback works in a similar vein; it helps you understand how your model is perceived in the wild. Perhaps the customers (i.e., users) think the slices are too thick or too thin, and adjusting based on their feedback not only improves your pizza but also makes you the Michelangelo of the machine learning realm.

This brings me to the concept of overfitting, a common and hilarious trap that even expert data scientists fall into! Overfitting is when your model learns the training data so well that it can't generalize to new, unseen data, that's like me trying to serve lasagna made exclusively with my grandma's secret recipe but forgetting that my guests have distinct tastes. Just because I love anchovies in everything doesn't mean everyone else does. Continuous feedback helps combat overfitting by pointing out the oddities in your dish. Maybe the data is telling you that, yes, your model is fabulous when trained on old data, but falls flat on its face like a chef attempting a soufflé at altitude. You need spaces for iteration, where feedback serves as your alembic, distilling only the finest features from the data cauldron.

The importance of continuous feedback doesn't stop at just improving performance. It fosters innovation, too! Imagine every cook who ever dared to change a traditional recipe and faced the wrath of traditionalists, think of them as the 'Pasta Purists'. Those who adapt based on what people love have a greater chance of creating culinary magic. In AI, this innovative spirit can lead to groundbreaking features, better algorithms, and ultimately, a model that just gets better, like a good pecorino left to age.

So next time you drop a fresh batch of spaghetti into boiling water, remember the parallel: continuous feedback isn't just a nice-to-have ingredient; it's a critical component that determines whether your machine learning model is a triumphant bowl of pasta primavera or a soupy disappointment that even your cat wouldn't touch. People, the diners, the users, are your ultimate judges, and feedback is the golden ticket to making that model a five-star experience! Bon appetit, and may your algorithms be ever in your flavor!

Analogies to Culinary Tasting Techniques

The exhilarating world of culinary tasting techniques, a territory where my inner food critic meets my inner data scientist! As I stand in the kitchen, wooden spoon in one hand and a glass of wine in the other (for research purposes, of course), it strikes me how similar the tasting process is to evaluating a machine learning model. Just as with adjusting a recipe, checking your AI's performance can require a delicate touch, an adventurous palate, and sometimes a whole lot of trial and error.

Let's dive into this delectable analogy. Picture yourself concocting a new risotto recipe. As the rice simmers, you can't help but dip your wooden spoon into the pot for a taste now and then. This is critical: one little taste test can tell you whether your dish needs more salt, an extra splash of white wine, or perhaps a whole new approach involving giant meatballs. Each taste is like running validation checks on a machine learning model; you're continuously assessing how it measures up to your culinary vision. Likewise, in AI, you regularly evaluate your model's predictions against real-world data. Tasting a dish is your way of learning if it lives up to the mouthwatering culinary journey you had in mind.

During this tasting escapade, we'll want to remember that tasting isn't just a formality; it's a celebration of flavors. You can't just ladle a spoonful of sauce directly from the pot into your mouth. No, no! That's the equivalent of blindly feeding your model data without understanding what you're feeding it! Instead, you must employ technique, swirling the sauce around your tongue, experiencing its flavor profile, and noting how the seasonings develop with each cycle through the taste buds. In machine learning, this meticulous approach echoes the process of evaluating model performance metrics, where you're assessing everything from accuracy to recall and F1 scores to evaluate how well a classification model performs on a dataset. Just as no one wants a risotto that tastes like wall paint, no one wants an AI that's about as useful as a weather app during a blizzard.

Now, let's talk about the critical concept of balance. As any seasoned chef will tell you, great dishes are a harmonious blend of flavors: salty, savory, tangy, and sweet. To achieve this delicate balance, you taste as you cook. Similarly, machine learning models thrive on balance: between bias and variance, between features and labels, and between overfitting and underfitting. When I prepare my famous carbonara (which, if you haven't tried, you're clearly missing out on a masterpiece), balance is essential, just as it is when tuning the parameters of your algorithm. One tablespoon too much cheese, and my pasta becomes a gooey disaster, akin to an AI model becoming overly complex when a simple solution would suffice.

That brings us to the value of ambiance, yes, ambiance! Imagine you've prepared a sumptuous feast, and as you taste, you notice it lacks a little flair. Perhaps it needs a squeeze of lemon to brighten the flavors, just like how an unexpected user insight can bring your AI model to life! Every chef knows that the joy of cooking isn't just about the sustenance; it's about the excitement and surprise, much like how a well-placed feature can surprise you by boosting your model's performance dramatically. The best recipes often include an element of spontaneity; sometimes it's that sprig of fresh basil that not only elevates your dish but redefines it. Similarly, integrating user feedback into your model can provide new dimensions you never anticipated.

Let's not forget about timing, the unseen but critical factor that determines whether your dish ends up being divine or a culinary catastrophe. With risotto, that perfect creaminess comes with patience, with each ladle-full of broth stirred in at just the right moment. In AI, the timing of feedback, whether in batch intervals or real-time adjustments, can profoundly influence the model's adaptability and accuracy, allowing it to reach peak performance like a perfectly creamy risotto. Timing is everything, my friends!

So, the next time you're whipping up a culinary masterpiece or refining a machine learning model, remember: tasting is not just a formality; it's both an art and a science. It's the theme song that plays in the background of your cooking adventures and your data adventures, reminding you to adjust, balance, and innovate. Whether you're tasting sauces or evaluating algorithms, take note of those complex layers of flavors and insights. Here's to the delightful journey of culinary and AI exploration, both of which, when done right, can make even your grandmother's lasagna seem like yesterday's leftovers!

Techniques for Effective Model Validation

Model validation, the proverbial taste test of the machine learning realm! If cooking were a competitive sport, model validation would be the judge holding up scorecards, ensuring that your dish not only looks phenomenal but also tastes fantastic. When I think of the thrill of validation, I can't help but draw parallels to my culinary escapades. Each time I whip up a new batch of pesto or, for the more adventurous souls, a truffle-infused mac and cheese. I'm not just throwing ingredients into a pot. No, I'm validating the flavors, testing the outcomes, and ultimately ensuring that what I serve will not only delight but inspire applause, just as our models should do within their respective domains.

To embark on a successful model validation journey, we first need to clarify our ingredients, our data. Just like a cook needs fresh basil, ripe tomatoes, or perhaps mysteriously abundant zucchini from a neighbor's garden to ace a dish, model validation begins with the right data split. We start by partitioning our dataset, usually into training, validation, and test sets. Think of the training set as your recipe's main ingredients; it's the foundational layer upon which all things tasty will sit. Your validation set? That's like your trusty sous-chef, helping you taste and fine-tune as you go. Finally, the test set is your "reveal" moment, where you confidently present your culinary masterpiece to guests, hoping everyone can scarf it down without realizing you forgot to add salt.

One technique that I find particularly useful for model validation is cross-validation. It's like putting your pasta to the test in several boiling pots at once! Traditional validation can sometimes feel as risky as diving into a deep fryer without a basket. Do you really want to find out your model can only perform well in one scenario? Cross-validation helps by repeatedly training and testing your model on different small portions of data. It's akin to inviting a group of discerning food critics to taste your latest creation and letting them give you feedback on various aspects. The more reviews you receive, the better! And if one critic thinks your tiramisu is too soggy, you'll know to swap out that rogue espresso for an insider-approved alternative.

Then there's the heartwarming concept of confusion matrices. Now, you may ask, "What on earth does a matrix have to do with pasta?" Well, my friend, a confusion matrix is your best friend when evaluating classification models! Imagine serving two different pasta dishes at an upscale restaurant and bewildering your customers by mixing up spaghetti and fettuccine on their plates. A confusion matrix helps visualize your model's performance, breaking down its true positives, false positives, true negatives, and false negatives. It's a bit like a snapshot of your table setting: are they served the right dish, or did someone accidentally garnish spaghetti with dessert sauce? It helps you identify where things went wrong and ensures that next time, everyone's dinner arrives at the table exactly as intended.

Of course, my love for culinary techniques wouldn't be complete without mentioning the importance of metrics. What's a good dish without proper plating? Likewise, what's a well-tuned model without relevant evaluation metrics? Precision and recall might sound like terms from an Italian opera, but trust me, they're vital in knowing whether your model meets the grade. Precision measures how many selected items were relevant, think of it as your beautiful, tantalizing soufflé that never deflates! Recall tells you how many relevant items were selected, like getting every last piece of sauce absorbed into those gnocchi. The real magic happens when you achieve the perfect balance between precision and recall, culminating in metrics that sing sweet symphonies of success.

And oh, let's not overlook the importance of user feedback! Picture a bustling Italian bistro where patrons share their thoughts on the mouth-puckering acidity of the limoncello, it can make or break your dining experience! Incorporating user feedback into validation provides broader insights, such as understanding which flavors resonate with your customers or identifying a seasoning that consistently raises eyebrows. This feedback loop is like a secret blend of spices, known only to you, that transforms a standard dish into something memorable.

So here's my call to action: whether you're simmering a sauce or fine-tuning a machine learning model, remember that validation is not just a one-time effort. It's an ongoing process, a culinary journey that requires open-mindedness, creativity, and the patience to experiment. With the right techniques, your models will dazzle clients and guests alike, just as my infamous eggplant parmesan brings joy with every cheesy bite. Bon appetit and model validation on!

Dealing with Overfitting: A Culinary Disaster

Overfitting, the Gordon Ramsay of the machine learning world! You thought you could elegantly craft a model ready to impress, only to realize it's as stubborn as a three-star Michelin chef refusing to adapt his signature dish. In both the culinary arts and machine learning, overfitting can lead

to disastrous outcomes, and trust me, neither of them will earn you a coveted nod from the food gods or make you the toast of Silicon Valley. It's like blending so many flavors together that the dish ends up tasting like a culinary crime scene; instead of sophistication, you land yourself in the realm of confusion and horror.

Overfitting is essentially the culinary equivalent of making a chili so complex that it requires a Ph.D. from Gastronomy University just to comprehend what went into it. You start with a basic bean base and think, "Hey, maybe some cumin, garlic, jalapenos," and before you know it, you've added saffron, chocolate, and twelve different types of chili peppers. Why? Because you think, "Why not?" Forgetting, my dear friends, that less is often more. Suddenly, your chili takes on the qualities of a villain from a cheesy action movie: complicated, overwhelming, and just waiting for someone to call in the culinary SWAT team to defuse the situation.

In machine learning, overfitting rears its ugly head when a model learns your training data so well that it fails to generalize to new, unseen data. Picture this scenario: you're training a model to categorize pasta types based on features such as sauciness, noodle thickness, and craving level. It becomes so fixated on the training examples that it memorizes every little detail, to the point that it struggles to identify a simple fettuccine amid a sea of lasagna layers. It's as if I'm so obsessed with crafting the ultimate focaccia with every exotic topping available that I completely forget the basics, and I either leave out the salt or throw in way too much.

So, how do we confront this culinary calamity? It all begins with the size of your dataset, like deciding whether to make an elegant dinner for two or a potluck extravaganza for fifty. Smaller datasets can lead to overfitting faster than you can say "lasagna with a side of existential crisis." To combat this, you want to ensure you have enough examples to give your model a well-rounded understanding without turning it into a paranoid overthinker. It's not unlike ensuring that your mom's lasagna recipe includes multiple test versions so that the cheese-to-sauce ratio is just right.

Enter regularization, this is where we apply a little culinary wisdom to prevent our model from forgetting its roots. In cooking terms, think of it as a mindful cook who prevents a sauce from boiling over by maintaining a watchful eye and occasionally adjusting the heat. Regularization techniques help in keeping models from becoming too complex. For instance, dropout is like saying, "Let's not use every ingredient this time; let's simplify." With dropout, you randomly exclude certain nodes from neural networks during training, helping all relevant flavors shine without overwhelming our palates. The next time you're tempted to toss in that fifth zest of lime, remember how just one can highlight your dish's essence!

Also, let's talk about one of my favorite gates to the culinary world: cross-validation. In my kitchen, cross-validation is akin to inviting a slew of friends over for cooking night. I get them to try my latest pesto concoction and provide honest feedback. "Too much garlic, John!" one might exclaim. This episodic help can save a dish from being so overly garlic-infused that it stuns unsuspecting guests like a rogue magician pulling a rabbit out of a hat. In the world of machine learning, it helps you gather insights from multiple validations, thus calibrating your model without lead weights dragging you down.

Ultimately, the key to preventing overfitting, whether you're whipping up an exquisite coq au vin or an intricate machine learning model, is to embrace simplicity. When experimenting, tap into your inner chef philosophers! When developing your next AI concoction, remember that elegant solutions stem from reducing flavors rather than complicating them. If you're thinking of scaling new culinary heights, or machine learning ones, it's crucial to pivot back to fundamentals. There's beauty in a simple, clean classic sauce, much like there is genius in a model that effectively balances complexity with generalization.

As you venture into the exciting yet treacherous waters of both cooking and machine learning, remember: overfitting can turn your culinary magic into an epic disaster. Keep things in check, maintain your flavors, and always ensure your guests leave your dining experience wishing they could have taken home seconds, because when it comes to pasta or algorithms, nobody should ever feel overstuffed!

The Role of User Feedback in AI Validation

User feedback, a powerful ingredient that can elevate your machine learning model from a bland concoction to a five-star Michelin masterpiece quicker than you can say "pasta al dente!" You see, my friends, it's one thing to build a snazzy AI model in a pristine lab, tinkering away in isolation, but another to unveil it to the wild world filled with eager, often unpredictable users. User feedback is like accepting a secret ingredient challenge on a cooking show. You think you've nailed your recipe, only to find out that it needs a splash of whimsy to truly shine, and that whimsy often comes straight from the dining table!

Picture this: you've diligently designed a predictive model that evaluates which type of pasta pairs best with various sauces. You're convinced you've cracked the code, "Fusilli goes with everything!" you proclaim. But when you release the model into the wild, what do you hear? "Fusilli with Alfredo, you say?! In this house? Never!" User feedback is the culinary sage that helps you grasp the realities of taste: people will surprise you, and what seems evident in theory can turn into a heated debate around the dinner table. Suddenly, your precious model runs headlong into the metaphorical wall of human expectation.

At its core, user feedback acts as the thermometer in your kitchen, letting you know whether your dish is simmering just right or reaching that precarious boiling point where chaos ensues! Incorporating feedback lets you assess your model's temperature, identify any discomfort, and make necessary adjustments. You could compare the model's initial predictions to the user's expectations and discover, much to your chagrin, that they expected tortellini rather than ravioli! Thus, user feedback shines the spotlight on what flavors really matter to your audience, guiding you to refine, season, and test again, because nobody likes a meal served cold!

So, what's an aspiring maestro to do? The key is to foster an ongoing dialogue between your AI model and its users. Much like cooking with seasoned chefs, you'll be gleaning wisdom from those who, every day, ask the burning question, "Should we drizzle balsamic over this, or stick to classic olive oil?" Stakeholders and end-users become your audience, providing a feedback buffet that helps shape your model's offerings, insight by delicious insight. They reflect not only preferences but also contextual nuances; a sprinkle of this or a dash of that can mean the difference between a jaw-dropping creation and disappointment.

But let's not kid ourselves; sifting through user feedback can occasionally feel like navigating a finely filtered cheese grater. Not all feedback is created equal! Is Aunt Gertrude's suggestion of adding pineapple to every dish valid, or a subtle way of expressing her unremarkable culinary misadventures? It's essential to cut through the noise. Focus your energies on constructive criticism that aligns with your model's core objectives. Noise can, of course, be overwhelming. Maybe half of your feedback boils down to people wanting a gluten-free pasta that tastes just as good as the wheat version! Be discerning with your ears wide open; sort through the gems and toss the smelly bits.

Often, with a bit of persistence, you'll notice themes emerge, a shared understanding of what works, what's more "eh," and what deserves place of honor in your AI kitchen. This iterative process, fueled by ongoing user input, is how we refine our models. It's akin to sharpening your best chef s knife: initially, you encourage every perspective while maintaining your own vision, but with each round of feedback, you strategically trim away the extraneous. Your dish, and by extension your model, emerges from the trial-tested and taste-approved!

But this is just the beginning. Celebrated chefs know they can take it a step further. Not only do they listen, but they engage! Why not host a feedback dinner where your users delve into delightful culinary experiences designed by your model? They can charm you with their opinions while sampling your latest creations, embodying the dynamic of active user engagement. Perhaps your restaurant will be graced by critics, like an elegant end-user summit showcasing your AI's culinary potential.

In a world where user feedback reigns supreme, it's crucial to remember that behind every data point lies a human desire to connect, taste, and share. User feedback should feel less like an obligation and more like a vibrant dialogue, lasting beyond the kitchen's opening night. If you can embrace it, listen, and adapt your model accordingly, you'll transform an ordinary dish, or an AI model, into a succulent, gold-star experience that everyone will clamor to enjoy. After all, cooking is about connection, and perhaps even more so, AI thrives when it knows the diners' preferences and cravings! So, my friends, let's celebrate user feedback as the culinary critic, cheering us on from the sidelines and guiding us toward gastronomic excellence!

Chapter 7

Layering Flavors: Ensemble Methods

Understanding Ensemble Learning

Ensemble learning is a concept that, much like the four seasons of Italian cuisine, thrives on variety and balance. Picture a family gathering for Sunday dinner; everyone brings their own dish, and together, they create an unforgettable feast. In the realm of machine learning, ensemble learning works in much the same way by combining multiple models to improve accuracy, performance, and generalization. But don't worry! I promise this won't turn into a culinary disaster where Aunt Maria accidentally brings her infamous "mystery meat casserole" - that's a fate I wouldn't wish upon anyone.

At its core, ensemble learning merges the strengths of several individual models, effectively creating a robust collective. Think of it as assembling a superstar band on a Saturday night; each musician brings their quirks, talents, and eccentricities to the stage. Individually, they may be great, but together, they create a symphony that can move mountains (or at least make you want to dance like no one's watching - especially if you've had one

too many glasses of Chianti). This collaborative spirit leads to improved accuracy; another's brilliance can outweigh one model's blunders. So if one guitar player forgets the chord, the rest of the group can still jam along, resulting in delightful melodies instead of a cacophony that resembles a cat fight.

A common analogy to illustrate ensemble learning is the "wisdom of the crowd." Just as people tend to make better decisions when drawing on pooled opinions and perspectives, machine learning models can benefit from the collective knowledge of individual algorithms. For example, if you ask a group of people to guess how many jelly beans are in a jar, you'll likely find that the average of their guesses is closer to the actual number than any single guess. You may have that one friend who insists he can guess the exact number because he had a jelly bean for breakfast. Spoiler alert - he's wrong. Ensemble learning leverages this principle, where multiple algorithms, often with different strengths and weaknesses, are combined to enhance predictive performance.

Now, let's delve deeper into the various types of ensemble methods. There are mainly two classes: bagging and boosting. Bagging, short for bootstrap aggregating, is like preparing multiple pots of sauce at once. You take your base ingredients, like tomatoes, garlic, and basil, and make a separate batch in each pot, then mix-and-match for the best outcome. It reduces variance, or that pesky overfitting problem, by helping the model become more robust. If one pot accidentally splatters sauce on the floor (hey, we've all been there!), you still have a few perfect sauces left to work with. Random Forest classifiers, for instance, employ this technique by creating a multitude of decision trees and averaging their predictions to produce a final output.

On the other hand, boosting builds one model on top of another, like layers of lasagna. You start with your bottom layer of pasta, and then each subsequent layer is filled with carefully selected ingredients that enhance the flavor and add complexity (hear that, Chef Ramsey?). Boosting techniques, such as AdaBoost and Gradient Boosting Machines, sequentially build models, focusing on the data points that previous models struggled to predict correctly. The goal is to reduce both bias and variance, and it might just result in the most heavenly lasagna ever tasted.

While ensemble learning has its benefits, it also comes with a spice of its own - increased computational complexity. It's as if you were preparing a grand feast for 40 guests and found yourself buried under a mountain of dirty dishes and pots, questioning your life choices (and your sanity!). Multiple models mean more calculations, more resources, and, unfortunately, more headaches. However, when done right, the outcome usually outweighs the cost, resulting in impressive predictive capabilities and a machine learning model that can handle the complexities of the world.

So the next time you're contemplating how to tackle a challenging dataset or wondering why your prediction model appears unbalanced (like a two-cheese pizza with only one side loaded), consider that ensemble learning can be your ticket to culinary (and analytical) bliss. By understanding the collaborative spirit inherent to ensemble methods, you can whip up a delightful combination of insights as rich and varied as Italy's flavors. And remember, sometimes the best results come from bringing together those differing flavors, just as we do when we gather around the family table for good food, laughter, and a healthy dose of chaos. Buon appetito!

The Power of Combining Models

In the grand kitchen of machine learning, combining models is akin to crafting a multi-course Italian meal that leaves your guests ecstatic and slightly confused about how many calories they've just consumed. You start with the antipasto of basic models, simple linear regression, decision trees, maybe a side of naive Bayes, and before you know it, you end up serving something that resembles a culinary extravaganza worthy of a Michelin star. The power of combining models lies in the ability to leverage diversity, much like putting together a ragtag band of family members for an epic cooking competition on a Sunday afternoon.

Let's face it; no one wants to watch a single ingredient take center stage at a feast. An entire evening of just plain spaghetti could lead to avoiding future family gatherings if there's no sauce in sight. Similarly, individual models possess their specific strengths and weaknesses; by combining them, we can celebrate the strengths while minimizing the weaknesses. It's like inviting Grandma to teach everyone how to make her famous walnut sauce while Uncle Guido tries to burn his pizza in the oven, a combination of talent and, well, chaotic charm.

Combining models fosters a level of robustness that is not easily achieved through standalone approaches. Consider, for example, the famous Italian dessert, tiramisu. What makes it so devilishly delightful? It's that tantalizing blend of espresso, cocoa, ladyfingers, and mascarpone cheese. Each element contributes to the final dish's flavor profile, building layers of rich complexity that elevate it from bland to spectacular. In the same way, merging various models, be it through bagging, boosting, or stacking, creates a final prediction that benefits from the strengths of its constituent parts. A decision tree's ability to classify can be bolstered by the probability distribution from a naive Bayes classifier, resulting in a fusion of insights that is far superior to either one standing alone.

Now, let's take a moment to talk about how this all works in practice, or at least, in the chaos of my kitchen experiments. When I decided to combine models for a project, it felt like hosting a family reunion. Everyone's invited, and everyone has their strengths. However, this venture could also lead to gastronomic havoc if not done thoughtfully. The key is finding the right blend, where models complement each other like warm bread and marinara, instead of clashing like Aunt Rosa and Cousin Tony over who makes the best sauce. It's a delicate dance of ensuring that each model's predictions mesh with the others and honing in on their unique advantages to create a harmonious outcome.

One of the more notable benefits of combining models is that it reduces overfitting, a problem that feels painfully familiar to anyone baffled by a relative's insistence that apple pie is an acceptable breakfast. Overfitting occurs when a model learns the training data too well, including its noise and outliers, making it less effective with new data (or 'guests'). However, when models are treated as a council of wise chefs, each with its own opinion on the dish being prepared, the outcome becomes a balanced affair. The individual quirks and blunders of one model are counteracted by the more refined suggestions of another, resulting in a final prediction that generalizes significantly better in the real world.

Let's not forget the amusing fact that the combination process can feel like an episode of a cooking reality show, complete with drama and suspense. Consider a boosting algorithm, for example: it's like competing under the watchful eye of celebrity chefs as they critique your every move. With each iteration, your initial model is, quite literally, "boosted" into shape, adjusting its approach based on the errors of previous attempts. Before you know it, you've gone from something resembling an unseasoned vegetable medley to a nuanced vegetable risotto that has your guests singing your praises, or at least not running away in horror.

But, be forewarned, there can be challenges. The combination of models can lead to increased complexity and difficulty in interpreting the fantastic fusion of flavors (I mean, isn't that why we avoid cooking for large groups?). The more models you add, the trickier the dish can become to handle. Like introducing a complicated dessert into the mix, one you've never attempted before, all you need is a slight miscalculation, and you end up with a boiling mess. And don't even get me started on hyperparameters; tuning them for each model is akin to trying to find just the right balance of salt in your dad's spaghetti sauce, an age-old debate that can ignite family feuds!

Ultimately, the power of combining models in machine learning reflects the spirit of Italian cuisine: it's about finding that delightful balance, where the whole becomes greater than the sum of the parts. By inviting different models to the table, we open up a world of possibilities, transforming our predictions from bland to bombastic, while keeping things flavorful and enticing. So grab your spatula, roll up your sleeves, and get ready to mix, mash, and merge your way to success, because in the kitchen of machine learning, the best results always come when we learn to collaborate together. Bon appetit!

Analogies to Layering Flavors

Layering flavors in cooking is much like orchestrating a well-timed performance in machine learning, where every ingredient has its moment on stage. Imagine preparing a classic lasagna, each layer, whether it's rich, gooey bechamel, robust marinara, or a gooey blend of cheeses, contributes to the final dish in a magical way. In the same way, machine learning models can be combined, layered, and refined to extract the most delicious insights from a dataset. The art of layering, whether it be sauce upon noodles or algorithms upon one another, can lead to a culinary symphony that dazzles the palate and the mind.

To start, let's talk about how each ingredient adds a unique flavor to the mix. In culinary lingo, think about the contrast between sweet and savory; the brightness of herbs against the depth of roasted vegetables. In machine learning, each model has its own strengths, weaknesses, and eccentricities, akin to a chef's assortment of spices and seasonings. You wouldn't toss a whole jar of pepper into a delicate panna cotta, and likewise, you need to be judicious with which models you stack and how you arrange them. Incorrect layering can lead to disaster, sending you down a rabbit hole of debugging that, I assure you, is harder to navigate than my mom's recipe book, the one where every ingredient is written in her rapidly fading handwriting and features vague instructions like, "Add a pinch of love."

When it comes to creating that perfect dish, layering involves not just the careful application of ingredients but also the timing of when to add each one. For instance, adding a sprinkle of salt right before serving will dramatically alter the final taste compared to mixing it into the base sauce hours prior. In machine learning, it's similar to introducing a model at the right stage of the development process. You may start with robust linear regression, then slap on a decision tree to divide your data into categories, and toss in a neural network on the last layer for that extra-creamy finish. It's a careful ballet of timing, precision, and maybe just a sprinkle of luck, because let's be honest, sometimes, even the best-laid plans can result in culinary chaos.

Now, let's not forget about the importance of balance in layering. If a lasagna is too cheesy, your guests may find themselves in a mozzarella-induced coma, while the absence of flavor could lead them to stare at their plates as if they were engaged in an existential crisis. Similarly, a machine learning model that combines too many algorithms without thoughtful consideration can result in radical overfitting or underfitting, two scenarios that tend to rock the proverbial boat in the classroom and beyond. Just as you would taste-test your sauce as you layer those flavors, adjusting along the way, so too must you evaluate model performances and calibrate parameters to achieve that delicate equilibrium.

What's delightful about the layering process is its potential for creative expression. You can adjust the amounts, swap ingredients, or even experiment with techniques, and the result will still feel like your own signature dish. Think of it like programming: you can play around with ensemble methods, new algorithms, and hyperparameter tuning, tuning each 'layer' to reflect your unique approach to the problem at hand. Like the chef who decides a hint of nutmeg will elevate a classic risotto, I encourage my students to think outside the box. After all, sometimes a bold mash-up can yield an utterly exquisite flavor combination, or at the very least, a conversation starter at dinner parties!

Of course, don't underestimate the aesthetic side of layering. The presentation of a layered dish can be just as crucial as its flavors. Just like a well-structured algorithm needs to be interpretable, a good looking lasagna demands to be both photographed and devoured. Layering not only impacts taste but visuals, which is something I often remind students when discussing the importance of data visualization. Think of it as laying out your ingredients in a way that even your grandma would be proud of it on a Sunday dinner table, where every layer peeks through begging for attention, just like that captivating plot waiting to showcase how your model is performing.

In conclusion, mastering the art of layering flavors in cooking can illuminate the way for combining algorithms in machine learning. Each model, much like its culinary counterpart, adds depth, balance, and richness to our understanding of the data. So the next time you find yourself in the kitchen (or the coding realm), remember: the secret to success lies in the thoughtful layering of flavors, whether you're tasting a delicious dish or balancing the strengths of multiple models in pursuit of the perfect prediction. And let's face it, sometimes it takes a bit of a mess to create something extraordinary. Now, who's ready for seconds? Buon appetito!

Aggregation Methods: A Recipe for Success

When it comes to combining multiple flavors in cooking, the magic often lies in the art of aggregation. Just as you might blend together various ingredients to whip up a sumptuous sauce, aggregation methods in machine learning create a dish of predictions that is infinitely richer than the sum of its parts. We're talking about a veritable buffet of analytical delights, where every model brings its own special touch to the table in perfect harmony. So grab your whisk, because it's time for me to serve you a hefty helping of aggregation methods, a recipe for success that could make even Nonna proud.

Imagine standing over a vast array of sauces, creme brulees, and gelatos, all vying for your attention. In machine learning, we face a similar cacophony of options when collating multiple predictions. We can go for averaging, voting, or even some fancy mathematical wizardry, each offering its own twists and turns. Voting is like gathering a jury of culinary experts to decide whether pineapple belongs on pizza: everyone adds their opinion, and the majority rules! In this case, you're blending predictions from several models to arrive at a final conclusion. If the majority says pineapple's a no-go, you probably should think twice before pulling out the chef's knife.

But aggregation methods aren't just about counting heads or going with the crowd. Consider the sumptuous world of averaging, a method that takes predictions from various models, gives them a gentle nudge, and sends them to the finish line as a collective bonanza. Just as good chefs often taste their sauces to strike the right flavor balance before plating, average predictions keep things grounded. The beauty of averaging is that it minimizes the impact of outliers that can skew results; just like tossing in a rogue olive that can ruin a perfectly good tapenade, we want to kick those outliers to the sidelines. So if one model goes berserk and passionately insists that the dinner requires 500 cloves of garlic (hey, we all have our quirks), averaging pulls back on that chaos and calmly suggests a more reasonable approach.

If you feel like jazzing it up a bit, you might turn to weighted aggregation methods, which act like the chef who has mastered the delicate art of seasoning. Here, each contributing model is given its due credit based on accuracy, and the final prediction is a combination where better-performing models have more influence. It's like awarding extra herbs and spices to a dish based on how well each ingredient cooked in the previous rounds. Did you know that the chef behind that heavenly rabbit ragu has a secret stash of saffron that requires special handling? For those delicate nuances that might hit differently on the palate, weighted aggregation lovingly lifts the best models to the limelight.

Another method that often garners attention in the realm of aggregation is stacking. This strategy is akin to the grand finale of an elaborate cooking show, where each dish contributes to a final masterpiece. In stacking, we build a meta-model on top of base models, capturing insights from their respective predictions. It's like creating a towering cake adorned with layers and flavors all destined to amaze, not forget that time I tried to impress my family with an eight-layer tiramisu. Spoiler alert: the layers collapsed under the weight of expectation. Nevertheless, stacking allows us to harness the hidden potential of our various models, layering them like a scrumptious meal as we aim for those softer, richer flavors in cooked pasta.

Let's not dismiss the challenges that come with aggregation methods. They can be complex, much like preparing an ambitious recipe during a family dinner, think of Aunt Rosa stirring a bubbling pot of sauce while trying to manage her three overly opinionated children. The overhead in terms of computation and the struggle to understand why a model didn't perform as expected can leave you scratching your head (or pulling your hair out). Fortunately, redundancy is a friend here. Aggregation methods have certain weaknesses, but their collective expertise often positions us well against unexpected uncertainty, like serving a balanced antipasti plate that makes even picky eaters feel satisfied.

Ultimately, aggregation methods are invaluable recipes for both culinary success and machine learning brilliance. When you pull together multiple models, mixing different predictions, you create something far more delectable than any single ingredient could inspire. So whether you're shouting, ''Mama mia!" over a glorious pasta dish or marveling at the intricate insights drawn from your aggregated model, it's the blending of those unique perspectives that leads us to the ultimate verdict: success! So, onward my friends! Take these aggregation methods into your kitchen and your code, and get ready to cook up something spectacular. Buon appetito, e buona fortuna!

Best Practices for Effective Ensemble Learning

When it comes to mastering the art of ensemble learning, there's no shortage of strategies that can elevate your models from ordinary to extraordinary, like transforming a basic bowl of bland spaghetti into a punchy plate of fun with vibrant pesto. However, as any seasoned chef worth their salt will tell you, success in the kitchen (or on the data battlefield) comes from following a handful of best practices. So grab your apron or your JavaScript framework, whichever fits your fancy, and let me guide you through the essential tips for effective ensemble learning, seasoned with a dash of humor and Italian flair.

First things first: diversity is the secret ingredient that sparks joy in the world of ensemble learning. It's akin to a wise chef recognizing that throwing every bibbed vegetable into a dish won't yield the best results. Instead, consider the myriad of textures and flavors you can conjure by mixing chewy, firm, or crispy ingredients together. In ensemble learning, using a variety of models or algorithms introduces an exciting array of perspectives into the mix. For example, combining a decision tree with a neural network and a support vector machine provides the nuanced insights we crave, much like tossing together your grandma's beloved marinara, bright basil, and rich pecorino cheese for that perfect caprese experience.

Next up is the importance of avoiding model overfitting. Just as no one wants to chew through a tough piece of meat that seems to be preparing for an uninvited duel, you definitely don't want your ensemble model to hinge too closely to the training data. Overfitting occurs when your model learns the nuances of the training set so well that it fails to generalize to new data. To combat this, I recommend tweaking hyperparameters and employing techniques such as cross-validation to ensure you aren't putting all your eggs, or in this case, sparkly pasta dough, into one basket. Always be honest with yourself. If that single-layer lasagna went wrong, it's best to accept it and adjust before your dinner guests call for a chef's hat and demand a refund, because nobody wants a meal that requires a culinary bailout!

Speaking of cooking something that requires finesse, let's talk tuning! Tuned hyperparameters are the secret sauce intrinsic to the performance of an ensemble model. Think of these hyperparameters as the elusive balance of salt and pepper. You can easily over-season a dish, leaving your guests reaching for extra bread to absorb the shock. In ensemble learning, tuning is crucial because combining models can introduce unintended variability. Invest some time and effort in figuring out the optimal settings, because let's be honest, nobody wants quinoa risotto that tastes like a salt lick.

Now, how about the art of blending results? Here's where you can channel your inner Italian grandmother and trust the process.

When aggregating predictions, don't underestimate the power of simplicity; often, a simple average or majority vote yields results as satisfying as your aunt's secret family recipe. But be cautious; don't fall into the trap of overcomplicating your predictions with every fancy averaging mechanism you encounter. Much like the "Too Many Chefs" syndrome, where too many competing flavors can lead to confusion, complicated aggregations can muddy the waters of an otherwise palatable model.

Another key consideration is monitoring and evaluation. Just as any chef worth their truffle oil would embark on a taste test before serving, you must adequately evaluate your ensemble model's performance. Each dish requires adjustment throughout the cooking process, just like each model needs to be critiqued on its performance metrics, be it accuracy, Fi score, or AUC. Utilize a validation set to monitor performance; if it tastes off, it's critical to go back and analyze which flavors need readjusting.

And let's not neglect the importance of scalability, especially when expanding your culinary horizons. It can be tempting to throw together more models with the hopes of achieving a Michelin Star-worthy prediction, but beware! Too many models can weigh down your computational efficiency like a stuffed cannoli. Keep an eye on the performance and ensure that your model scales gracefully, whether you're working with a small dataset or you've got a banquet feast ahead.

At the end of the day, effective ensemble learning is akin to crafting a delicious meal: a medley of flavors, textures, and techniques carefully balanced to create a sensational dining experience (or, in our case, a powerful predictive model). So embrace the art of gathering diverse models, avoid the pitfalls of overfitting, and cultivate the spirit of experimentation in your kitchen (and coding environment). Like a well-prepared plate of pasta, the careful integration of ensemble learning knowledge can lend itself to a feast for the senses. Now, shall we dig in? Buon appetito!

Chapter 8

Finding the Right Pairing: Feature Selection

The Importance of Feature Selection in Machine Learning

When it comes to machine learning, there's a mantra that echoes among data scientists: "Garbage In, Garbage Out." This quaint little phrase reminds us that the quality of our model's output is heavily influenced by the quality of the data we feed it. And guess what? The same goes for the features we choose! Feature selection is like picking the right ingredients before preparing a top-notch Italian dish. Don't just throw whatever you have into a pot, I mean, unless you're auditioning for "Chopped" or something. The proper selection of features can make the difference between a Michelin-starred AI system and one that crumbles faster than a soggy lasagna.

So what exactly are "features," you ask? Well, think of them as the attributes or characteristics of your data that you believe will help your model understand the problem it's trying to solve. In the world of cooking, if pasta is the foundation, your features are the spices, herbs, and proxies that elevate your dish from "meh" to "magnifico!" Just as you wouldn't toss in six different types of cheese just because they're there (unless you have lost all sense of culinary decency), in machine learning, you can't just slap every data point into your model willy-nilly. The wrong features lead to confusion, just like throwing a pineapple on your Margherita pizza, and trust me, folks, that's a crime that should be punished by having to listen to a two-hour lecture on the importance of cultural respect in cuisine.

Choosing features wisely is crucial for several reasons, not the least of which is that the more irrelevant features you throw into the mix, the higher the chances your model will overfit. Overfitting is when your model learns the training data too well, like a student who memorizes a textbook but can't hold a conversation about the subject. It might get a fantastic score on the exam, but when faced with a real-world question, it's about as useful as a breadstick in a gluten-free diet. By carefully vetting your features, you're essentially teaching your model to become a discerning chef, capable of making nuanced decisions rather than just throwing everything into the simmering pot.

Ah, but the culinary analogy goes deeper! Let's imagine you're tasked with cooking for a group of diners with diverse tastes and dietary restrictions. If you were to choose a feature set that included only spicy ingredients like jalapenos and cumin, you'd certainly end up with a table of unhappy eaters, unless your crowd happens to comprise die-hard chili enthusiasts (which would only further drive home my point about context and feature selection). Similarly, in machine learning, we must consider the demographics and primary characteristics of the audience our model is directed toward. Is it a financial algorithm trying to predict loan default risk? You might want to include income levels and debt-to-income ratios rather than the number of times a person has posted a meme about avocado toast. After all, nobody is currently defaulting on their loans due to a craving for brunch.

But how do we go about identifying the right features? Well, there are some spicy methods for selection! Techniques like Recursive Feature

Elimination, Lasso Regression, and even good old-fashioned correlation matrices often come to the rescue. It's like tasting your marinara sauce throughout the simmering process; you ensure you have just the right amounts of garlic and oregano, rather than going overboard with either. Your data insights and evaluations will guide you to the most important features. But be wary, it's a process that can very quickly devolve into a cook-off of epic proportions, where your one cousin who insists on adding "just a little more" garlic proves to be an adversary of the highest caliber!

At the end of the day, feature selection isn't just an important step; it's a rite of passage. It molds your approach to the task, like how mastering the skill of rolling out pasta makes you a bona fide Italian nonna. The power of discernment differentiates the amateurs from the culinary wizards, and trust me, in the world of machine learning, you want to be the wizard. So the next time you embark on a machine learning project, channel your inner Italian chef, choose your features wisely, and let your data dish achieve that perfect blend of richness and depth. Buon appetito!

The Art of Pairing: Analogies from Italian Cuisine

The fine art of pairing! Whether we're talking about cheese and wine or selecting features in a machine learning model, the principles remain remarkably similar. Both pursuits require a keen sense of balance, synergy, and an appreciation for the complexity that emerges when seemingly disparate elements come together. In Italian cuisine, the joy of pairing ingredients is akin to conducting a harmonious orchestra; every note must complement the others to create a masterpiece that elicits sensations of love and joy, possibly even spontaneous bursts of enthusiastic song and dance. No one wants the tortellini clashing with the tomato sauce, any more than I want to witness an algorithm throwing wild predictions because it mixed irrelevant features into a data salad!

Take, for instance, the classic pairing of a rich, creamy Alfredo sauce with simple, al dente fettuccine. Here, the creaminess of the sauce hugs the noodles in a way that would make any pasta lover weep tears of joy. It's a match made in culinary heaven, one that emphasizes the importance of not just what you put on your plate, but in what quantities and in what relationships. In the machine learning universe, this calls for a delicate selection of features that work together to support the final output. You wouldn't just pair fettuccine with maple syrup and call it a meal; likewise, in your dataset, the relationships among features dictate how accurately your model learns and predicts. A feature that stands alone or works against the others can ruin the entire dining experience, or presentation of your model's output!

Think about wine, that other grand staple of Italian cuisine. Pairing a robust Chianti with a flavorful Bolognese can elevate the dish from ordinary to extraordinary. However, serve that same Chianti with a delicate dish like chicken Piccata, and you've ruined the whole meal while simultaneously offending the chicken! In the world of machine learning, certain features might be exquisitely suited to enhance certain types of models but disastrous when paired with others. A feature that brings clarity to a decision tree may turn a neural network into that feeling of constantly grappling with tangled spaghetti. It's crucial to pay attention to the nuances. Does your model prefer a structured set of features, or does it thrive in a more chaotic environment? More importantly, does your algorithm have a sensitive palate?

Then there's the timeless combination of tomato and basil, a pairing so iconic that it inspires sonnets and urges people to venture into Italy just to taste it with their own tongues. These two greats highlight a truth in data science: the strongest features don't always come from strict numerical values or elaborate calculations. Sometimes, simplicity reigns supreme. You can have the most complicated ingredients, exotic spices, artisanal cheeses, but if they don't play nicely with each other, they'll taste like a halfhearted attempt at fusion cuisine. In machine learning, if you continue adding features to achieve complexity while ignoring the inherent relationships, you might end up with a model that resembles a three-cheese pizza topped with gummy bears, absolutely confusing and not what anyone ordered.

Let's not forget about timing; the moment when ingredients come together can affect the entire outcome. Do you add the garlic at the beginning of your saute or closer to the end for a punch of flavor? That decision has a profound impact on the dish's final taste. Similarly, the timing of feature introduction into a model influences its ability to learn effectively. Throw everything in at once like a haphazard cook who's skipped the prep step, and you may end up serving your audience something that has all the right ingredients but tastes like a regretful disaster. A thoughtful approach to feature pairing allows your model to adapt and refine over time, learning the value of nuance, much like learning to eat spaghetti without wearing half of it.

In the end, mastering the art of pairing is an enchanting blend of intuition, experimentation, and a genuine love for the craft, whether it's fine dining or fine-tuning a machine learning model. So, as you step into the realms of data discovery, don't just think about what features you can throw together. Channel your inner Italian chef, taste-test, adjust, choose wisely, and, for goodness' sake, make sure they complement each other beautifully! With a little practice, you'll be creating delicious, predictive models that make even the most seasoned data scientists rethink their approach. After all, just as spaghetti deserves a perfect marinara sauce, your data deserves the best feature combinations to delight both the algorithm and the end-user! Buon appetito and happy pairing!

Methods for Feature Selection

Selecting the right features for your machine learning model is a bit like deciding what goes into your Sunday sauce, there are a plethora of options, but only a few will harmonize beautifully to create a dish that everyone raves about. While I could wax poetic about the artistry of choice, let's cut to the chase: the world of feature selection has culinary-worthy techniques that help us sift through the endless buffet of data. So, grab your aprons and let's dive into the methods of feature selection that can save your model from being a saucy disaster.

First up, we have **Filter Methods**, think of these as your fine sieve, filtering out the good from the bad before the ingredients even hit the pot. Filter methods evaluate the importance of each feature independently, without regard for the model they may be used in. This approach is akin to assessing ingredients solely by their flavor profiles, without considering how they might interact during cooking. Take that glorious parmesan cheese: when standing alone, it's magnificent. But dump an entire block of it into a light, delicate risotto, and all you'll end up with is a gooey, overcooked mess. By using statistical techniques, such as correlation coefficients, chi-squared tests, or mutual information, filter methods allow you to shortlist candidates, making it easier to see which features should be avoided.

Next, let's stir in **Wrapper Methods**. Now, these are for those who love to experiment in the kitchen, testing everything to find the perfect combination. Wrapper methods assess a subset of features based on the model's performance, which means we are actively cooking and adjusting as we taste. It's like whipping up a fresh pesto while casually tossing in different quantities of basil, garlic, and olive oil until you hit that sweet, aromatic spot. While wrapper methods can lead you to discover a delightful combination, they can be computationally expensive, sometimes leaving you with a pasta dish that took way too long to prepare. The primary culprit here is the exhaustive search technique, which evaluates every possible feature combination. Beware: if you don't have a pot full of patience and a spare sense of humor, you might be stuck waiting longer than it takes to make a traditional ragu sauce.

Then we have the **Embedded Methods**, the dynamic duo in which feature selection occurs during model training. Think of these methods as the proverbial sous-chefs, busy preparing simple yet brilliant dishes while the main chef (your model) does all the heavy lifting. This method combines the best of both worlds: it evaluates feature relevance while actually training the modelz. Techniques like Lasso Regression and Decision Trees come into play here. They automatically select the most influential features while leaving the rest of the ingredients off the table, like a wise cook deciding which flavors complement the overall dish. Just as a trained chef can instantly spot fresh basil from wilted leaves from last week, embedded methods ensure that only the freshest ingredients influence the model's learning.

Of course, we can't overlook the importance of **Dimensionality Reduction** techniques like Principal Component Analysis (PCA). Think of these methods as the culinary equivalent of a blender that turns a multitude of ingredients into a velvety soup. By transforming features into a smaller set of uncorrelated variables while preserving as much information as possible, dimensionality reduction can streamline your model and eliminate complexity, kind of like how a good risotto is much more about the creamy goodness than the ingredients floating around in it. But here's the catch: sometimes, in the pursuit of a smooth finish, that signature ingredient might lose its unique character. So tread carefully; while PCA can simplify, you want to ensure you've not left out the critical flavors that create the essence of the dish.

Lastly, we can't leave out good old **Domain Knowledge**! Sometimes the best method is simply understanding your ingredients as well as the dishes you seek to create, as you would with a traditional Italian recipe your grandmother handed down. Channeling that knowledge can help you recognize which features are likely to be significant and eliminate those unnecessary fillers, like the time I discovered that coriander doesn't work in everything (seriously, it can taste like soap on my palate!). Combining domain expertise with the aforementioned selection methods can yield a dish that's both delicious and predictive.

In conclusion, the methods of feature selection do not merely serve as tools for data scientists; they are the culinary techniques that elevate a dish from "meh" to "magnifico." As chefs in the kitchen of machine learning, we must wield these methods wisely, embracing a holistic approach to feature selection in order to create models that truly resonate. So go forth, play in the world of features, and remember: the right selections make all the difference in a flavorful outcome! Now, if you'll excuse me, I'm off to perfect my own Sunday sauce; there's no time to waste in the kitchen of machine learning!

Evaluating Feature Importance

Evaluating feature importance is like ensuring you know which ingredients in your pasta primavera are truly essential to that glorious dish rather than just collecting random vegetables because they were on sale. After all, you wouldn't dream of showcasing a delightful, crisp zucchini surrounded by a cast of vegetables that resemble a sad, droopy assortment pulled from the depths of your crisper drawer after a week of neglect. Understanding which features add substance to your predictive model, much like choosing only the freshest and most vibrant vegetables, can often mean the difference between creating a beautiful presentation that has your audience licking the plate clean or leaving them with a face scrunched up in culinary horror.

Just how do we go about determining which features earn the right to simmer in our beloved cauldron of data? One of the most appealing methods is to use *feature importance scores* obtained from various machine learning models. Imagine you're whipping up a delightful marinara and assessing how essential each ingredient is to the overall dish; perhaps you discover that the quality of the crushed tomatoes provides an unparalleled base flavor, whereas the basil might sparkle as a lovely finishing touch. Similarly, feature importance scores can be derived from decision trees, random forests, or gradient boosting techniques, giving you a culinary-style rating of which features to keep front and center. A score of 0.8 beside your 'number of garlic cloves' might send you rushing to add more, while a feature hanging on with a measly 0.05 could very well be an "add when you're desperate" ingredient.

Yet using feature importance scores isn't without its complications. If you're akin to a chef who's only ever cooked minestrone, you'll need to be careful about misinterpreting these scores. You may find a feature gets a high rating because it correlates with another, more significant feature, much like a garnish that looks fabulous but doesn't add any value to the overall dish. In these scenarios, our dear old friend multicollinearity can sneak in like an unwelcome guest at a dinner party, leading us toward false beliefs about which features truly hold sway in transforming our projections from humble to haute cuisine.

Another enticing avenue for evaluating feature importance is to employ *permutation feature importance.* Think of this as an exciting game of musical chairs where you shuffle the ingredients around to see how the flavor changes. To gauge a feature's true significance, you can randomly shuffle the data for that feature while keeping the other features intact. If your model's performance takes a nose dive after the shuffle, congratulations! That ingredient is crucial to the flavor of your entire analysis. But if the performance remains the same, well, my friend, it's time to reconsider its place in the culinary lineup. It's like watching someone sprinkle salt into a recipe: if it doesn't even cause a stir, it's probably not enhancing the overall experience!

Let's not overlook models that inherently indicate the importance of features during training, such as *Lasso Regression and Regularized Techniques.* Using linear regression with regularization can help us shrink the coefficients of less important features, effectively banishing them to the land of non-essential ingredients. We don't need baby carrots pontificating about their role when they're clearly just meant to be cut, sauteed, and blended into the dish. When a feature's coefficient reaches a near-zero value, it's an indicator that it's time to find it a less significant role, like debuting as a garnish rather than a taste hero.

Now, a little word of caution: while evaluating feature importance can help elevate your model, don't be blinded by the allure of a flashy ingredient. Just like that vibrant, neon-hued ingredient that seems to do wonders for your eyes but leaves a questionable flavor on your palate, a high-ranking feature may still not provide the most meaningful insight. Context is critical in interpreting these scores, especially when dealing with vastly different datasets or when features vary in scale.

In closing, evaluating feature importance is an essential ingredient in the recipe for successful machine learning modeling. It helps us distill what contributes to the best results and eliminates those pesky predictors that give me more of a headache than hearty satisfaction. So, as you embark on this crucial journey, know that, similar to crafting the perfect risotto, it requires patience, consideration, and the courage to let go of ingredients that aren't playing well together. In the world of data, feature importance is what spices up your analysis and gives it that kick that keeps everyone coming back for seconds! Remember to bring your taste buds along for the ride; after all, a well-informed chef is a happy chef! Bon appetit and happy feature evaluating!

Challenges and Pitfalls in Feature Selection

Feature selection! The glittering promise of optimal performance and simplified models. It's like cooking a delicious risotto: every grain of rice counts, and neglecting even one facet can turn your dinner party into a simmering disaster. While the process of selecting the right features can lead to delightful results, it's not without its share of challenges and pitfalls that can turn your joyous data endeavor into a kitchen nightmare! So, conjure up your best apron and prepare for a recipe that highlights what can go wrong when picking features, you know, just in case you ever find yourself in the wine-soaked trenches of machine learning.

First off, let's talk about **overfitting**, the culinary equivalent of producing the perfect soufflé that, when removed from the oven, collapses into a flat pancake of disappointment. Overfitting occurs when your model learns patterns too well, including noise and irrelevant features in your training dataset. It's like becoming so attached to a particular recipe that you insist on adding every single component on your spice rack, even if rosemary doesn't go with chocolate cake! When your model overfits, it may perform beautifully on the training data but flop dramatically on new, unseen data. Therefore, one must exercise caution; after all, the airy nature of cooking often demands balance, a clue that should not be ignored in the world of data science! Selecting too many intricate features can cause our model to overindulge, much like an Italian grandmother who can't resist adding just one more layer of cheese.

Let's not forget **multicollinearity**, an insidious foe lurking in our kitchen. Picture a family dinner where everyone is vying for attention at the same time; it can become maddeningly difficult to hear any one voice. Similarly, when features are highly correlated, they can dilute the value of individual features and lead to confusion in model predictions. You might think that including more related features would provide richer context. Still, instead, they create such a cacophony that the model struggles to discern which ingredient truly contributes to the flavor profile. You wouldn't add both basil and bay leaves to a caprese salad and expect the fresh basil to sing! In machine learning, reducing complexity is key. Using techniques like variance inflation factors, you can assess multicollinearity and carve out those redundant features before they become a culinary catastrophe.

Then we stumble upon **biased assumptions**, the invisible hands that guide our feature selection decisions. When we allow our preconceived notions to dictate which features we incorporate, we open ourselves to bias, overlooking the finest truffles because we think they won't work with a simple pasta dish. While domain expertise is undeniably helpful, clinging to outdated beliefs can stifle your predictive potential. It's like insisting on using only elbow macaroni because that's what your mother always used, even if the dish could be bolder and brighter with those delicate farfalle instead! Be willing to explore and experiment with alternatives, ensuring that your features aren't limited to what's familiar but rather are genuinely assessed for their value.

As we dive deeper, we must acknowledge the excruciatingly tedious and ever-frustrating challenge of **feature engineering**. Both creatives and mathematicians can feel like they're riding a rollercoaster of joy and despair, churning through potential combinations. However, when the kitchen becomes overwhelmed with options, it can lead to "analysis paralysis", an agonizing state where you can't decide which feature to use or discard. You might look at your dataset, tempted to flavor up your model by combining ecstasy with olive oil, only to find yourself grappling with the realization that some features might not be inversely correlated with your target at all! Feature selection should be a lovely dance, not a drag race. Don't get lost in the whirl; let the sizzle of excitement guide you toward clarity.

Lastly, we face the looming specter of **lack of interpretability** in high-dimensional spaces. This complex dish presents us with a platter that bears an uncanny resemblance to a fusion cuisine gone awry, where you can't quite discern which ingredients made the meal palatable. As we incorporate complex feature selection techniques, we must tread carefully to ensure we don't sacrifice the elegance of interpretation in our quest for accuracy. Just as a layered tiramisu pleases the eyes while delicately blending flavors in each layer, our model should remain comprehensible. Choose techniques that allow for simplicity rather than relying on black-box algorithms that spit out results without explanation, because let's be real, your audience wants to know what they're savoring!

In conclusion, while the journey of feature selection brings with it the potential for a truly delightful outcome, it's paved with hurdles that could leave even the most seasoned chefs scratching their heads. By respecting the intricate dance of predictive modeling and maintaining a critical eye while overcoming challenges such as overfitting, multicollinearity, and bias, you'll become a master of your culinary craft. Embrace the imperfections that arise, for they're often another opportunity for growth, so as you explore the wonderful world of data, remember that the best dishes (and predictions) stem from a blend of analytics, intuition, and the undeniable spirit of adventure in cooking! Buon lavoro e buona fortuna!

Chapter 9

Cooking Under Pressure: Tuning Hyperparameters

Understanding Hyperparameters: The Key Ingredients

When diving into the complex world of machine learning, one often stumbles upon a term that sounds like something a chef would sprinkle into a bubbling pot: hyperparameters. You may imagine them as tiny, mischievous fairies flitting about an ambiguous cooking class, adjusting the temperature of the oven without so much as a warning. But no, dear reader, hyperparameters are not the pixies of the computational realm; rather, they are the key ingredients that can make or break your model. Much like the perfect garlic clove or the ideal sprinkle of Parmesan can rescue an otherwise mediocre plate of pasta, hyperparameters can act as your sauce's secret weapon, or a potential disaster waiting to happen.

A hyperparameter is essentially a configuration you set before training your model. It's the equivalent of deciding how much salt to throw into that pot of water before you boil your pasta. Are you throwing caution to

the wind with a hefty pinch, or are you cautiously adding just a hint? In the grand scheme of algorithmic dining, hyperparameters include settings such as the learning rate, batch size, and the number of layers in a neural network, among others. Each of these options works silently in the background, but adjusting them can lead your model either to culinary success or an unfinished dish left strewn across the kitchen floor.

Let's talk about the learning rate, one of the most critical hyperparameters and perhaps the diva of our hyperparameter banquet. If it's too low, your model may take its time and meander through the training process, like a slow-baked lasagna that just isn't quite ready to emerge from the oven. If it's too high, you'll see the equivalent of a runaway chef tossing ingredients without measuring, hello overcooked pasta! A learning rate that's in the Goldilocks zone leads to a well-trained model, as it balances between moving too fast and burning down your neural network.

Now, let's not forget the batch size, which is akin to preparing dinner for a small gathering versus a family feast. Preparing a meal for one may allow you to experiment without panic, but when multiplied by twenty guests, you'd better hope that everyone likes al dente. In the machine learning realm, a small batch size can enable more frequent model updates but often introduces more noise, while a large batch size can smooth things out but may slow convergence. In essence, determine if you're cooking for a quaint dinner party or the entire extended family before you disburse the pasta!

But hold on! There's more! Let's stir in the number of layers in your neural network, because if we don't include this, it's like forgetting to add the basil to a Caprese salad, what's the point?! More layers can often mean a more complex model that can capture intricate relationships. However, it can just as easily lead to "overfitting," which is like making lasagna with too much cheese, delicious at first but ultimately overwhelming. Finding the right balance is crucial, akin to achieving the precise harmony of flavors in an authentic Italian meal.

The beauty of hyperparameters lies in their ability to turn the mundane into the magnificent. These fine adjustments are precisely what elevate a simple tomato sauce to a five-star culinary experience. But be prepared, since tuning hyperparameters requires patience. It's not as glamorous as tossing around a pizza dough as if you were in an Italian pizzeria. Instead, it often involves a lot of trial and error. Get ready for a task akin to perfecting your grandmother's secret Bolognese recipe while navigating a maze of distracting relatives willing to offer unsolicited cooking advice.

The journey of hyperparameter tuning ultimately reflects a core truth of both cooking and machine learning: simplicity can be the ultimate sophistication. Too often, we tend to over-complicate things; recipes and algorithms alike can become bloated with unnecessary adjustments. Remember, just as a simple pasta dish can steal the show, a straightforward model with well-tuned hyperparameters may yield the richest insights. So, as you navigate the hyperparameter landscape, think of yourself as a chef creating a masterpiece, juggling ingredients, tweaking, and tasting, until, finally, you serve up something that shines as brightly as a perfectly cooked plate of spaghetti. Bon appetit!

Timing is Everything: The Role of Pressure

Timing! The unsung hero of both the culinary and machine learning worlds. It's that magical moment when al dente pasta meets the sauce for the first time, a crescendo of harmony that leaves dinner guests swooning. In the realm of machine learning, however, timing takes on a whole new meaning, especially when we talk about the role of pressure, yes, pressure! But don't worry; it's not about your mother-in-law arriving unannounced or the clock ticking down to midnight. Instead, we're diving into the metaphorical pressure cooker that is the process of model training, where timing can separate the seasoned chefs from the wannabe microwave aficionados.

Imagine, if you will, a giant pot of boiling water. Your pasta is in there, swirling around like a frantic hypothesis searching for validation. Too much pressure (as in keeping it on the heat too long) and you've got a mushy mess nobody wants to eat, not to mention some perplexed neural networks that can't make sense of your data. Likely, your model will either crash and burn or leave you with results boring enough to put even the most patient of investors to sleep. On the other hand, if you pull the pasta too soon, you're left with crunchier results than a "perfect" car-tire pasta, and you might find yourself confronted with an unyielding audience that promptly demands a refund (or at least a more edible side of bread).

Much like cooking, machine learning demands an awareness of time and pressure to optimize results. The training process has its own rhythm, and understanding this dance can mean the difference between a culinary delight and a dreaded disaster. As you train your model, each epoch is a new iteration, an opportunity to revisit the dish. However, it's vital to know when to let the model stew and when to strain it from the boiling sensations of overfitting. Too few epochs, and your model will be like a chef who never bothered to read the recipe; too many epochs, and you risk the dreaded phenomenon of overcooking, creating a model that performs wonderfully in training but struggles to find its footing in the real world.

Let's also discuss how batch size affects the timing of your training. Like the home cook who insists on using only the freshest garlic, a smaller batch size means more time spent adjusting to the flavors as they're mixed. It allows for a more granular examination of how the algorithms react to each adjustment, akin to tasting a sauce spoonful by spoonful, until you find that heavenly balance. However, we must consider the flipside: increasing the batch size is like tossing a bucket of garlic into the mix; while it might taste good to you, it's likely to overwhelm your dinner companions. Balancing the amount of data fed to a model is crucial to achieving the right training pressure without letting it bubble over.

Now, timing and pressure aren't just about the cooking process; they also play a significant role in model evaluation and validation. Think about the moment you taste your dish: it's not merely an exercise in culinary masochism, but a crucial test to see if everything is just right. This step helps you adjust flavors and ingredients in the kitchen, and similarly, a well-timed validation process helps you evaluate your model's performance. The trick lies in knowing when to taste, what to adjust, and how long to let your creation develop its flavors. Too little testing could lead to mortification when you unveil your model to the world, and nobody wants to serve an undercooked dish or an algorithm full of bugs!

And let's face it, anxiety levels can escalate quickly when you're anticipating those results, especially if you're running what feels like a thousand iterations of parameter tuning while the clock ticks. You start feeling like you're opening the oven every five minutes, unable to resist peeking just to see whether the soufflé will rise or collapse. Spoiler alert: it's a lot harder to manage the oven's heat than it is to manage the pressure cooker of life, or your upcoming dinner party. But with practice, you'll develop an innate ability to sense when the time is ripe for validation and when to put your trust in the machine.

In closing, just as a great dish is a delicate balance of heat, timing, and artistry, so too is a successful machine learning model dependent on the art of timing and the management of pressure. So next time you find yourself staring at a simmering pot of data, remember that the secret to success lies not just in the ingredients, but in how you orchestrate them together. Time may be of the essence, but let's not forget: the flavor is everything. Stay tuned in your culinary journey, or, let's face it, you might just serve up a heaping helping of regret!

Finding the Perfect Temperature: Balancing Bias and Variance

Bias and variance, the culinary pairings of the machine learning world. Picture this: You're in the kitchen, trying to perfect your creamy risotto. You've got your broth simmering, your arborio rice awaiting its moment of limelight, and now, you need to balance the temperature, too hot, and you risk burning; too cool, and you'll end up with an undercooked disaster begging for liquid. Similarly, in the vast expanse of model training, finding that perfect temperature to balance bias and variance can feel akin to mastering the art of risotto while a very particular food critic (ahem, your stakeholders) is lurking nearby with a discerning palate.

Bias, in this context, is like the cook who occasionally drops a can of tomato sauce in place of freshly diced tomatoes; sure, it'll give you a unified flavor, but it lacks the depth and character that come from real, home-grown ingredients. A model with high bias is overly simplistic. It's the classic one-size-fits-all attire that everyone's shoehorned into but somehow just doesn't fit right. It fails to capture the complexity of the data set, like trying to make a gourmet dish out of frozen pizza, boring and disappointing! The result, my dear pasta aficionados, is underfitting, where it goes through the motions but misses the subtleties of flavor.

On the flip side, we have variance, an elusive troublemaker that flourishes in chaotic kitchens and introduces randomness like a chef who can't stick to the recipe. High variance indicates overfitting, akin to a sous chef going rogue and adding an unnecessary amount of saffron to the dish just because they can. In doing so, they create a melange of tastes that, while they may dazzle the taste buds momentarily, ultimately leaves diners shaken and bewildered. The model becomes overly sensitive to noise in the training data, often performing spectacularly during training but poorly in real-world applications, much like that unexpected extra ingredient that ruins the dish.

Now, what you're really looking for is that Goldilocks zone, the sweet spot where bias and variance coexist peacefully, like a skilled chef and an efficient sous chef working in tandem. Ideally, you want a model that's complex enough to capture the nuances of the data (no more frozen pizza!), while remaining generalizable enough to handle new scenarios that come tumbling in, think guests suddenly requesting vegan alternatives. Achieving this balance can symbolize the heart of culinary artistry, and, surprisingly, the perfect algorithmic approach.

How do we find that ideal temperature? Enter our trusty hyperparameters to the rescue! These little darlings can be adjusted to control the complexity of your model, just as the heat on your stovetop determines how your ingredients cook. For instance, if you feel like your model is experiencing high bias, you could crank up the complexity by adding layers to a neural network or increasing the features fed to your model. But wait! If you go too far and the variance skyrockets, you might just create a melty mess that no one would dare touch.

Picture this: You're monitoring the pot of risotto. Should you let it cook longer or add more broth? The decision feels monumental, doesn't it? The same thought processes reign supreme when tuning your model. Avoiding underfitting requires dialing up the temperature (a bit more complexity!), but you must tread carefully to avoid the impending explosion of overfitting when crankiness bubbles over. It's normally a dance between what you've created and what you want to achieve, and this delicate navigation often dictates whether your data emerges as a Michelin star-worthy meal or just another underwhelming plate.

And here's where the curious concept of cross-validation steps into the kitchen, providing a solution more elegant than your Aunt Rosa's secret sauce recipe. By validating your model against separate data sets, much as you'd taste test your risotto in a clever battle against the impending food critic, you can verify how it handles different scenarios. This strategy can mitigate both bias and variance, ensuring that your culinary creation shines on both the training table and in the actual kitchen.

In conclusion, achieving that perfect temperature between bias and variance is not a one-time gig, oh no! It's an ongoing culinary crusade. Remember that, like skilled chefs, we must never stop experimenting and refining our dishes or our machine learning models. With practice, patience, and perhaps a sprinkle of humor before the critics arrive, we can muster the courage to make that risotto future gourmet-worthy. So, throw on that apron, keep cooking, keep learning, and never forget that the masterpiece you create can shine, whether in a pot on the stove or a neural network in the cloud. Buon appetito!

Adjusting the Seasoning: Strategies for Tuning

The delicate art of seasoning, one might say, is the heartbeat of every great dish, and when it comes to machine learning, tuning is strikingly similar. It's what separates a dish that grabs the rambunctious attention of an Italian grandmother from one that elicits a shrug and a polite smile. You see, just as each pinch of salt transforms a bland pasta into a tantalizing creation, precisely tuning hyperparameters can breathe life into a machine learning model, turning it from a monotonous collection of algorithms into a veritable fountain of insights. So, let's grab our aprons (and maybe a glass of wine) and explore how we can master the seasoning of our models!

First off, when tuning, it's essential to understand that there isn't a magic fairy dust you can sprinkle to solve all your model woes. Think about it: Would you ever rely solely on salt to carry an entire dish? Far from it! Like a true Italian chef, you need to experiment with a medley of spices, flavors, and techniques. In machine learning, this means using optimized strategies such as grid search, random search, and Bayesian optimization, each offering a unique blend of 'seasonings' to perfect your model.

Take grid search, for instance, imagine it as a buffet where you can sample each dish but risk finding yourself overstuffed before dessert. You create a grid of hyperparameter values and 'taste' each combination, exhaustively evaluating them against your training data. However, beware! While grid search allows you to taste everything, it can also lead you on a calorie-laden journey that leaves you in a food coma, read: extremely slow and computationally expensive. After all, we don't want our model to be featherweight yet overly stuffed with parameters that lack flavor.

Then there's random search, a little less conventional but oh-so-fun, akin to a game night where you aren't sure whether you'll discover a hidden culinary gem or end up with a plateful of befuddlement. With random search, you select random combinations of hyperparameters rather than systematically testing them. It has been found that this technique can sometimes yield better results in a fraction of the time, revealing excellent 'seasoning' suggestions sans the rigorous culinary gymnastics of grid search. Like a good Italian dinner party, sometimes improvisation can lead to delightful surprises!

And who could forget Bayesian optimization, the sophisticated maestro of tuning? This method turns your search into a strategic game of chess, where prior knowledge of your model's performance is used to inform decisions about which hyperparameters to sample next. Imagine it as having a Michelin-starred chef guiding you through the kitchen, preventing you from adding that ridiculously heavy layer of cheese that looks appealing but overpowers the actual dish. By learning from past experiences and narrowing down, Bayesian optimization helps you maximize performance while minimizing 'oven time', pure culinary gold!

As we adjust the seasoning, we also need to pay close attention to the accompanying ingredients, the data itself. A thrilling part of model tuning is understanding how inputs affect outputs and how even a seemingly innocuous new feature can tip the balance of flavors either way. Think of it as adding a surprise ingredient to your grandma's spaghetti sauce, it might just transform that dish into something ethereal, or you could wind up with a kitchen catastrophe that leaves guests gasping for water! Feature engineering is your ally, allowing you to incorporate the right flavors into the model, while also managing the tension and interplay of bias and variance.

The key to successful tuning, however, lies not just in the elimination of blandness but in finding that harmony. Your goal is to achieve a symphony of flavors, like a perfectly harmonized pasta dish that lingers delicately on the palate. Each hyperparameter is a variable that adds its unique note to the composition. When tuned correctly, the amalgamation creates a delectable dish, or, in our case, a well-functioning model that delivers the insights we crave.

And finally, let's not overlook the importance of patience! Just as Rome wasn't built in a day, neither are the best machine learning models concocted overnight. Embrace the iterative process of seasoning; taste, adjust, and repeat until you reach a balance that makes your taste buds sing. In this dynamic realm of tuning, don't just throw a handful of this or a dash of that into the model and hope for the best, you'll end up with a bit of a horror show resembling an Italian food fight gone awry!

So, don your chef's hat, not just for the kitchen but for the coding environment as well. Adjust your seasoning judiciously, sprinkle your tuning methodologies in with care, and you'll soon find that your model flirts charmingly between perfection and culinary chaos. When you finally unearth that ideal combination, the fruits of your labor will serenade you with insights previously hidden. Now that's a dish worthy of a standing ovation! Buon appetito!

Serving Up Results: The Effects of Hyperparameter Tuning on Model Performance

It's a magical moment when traditional Italian cooking meets machine learning, a union destined for greatness! Picture yourself in a rustic Italian kitchen, immersed in the aroma of fresh basil and simmering garlic, ready to serve a sumptuous dish. Similarly, in the world of machine learning, the dramatic effects of hyperparameter tuning on model performance can spark the same excitement! With the right adjustments, your model can transform from a somewhat lugubrious performer (think overcooked pasta) to an agile maestro, ready to dazzle your stakeholders' dining experience with delectable insights.

Let's dig deep into the metaphorical pot of hyperparameter tuning: it's akin to the meticulous adjustments you make when cooking that perfect marinara sauce. You don't just dump in everything at once and call it a day, no, dear reader! You taste, you adjust, and you find that ideal blend of flavors that sings in harmony. In machine learning, hyperparameters play a significant role in that fine-tuning process. For example, a slight change in the learning rate can propel your model from a sluggish pace to a lightning-fast learning cycle. But beware! A poorly chosen learning rate might leave your model tripping over itself, unable to grasp patterns and clues nestled within the oceans of data.

Hypothesize for a moment, what happens when hyperparameters are finely tuned? A breakthrough! A well-tuned model can achieve higher accuracy, grasping the complexities inherent in the data with finesse. Consider your latest creation; the difference is akin to the bold strides of a well-marinated osso buco, cutting through with depth and flavor. The satisfaction that comes from a well-optimized model mirrors the gritty joy of digging into a meal prepared with love, revealing layers of flavor while serenading your taste buds.

Now, let's talk interactivity! Just as adjusting ingredients invites new flavors into the mix, tuning hyperparameters opens the door to a world of interactions within your data. Many models encapsulate important relationships that aren't immediately detectable, but with careful tuning, you're playing matchmaker! Imagine trying to enhance a simple pasta primavera, a strategic sprinkle of fresh herbs or a twist of lemon can elevate it to culinary glory. Similarly, feature selection can bring forth hidden treasures, illuminating patterns that were previously mundane and giving your model the zing it so desperately craves.

However, with great power comes great responsibility! Navigating the world of hyperparameters is like dancing on a tightrope while juggling! Over-tuning can lead to overfitting, where your model becomes obsessed with fitting the training data so tightly that it stumbles when faced with new data. It's like serving a risotto that's so creamy and decadent that it simply collapses. You're left with a delightful dish, no doubt, but it fails to stand strong at the dining table of life. Wholeheartedly tuning means exercising caution and moderation, allowing your model to be adaptable while retaining its core flavors.

And here's a delightful twist: the impact of hyperparameter tuning doesn't stop at mere accuracy; it can also reduce computational costs. Yes, ladies and gentlemen, we want that beautiful soufflé without cranking the oven to overload it! An optimized model with well-tuned parameters can reduce the time and resources required to produce results, ideally serving up insights that let your stakeholders feast on success. Just as cooking shouldn't feel like a laborious uphill battle, your machine learning models shouldn't require excruciating amounts of energy to churn out precise predictions.

As we delve deeper into the effects of tuning, remember that the stakes are high! The results of your efforts can spell success or disaster. Like a chef preparing a dinner for important guests, inconsistent tuning can lead to distinctly mixed reviews that leave your diners puzzled, or worse yet, hungry for something better. Thus, each tuning session must be treated with the diligence it deserves, addressing not only the performance metrics but also the specificities of the business objectives the model aims to address.

To wrap up, successful hyperparameter tuning transforms your model from a humble ingredient list into an extraordinary culinary creation, capable of mesmerizing the dining crowd with its finesse and flavor. Trust in the process: learn to stir, taste, adjust, and repeat, savoring the results as you serve them up to stakeholders eager to feast on your hard work. With patience and a passion for flavors, whether in the kitchen or on your computer screen, you will soon find that the world of hyperparameter tuning can unveil a banquet of breathtaking model performance. Mangia bene!

Chapter 10

The Art of Presentation: Visualization Techniques

The Importance of Visualization in Understanding Complex Data

In a world where data flows like spaghetti from a pot that's been tipped over by an overzealous chef, it's no surprise that we often find ourselves tangled in a messy web of numbers, figures, and chaotic spreadsheets. Just as a good marinara sauce requires blending a myriad of ingredients into a harmonious concoction that sings on your palate, understanding complex data demands clear and effective visualization. You wouldn't serve lasagna with a side of existential dread, would you? Similarly, the key to making data palatable is to present it in a way that even your non-techie uncle, who still believes that the cloud is where the rain comes from, can digest it.

Visualization is the secret sauce of making sense out of madness; it's the chef's kiss that elevates data from drab to fab. Think about it: when faced with rows of numbers that resemble my Aunt Maria's grocery list (which, by the way, contains a lot more garlic than most algorithms can handle), it's easy to shut down and lose the will to understand anything. But throw those numbers onto a neat little graph or a colorful chart, and voila! Suddenly, you can see trends, patterns, and relationships materialize before your very eyes, like the magic moment when your pasta transforms as it cooks. It establishes a visual narrative, providing context in which data breathes and thrives. Data visualization helps us take a step back and look at the bigger picture, rather than drowning in an ocean of digits.

Just like every chef knows that the right plating can make or break a dish, a well-designed visualization captures the essence of what you're trying to communicate and engages your audience. When I prepared for my last dinner party, I arranged my antipasti on a platter like an artist painting a canvas, ensuring that every prosciutto-wrapped melon ball sparkled with visual delight. Similarly, in the realm of machine learning and artificial intelligence, visualizations act as the stylish chef of your data story. They help highlight important findings and insights, allowing your audience to engage with the story. Who wouldn't want to see the "spaghetti phenomenon," where the amount of pasta consumed correlates with the number of Italian restaurants within a z-mile radius? Visualization makes those connections deliciously apparent.

Moreover, good visualizations help in navigating the treacherous waters of complexity, much like a well-placed buoy that steers enthusiastic sailors away from hidden reefs (or, you know, data misinterpretations). A scatter plot can reveal correlations that might go unnoticed in a data table. The same way you might spot that missing ingredient in beloved family recipes, visualization helps identify outliers, trends, and anomalies. Who would have suspected that my old friend Giovanni's calorie-infused pasta could have led to an increase in my cholesterol? A dot here and a line there, and I began to see it clearly, like a well-prepared sauce bubbling away, signaling that it's almost time for dinner.

Now, let's pause and acknowledge that not all visualizations are created equal, akin to the fact that not all meatballs are prepared with love. Badly designed visualizations can lead your audience down a rabbit hole of confusion, just as my first attempt at preparing gnocchi led to what can only be described as potato-based hockey pucks. Everyone can be an "artist" with a click and a choice of chart style, but always remember that clarity and accessibility are paramount. After all, if your visualization is as intricate as my Aunt Lena's family recipes (trust me, they are legendary), you've just lost your audience. Data storytelling competes with a well-prepared meal; it needs to be digestible, engaging, and appetizing with just the right amount of seasoning.

The importance of visualization also extends beyond merely decoding complex data; it's about creating an experience. It's akin to enjoying a beautifully arranged charcuterie board while sipping on a bit of Prosecco. When data is visualized effectively, it evokes emotions. It stimulates curiosity, two essential ingredients when you're trying to understand the bizarre behaviors of AI, or why your last batch of lasagna tasted a bit off. It's through visualization that insights become actionable intelligence, informing decisions that can lead to success, much like the triumphant feeling after mastering the perfect al dente pasta.

As I reflect on the vibrant connection between cooking and data visualization, I am once again reminded that understanding complex data should never be a conundrum or a culinary disaster. Instead, it should be an adventure, where visualization is your chef's knife, cutting through ambiguity and bringing clarity to the table, ready to engage and enlighten. Just remember: the next time a haphazard data sheet looks like it jumped out of a clumsy chef's kitchen, pull out your visualization skills and make that pasta twirl!

Common Visualization Techniques in Data Science

Welcome to the world of data visualization, where colors, lines, and shapes come together to tell tales that might otherwise remain mute, like my cousin Roberto's post-pasta feast. Just as every good Italian chef has a repertoire of trusted recipes, data scientists have an array of visualization techniques at their disposal. These techniques help them sauté the complex flavor profiles of data, transforming raw numbers into delicious insights. With a flick of your wrist or a couple of clicks on some software, it's possible to create a visual feast that will have your audience saying ''Mamma Mia!" or, hopefully, ''Eureka!" depending on your flavor of data discovery.

First on our gastronomic journey through visualizations, let's talk about the humble **bar chart**. Think of it as the meatball of visualizations: reliable, universally recognized, and satisfying to a fault! When you want to compare different categories of data, the bar chart steps in like a true Italian grandma, waving her wooden spoon, ready to show you who's the most popular at the dinner table. Popularity checks aside, they can display quantities such as pasta brands, customer preferences, or even the number of gelato servings consumed during summer. Best of all, bar charts don't throw fancy shapes or convoluted designs at you. They simply present the data in a straightforward, digestible format that's as easy to parse as a good spaghetti Bolognese.

Next up, we have the **line chart**, which may remind you of a long ribbon of tagliatelle unfurled on your kitchen counter, waiting to be cooked. Line charts are perfect for showing trends over time, revealing delightful revelations about how things evolve, like how my waistline changes during the holiday season. Picture a line chart depicting the rise and fall of pizza sales during different months of the year. It highlights those peak "pizza party nights" while letting you know when to keep the dough in the fridge. It's all about visualizing how pasta consumption correlates with your mood or perhaps weather changes. Spoiler alert: when it's cold and raining outside, eat pasta, and do not skimp on the Parmigiano!

Enter the charming **scatter plot**, think of this as the unconventional cousin at the family dinner who just loves to mix things up. Scatter plots showcase relationships between two variables, throwing points on a grid like confetti at a wedding. For instance, it can reveal whether there's a relationship between the amount of garlic used in a dish and its perceived deliciousness. The beauty of a scatter plot is that it doesn't shy away from the awkward data points that could represent brisket gone wrong or a lime that looked excellent in the store but failed to deliver at the kitchen. With scatter plots on hand, it's easy to spot those outliers that so many people try to hide away, sort of like the overcooked lasagna layers that no one wants to acknowledge at a family gathering.

As we delve deeper into the colorful kitchen of visualization recipes, let's not forget the **pie chart**. Ah yes, the classic pie chart, visually fragrant like a freshly baked pizza, except hopefully not a burnt one. The pie chart is brilliant for showing proportions and percentages, like a well-balanced Italian feast: garlic bread, salad, pizza, and, yes, even dessert. But be careful! Too many slices can make it look like my Aunt's Thanksgiving turkey, which is usually stuffed with the whole kitchen. When used correctly, pie charts can provide a brief overview of the various components and improve your audience's understanding. Just remember that, like most things, moderation is crucial!

Now, we can't skip the more advanced techniques, such as **heat maps**, which resemble a rich lasagna bubbling in the oven, revealing layers of flavor. Heat maps provide a rich visual representation of data density or intensity, highlighting areas of interest. Imagine using a heat map to display customer activity on a website, where 'hot' areas depict where users enthusiastically click through various pasta recipes. It's like finding the perfect time to cook a dish, adjusting ingredients based on the heat tells you where the action is happening, making it a great strategic tool for a data scientist.

Lastly, let's sprinkle in the importance of **dashboards**. Think of dashboards as the grand buffet table, showcasing an array of delicious options and offering a comprehensive view of all the delightful dishes. A well-designed dashboard can consolidate multiple visualizations, offering a single glance at performance indicators, statistics, and data insights. Whether you're monitoring the number of pasta dishes ordered at your local trattoria or tracking AI model performances, dashboards can be your best ally, similar to a trusted sous-chef who keeps everything organized while you focus on whether or not to add another pinch of salt.

In conclusion, just as every Italian meal has its unique essence, the diverse range of visualization techniques has something for every dish, or dataset, for that matter. With the right visualization, you can transform your data from bland and confusing to flavorful and engaging. So, grab that ladle, embrace your inner Picasso, and serve your insights with flair because, let's face it, nobody wants to be stuck with a plateful of boring numbers when there's a whole buffet of visual options waiting. Buon appetito!

Choosing the Right Type of Visualization for Your Data

In the vast culinary landscape of data visualization, choosing the right visual for your data is akin to selecting the perfect pasta shape for a particular sauce. You wouldn't dare drown delicate angel hair in a chunky bolognese, nor would you smother rigatoni in a fragile herbal emulsion. Similarly, when communicating data insights, matching the right visualization to the specific dataset is essential to achieving a deliciously engaging outcome. So, let's roll up our sleeves and get ready to explore how to pick that ideal visual, just as you'd choose the finest ingredients for a signature dish.

Imagine for a moment that you're at a bustling Italian market, surrounded by various fresh produce, aromatic herbs, and gleaming olives. Now consider your data as the ingredients you've gathered. The secret is knowing what you're working with before you start chopping and tossing. The first question you must ask yourself is: What story am I trying to tell? Are you attempting to show a comparison, a trend, or perhaps a relationship between variables? This is where your inner chef must come to life, examining what flavors work best together. Just as certain pasta shapes complement specific sauces and dish types, different kinds of visualizations serve their respective purposes.

Let's say you want to compare the sales of your pasta dishes over the last few months, perhaps the spaghetti carbonara is facing fierce competition from the mushroom fettuccine alfredo. In this case, a **line chart** is your trusted ally. Picture it seamlessly tracking the ups and downs, showing rises as luscious noodle waves and dips as unfortunate pasta mishaps. Line charts are perfect for illustrating trends over time, helping you visualize whether the carbonara will become a perennial favorite or is destined for a dark, forgotten corner of your menu.

Now, what if your aim is to showcase sales by type for a big event like the Feast of St. Giuseppe? It's all about proportions! In this scenario, the **pie chart** or **donut chart** comes to the rescue, presenting an appetizing overview of all sales as individual slices of deliciousness. Just like a well-made pizza, everyone loves those tempting segments representing each dish, allowing viewers to visually grasp market shares or ingredient preferences at a glance. But remember, too many slices can overwhelm even the hungriest of guests, so keep it juicy and straightforward!

What if you want to highlight the relationship between variables? The classic **scatter plot** steps in, looking dapper like a suave Italian waiter balancing a tray of bruschetta on his fingertips. Perhaps you're interested in exploring the correlation between the amount of basil used in your pesto and the customer satisfaction ratings. Here, the scatter plot allows you to identify whether there's a positive relationship (i.e., more basil, happier diners), or reveal those occasional outliers, like the poor soul who doesn't appreciate fresh herbs or believes that sauce should only come from a jar labeled "Red." Scatter plots can unravel mysteries buried in the data, shedding light on unexpected connections.

Let's not forget the powerful and visually stunning **heat map**. Imagine you are preparing an ambitious dinner party and trying to grasp which dishes drove the most sales in your restaurant. The heat map could represent data density in a vibrant way, allowing you to identify which meals people were raving about, right down to the very grain of salt sprinkled on top. With a heat map, you can visualize the "hot" items that create culinary fireworks, while avoiding those poorly received experimental dishes that left a lingering taste of regret.

Beyond the basics, in a world where dashboards reign supreme, think about how multiple visualizations can work in harmony. If you're managing a kitchen brigade for pasta orders during rush hour, having all your essential metrics displayed at once can make a world of difference. Combine charts, graphs, and key performance indicators into a dashboard that looks like a vibrant family feast, so you can make quick decisions without overselling the lasagna... again.

Before diving headfirst into the world of visuals, remember that clarity should always reign supreme. You wouldn't serve a dish in a way that leaves diners guessing what on earth they're eating, and neither should you do that with your data. A beautifully crafted visual can lose its impact if it's too cluttered or convoluted. Think of your visual design as arranging a delightful plate of caprese salad: the components should complement each other and be distinct enough that diners (or viewers) immediately grasp what's on the menu.

In the grand buffet of data visualization, the ultimate goal is to make your story resonate, providing insights that linger in your audience's minds long after the last course. So, whether you're tossing spaghetti into a simmering sauce or laying the foundation for impactful visuals, always ensure the flavor profiles blend seamlessly. Just like in cooking, take your time, and don't be afraid to experiment a little until you've found that perfect plateful of data presentation! Buon appetito!

The Role of Data Storytelling in Visualization

When you think about great meals that reverberate through time, you realize it's not just about the food; it's about the experience, the story that wraps around it like the perfect layer of cheese on a baked ziti. The same holds true for data visualization. At its core, the art of storytelling plays a crucial role in transforming abstract numbers into relatable narratives, making us care about trends and insights as if they were our dear nonna's family recipes. And let's be honest: nobody wants to sit through a lecture on data without a bit of pizzazz, much like eating plain boiled pasta without so much as a dab of olive oil.

Data storytelling is the enchanting process that breathes life into numbers, turning them from mere statistics into compelling tales. Just as a rich tomato sauce evolves and thickens over time and with tender attention, data storytelling requires a deep understanding of context, audience, and the message you want to convey. Think of it as cooking for your family, a good meal isn't just thrown together blindly; you consider your guests, their preferences, and the memories you want to create. In the realm of data visualization, your audience is your family, and they're hungry for insights that you can serve up with flair.

Consider a line chart that tracks the number of spaghetti servings consumed over a year. On its own, it's just a hodgepodge of data points dancing across a grid. But add context to it, and you transform this mundane graph into a riveting tale of spaghetti supremacy that rivals even the best Hollywood scripts. Imagine highlighting that key moment, February, the month when everyone decided that pasta was the solution to their winter woes, leading to an unprecedented surge in consumption. By weaving individual data points into a narrative thread, you can evoke emotions, curiosity, and even laughter, drawing your audience closer to the experience you're presenting.

Just as any good chef knows that the ideal meal includes a pinch of flavor and a hearty dose of aroma to entice guests, effective data storytelling captures more than just numbers; it engages our senses and sparks curiosity. A well-crafted data story conveys purpose and enables the audience to forge connections and take away valuable insights. You wouldn't drizzle balsamic glaze artfully on a pile of muddy potatoes, would you? Similarly, without a narrative thread anchoring the visualization, metrics can leave your audience bewildered and lost, wondering where the all-important pizzazz went.

Let's face it, trying to communicate results without a cohesive story is like serving up pasta and expecting it to sell itself; it's not going to happen. If you throw random graphics and charts onto the table without a rhyme or reason, it's as confusing as my Uncle Rocco trying to explain the intricacies of Italian dialects while simultaneously talking over the family cat. Data storytelling allows your visuals to flow seamlessly, guiding the viewer through the "ingredients" of a narrative, from initial insights to their implications, transformations, and conclusions.

To spice things up, you can also integrate emotions into your storytelling by reflecting on real-life human experiences. Consider a scatter plot demonstrating customer satisfaction ratings vs. the number of garlic cloves used in a dish. Injecting a pinch of humor, perhaps referencing that dazzling garlic bread that left diners in love, creates an inviting atmosphere. People don't just want hard-hitting statistics; they want the emotional pull that comes from relatable experiences, enjoyment, and the delight of learning something new along the way.

Moreover, leveraging visuals as characters in your story can make a significant impact. Each element of your visualization, be it a bar chart, pie chart, or line graph, plays a role akin to a carefully cast actor in a cinematic masterpiece. A bar that towers above the rest, showcasing sales of lasagna, can be the hero, while another diminutive pie slice of novelty salads takes on the role of the sidekick, humorously lurking on the edge of relevance.

Through this interaction of visuals, you unfold a more complex tapestry of data that users are likely to connect with far more meaningfully.

In the end, powerful data storytelling is all about turning the ordinary into the extraordinary. Smoothly integrating visuals with compelling narratives creates a feast for the eyes and the mind. As you uncover insights and wrap them in the warmth of a story, you enrich your audience's dining experience and encourage deeper connections to the data and the knowledge it conveys. So, the next time you sit down to craft a visualization, ask yourself not just how to present the data, but how to make it sing, like a perfect aria that flows through the kitchen while pasta boils on the stove. In the grand kitchen of data, storytelling allows us to whip up delightful stories that tantalize the mind just as a plate of creamy risotto enchants the taste buds. Buon appetito!

Best Practices for Creating Compelling Visualizations

Creating compelling visualizations is not just an art form; it's a culinary adventure that requires a sprinkle of technique, a dollop of creativity, and a whole serving of best practices. Just like preparing a perfect risotto, creating an impactful visualization requires patience and precision, jumping the gun or skimping on the requisite steps can leave you with a plateful of regret! So grab your apron, preheat your creative juices, and let's dive into the flavorful world of visualization best practices that will leave your audience craving more!

First and foremost, clarity should always be your guiding star. A visual shouldn't feel like trying to read a family recipe scribbled in a mix of languages at an Italian Sunday dinner, often confusing and likely to lead to culinary chaos. Simplicity is the name of the game! The broadest brush strokes need to be used to convey your message. Imagine attempting to showcase the popularity of pasta dishes with a bar chart cluttered with unnecessary embellishments or colors that could make even a rainbow cringe. Less is definitely more; emphasize the essential elements and let your visuals breathe. A clean, straightforward presentation will elevate your data above the noise, placing your insights front and center.

Now let's talk about color, our beloved seasoning in the art of visual storytelling. Much like your favorite marinara sauce, a splash of color adds zest and appeal. However, tread carefully! You don't want to unleash a tornado of clashing colors that would cause even the sharpest palate a headache. Select a cohesive color palette that aligns with your theme and enhances the data's narrative. Colors should be used purposefully; for example, use warm colors to signify urgency (perhaps those calories creeping up on your favorite pizza) and cooler tones for restful, soothing visuals, think of a calm basil pesto as you unwind from a long day. The right color choices can make your visuals pop while keeping viewers engaged without overwhelming them.

Now, let's address the tried-and-true principle of **labeling**. It's vital to provide context so that your audience knows what they're feasting upon! Imagine sitting at a beautifully set table, only to find out that the enticing dish you're staring at is actually canned tuna in olive oil instead of Nonna's homemade ragu. Labels and annotations are the culinary touchstones of visualization. They go beyond mere eye candy; they explain the essence of what the audience is seeing. Every axis, legend, and title must be meticulously crafted to ensure viewers don't just admire the visuals but can also digest the information meaningfully.

In this digital age, interactivity also plays a pivotal role in creating engaging visuals that are akin to the surprise ingredient hidden in your favorite dish. Just as diners appreciate being part of the cooking process, mixing, tasting, and adjusting, the viewers of your data visualizations crave the opportunity to interact and explore. Utilizing interactive charts, sliders, and filtering options will entice users to dig deeper and experience the data firsthand. Let them navigate the nuances of their curiosity, akin to letting a family member taste your marinara to see if it needs just a pinch more salt!

Moreover, remember the power of **storytelling**. All great dishes tell a story, and so should your visuals! Embed your data within a narrative that follows hygiene: start with your premise and dive into the "why" behind the data. What problem are you solving, and how can your insights lead to a satisfying resolution? Use your visuals as the culinary plot twist: showcase key trends or surprising findings that keep the audience hungry for more. Guide them along the way, leading them through an experience, rather than being just a dry presentation of numbers and graphing minutiae.

The hallmark of compelling visualizations lies in **testing and refining**. Just as no chef serves up their first attempt at a new recipe, every data creator must be willing to experiment and iterate. Solicit feedback, embrace critiques, and be open to revision. What seems whimsical or clever to you may resemble a culinary disaster to your audience, and that's okay! Perfection takes time, and along the way, you will refine your visuals and messaging until they resonate and delight.

Lastly, always consider the **context** in which your visuals will be presented. Different audiences require different levels of detail; serving a simple dish at a family gathering is very different from preparing an elaborate banquet for VIP guests. Understand your audience; ask yourself, "What do they care about?" Tailor your visualizations accordingly, whether they're colleagues, clients, or curious relatives eager for new insights. This consideration will allow you to meet them where they are in their data journey, making your presentation feel more like a well-cooked meal rather than an indecipherable culinary experiment.

In conclusion, creating compelling visualizations is both a labor of love and an art. By adhering to best practices that enhance clarity, color, labeling, interactivity, storytelling, and context, you'll elevate your work to a delightful feast for the senses. Remember, the ultimate goal is to engage your audience and spark curiosity, so they walk away with insights and are eager for a second helping. Now go forth and create visuals so delicious that your audience will crave the next course. Buon appetito!

Chapter 11

Continuous Learning In AI

The Concept of Continuous Learning in AI

Probability Continuous learning in AI, the concept that makes machine learning models feel like that highly ambitious cousin who just can't stop refining their talent for cooking ravioli. I mean, while the rest of us are satisfied with our tried-and-true, slightly lumpy noodles, he's busy signing up for classes in molecular gastronomy, thinking he can turn flour and water into culinary masterpieces. In the realm of artificial intelligence, this notion of continuous learning isn't just a fancy buzzword; it's akin to having a recipe that evolves and improves each time you use it. So, let's dig into this delectable concept and see how it parallels the art of cooking.

To understand continuous learning in AI, think of it as an ever-evolving recipe for your famous lasagna, one that not only accommodates changes in flavor preferences but actually learns from the past experiences of your diners. You know those moments when Aunt Maria tastes your lasagna, she

raises an eyebrow, and says, "Hmm, it's good, but maybe a little more nutmeg?" Well, imagine if every time she said that, your lasagna developed a memory of that feedback, adjusting the recipe for the next family gathering. In the world of AI, models need to learn from their experiences just like I learn from Aunt Maria's critical (yet constructive) feedback. This iterative process of learning from past performance is what makes continuous learning essential.

In machine learning, continuous learning helps algorithms improve themselves by adapting to new data over time. It's somewhat akin to that awkward yet lovable uncle who eventually learns how to use social media, not without some fumbles along the way, of course. When the algorithm encounters new data, it doesn't just discard the old knowledge; instead, it uses that information to fine-tune its predictions, much like how I'd adjust my grandmother's pasta recipe every time I manage to actually remember to buy the right kind of cheese! This adaptability is crucial, especially when models face new and unforeseen scenarios. Imagine an AI that learns from its mistakes each time it encounters a surprise ingredient or finds itself in an unexpected dinner conversation. Isn't that what we all wish for during the holidays?

You must be wondering, "So, John, does that mean every model is like a perfect chef, continually updating their recipe book?" Not quite. Continuous learning also carries the risk of overfitting, much like the chef who gets so adventurous with the spices that they end up creating something more jarring than harmonious. As AI systems consume new data, they can sometimes become overly complex, trying to accommodate every single flavor of experience tossed their way. These models need to strike a balance between learning from new data and maintaining their foundational knowledge, just like I must be careful not to drown my marinara in an avalanche of garlic.

There's also this wonderful idea of 'forgetting' within continuous learning. Like that time I decided to temporarily forget how my Italian nonna used to make spaghetti just so I could try and develop my own unique version where lemon zest somehow fit in (and trust me, it didn't). Well, in the AI landscape, this 'forgetting' allows models to discard outdated knowledge that could cloud their performance. It's like getting rid of the last three-week-old leftovers in your fridge that are just one cough away from starting their own social media account. What's important here is understanding that while an AI model needs to learn continuously, it also needs an efficient way to reassess which information to keep and which to toss, just as I should learn to reassess which culinary experiments deserve a second chance.

In essence, continuous learning in AI is about perpetual improvement, adjusting to the flavors of the moment while respecting the time-honored traditions of cooking, just like my joyously stubborn adherence to the notion that there's a right way to make carbonara. And as I delve into this confluence of culinary and computational philosophies, I come to one clear takeaway: whether we're talking about lasagna or algorithms, success isn't just about a great start but about an ongoing commitment to learning, adapting, and, eventually, serving something truly unforgettable. Now, excuse me while I go ponder my next culinary AI experiment: the Sentient Spaghetti, your noodles have never been so self-aware!

Repurposing Leftover Data: Lessons from the Kitchen

Repurposing leftover data; it sounds like something only a true cooking aficionado, or perhaps a data scientist with a flair for the dramatic, would appreciate. Picture it: you've successfully churned out a sumptuous spaghetti dish, but in the end, you find yourself facing a somewhat intimidating surplus of exquisitely tangled noodles and an improbably large vat of marinara. Your first instinct may be to toss it all in the fridge and worry about it later, but before you know it, you're stuck with a mysterious Tupperware full of what was once delicious, now rapidly descending into a source of culinary anxiety. Well, like any resourceful chef worth their salt, or rather spaghetti, would tell you, there's gold to be found in leftover data. Let's dig into the marrow of the subject and discover how those bits and bytes of data we didn't think we'd need can be recycled into something spectacular, much like a classic Italian dish!

When we talk about data in the realm of AI, we often think of it as a raw ingredient, meticulously collected and prepped, ready to share its bounty in a glorious analysis. However, once the initial excitement wears off, it's common to encounter a comprehensive pile of leftover data, those bits we never ended up serving, similar to the half a loaf of bread lingering at the back of the pantry. Instead of tossing everything aside and pretending it never existed, we can use those leftovers to whip up something remarkable. Just as no Italian grandmother would let good bread go to waste, neither should we. What can we do with those "leftover" data sets? The opportunities are more enticing than the word 'spaghetti' can ever be in a three-Michelin-star restaurant!

Think of leftover data as the culinary equivalent of a fridge full of uncertainty. Maybe there's that half cup of pesto you forgot about, or the ogling jar of sun-dried tomatoes, patiently waiting for their moment to shine. In the same way, leftover data can provide new dimensions and fresh insights when we're trying to characterize a problem or build a machine learning model. It's not just about discarding the unusable bits; it's about taking a good look at what remains, stirring it up, and transforming it into something that will leave your audience raving about your ingenuity, if only to distract them from that overly firm piece of meatloaf you served last Sunday.

As we dive into these wasted bits, remember that every squished piece of data carries the potential for discovery. Much like you might creatively toss mushrooms into that extra marinara to make pasta primavera with what you thought was forgotten Spanish rice, we can use leftover data to enrich our models and make our algorithms robust. Whether it's historical data we never used or recent data sitting completely unapproved at the door, repurposing these leftover ingredients can unlock insights we previously overlooked. As I'm fond of saying, "one man's trash is another man's trendy risotto."

Remember, though, that just as an overenthusiastic chef might try to mix far too many flavors in one dish (cue the horror of chili chocolate gelato), data repurposing must be handled with care. Too many disparate data sources can indeed be worse than a soggy pizza crust. In the AI realm, this means terminologies like "dimensionality reduction", like a chef strategically trimming down their ingredient list to keep things elegantly simple. By carefully selecting which leftover data to combine, we can craft powerful algorithms that draw on past experience without inadvertently creating a mishmash of mediocrity.

Let's not forget the true heart of the matter: creativity is at the core of repurposing leftovers. As every Italian mama will tell you, the best meals don't always stem from brand-new ingredients; they come from a willingness to innovate and be free with those culinary accidents we might normally toss aside. Transforming leftover data might begin with the predictable options, but real innovation happens when we mix and match in unexpected ways. Are you introducing a new feature you once disregarded? Perhaps you're leveraging specific insights that were barely perceptible before? Voila! You're now cooking with some serious zest!

In the end, repurposing leftover data is a routine we can all embrace, especially if you've ever dug into the depths of your fridge, resisting the urge to scream, "Why on earth do I have thirty jars of mustard?" As a thoughtful chef does with a revered yet unconventional food item, finding ways to breathe new life into leftover data will transform your results, leading to extraordinary discoveries that can surprise and delight. So, the next time you find yourself knee-deep in untouched data, channel your inner chef, embrace creativity, and remember: sometimes the best dishes emerge from the most unexpected ingredients. All it takes is a pinch of flair and a dash of daring!

Feedback Loops in Machine Learning and Cooking

Feedback loops in machine learning are a fascinating (and sometimes baffling) concept that resonates remarkably well with the lifelong culinary journey most of us go through, whether or not it involves that off-brand pasta sauce incident. Think of feedback loops as the cosmic spaghetti strand connecting your taste buds to your cooking prowess, forever twirling and spinning into an intricate dance of learning and adapting. In the world of cooking, it's not just about following the recipe to the letter; it's about tasting, adjusting, and refining your dish based on taste tests (typically provided by friends or family, desperately hoping you're not about to poison them with an underseasoned risotto). Similarly, in machine learning, feedback loops help algorithms improve through cycles of learning, evaluation, and adjustment. So, let's dig into how these deliciously dynamic cycles can elevate both your cooking game and your machine learning models!

The essence of a feedback loop is making adjustments based on results to achieve the most pleasing outcome, like whipping up a batch of lasagna, realizing the noodles are overcooked, and swearing you'll never repeat that culinary atrocity again. As an aspiring chef (and yes, a technology risk manager), I can tell you that cooking is rife with feedback loops. It's all about the constant interplay between your culinary instincts, the responses of your ingredients, and the unvarnished critiques lobbed at you from taste testers who may or may not be too polite to let you know they'd rather eat a bowl of chalk dust than try your experimental pumpkin carbonara.

In machine learning, feedback loops work similarly: algorithms learn from previous outputs by assessing how well they achieved the desired objectives and adjusting their internal parameters accordingly. It's like the time my aunt served tuna salad at a family get-together and, upon discovering significant face-pulling from her beloved cousins, promptly decided to stick to the safer territory of her renowned veal parmesan. Algorithms are in the same boat, only they have the advantage of crunching data faster than any family member can say, "Please don't make that again." Whether it's tuning hyperparameters or evolving decision criteria, feedback loops enable AI to optimize its performance through iterative learning.

However, the challenge lies in understanding where to apply these feedback loops effectively; the all-too-common pitfall of overcooking a dish would pale next to an algorithm trapped in a feedback loop, going in circles and ending up in an infinite spiral of some kind of culinary limbo. In machine learning, this endless repetition can lead to overfitting, where the model becomes too specialized to the training data and loses its ability to generalize to new data. In my case, I once made a mushroom risotto so exquisite that I vowed to apply the very same technique to every rice dish I encountered, only to be reminded that not all rice dishes thrive with a heaping of mushroom stock. In short, staying attuned to the risks of feedback loops is essential in both cooking and machine learning.

Of course, no kitchen or lab has ever thrived on strictly formulaic practices. So, when it comes to feedback loops, there's a necessity for intuition and creativity. Just as I wouldn't shy away from experimenting with a mystical blend of rosemary to zest up my next chicken dish (cue the raised eyebrows of my culinary watchdogs), similarly, machine learning models benefit from experimentation. This exploration within feedback loops could mean trying different feature sets or model architectures to find the ideal combination for your specific needs. It allows us to break free from the traditional molds and dive into the thrilling whirlpool of culinary creativity, where every twist and turn leaves us scratching our heads, wondering how to balance onions and, perhaps, a healthy dose of herbs.

Moreover, effective collaboration can bolster both cooking and machine learning feedback loops. In the kitchen, sharing your delicious innovations (or, yikes, disasters) can inspire and refine ideas among your fellow culinary adventurers, reshaping how you approach future dishes. Similarly, team collaboration in AI projects ensures that feedback doesn't come from a single perspective, opening the door to new insights and invigorating discussions about potential model improvements. We'd all secretly like to think we're exceptional solo cooks, but nothing beats the experience of refining a dish together, just as nothing beats multi-disciplinary teams refining algorithms through constructive critique.

Ultimately, feedback loops to both cooking and machine learning encapsulate the magical interplay between learning, experiencing, and adapting through iterative trial and error. Whether you're flipping that pan of carbonara or fine-tuning your neural networks, remember that every setback is but a seasoning that can be adjusted for future culinary adventures. Embrace the delightful chaos and don't hesitate to tinker with what you've got; after all, every burnt dish or overfitted model is just an opportunity waiting to be transformed into something spectacular. Onward, dear readers, to a future where your spaghetti sauce is robust, your AI is astute, and the world is your flavor-tasting laboratory!

The Importance of Adjustability in Recipes and Algorithms

Adjustability in recipes and algorithms is akin to the dance we all do during the holiday season, when your family insists on the classic lasagna recipe but you secretly want to infuse it with a touch of modern flair, like an unexpected sprinkle of kale or, heaven forbid, a non-traditional cheese blend. It's in moments like these, where the push and pull of culinary tradition clash shamelessly with innovation, that we truly appreciate the necessity of adjustability. Much like testing the waters, how much salt do you dare add before Cousin Roberto starts to sweat at the mere mention of "salt content"? The ability to adapt is crucial whether we're working with a cherished family recipe or a complex algorithm. So let's dive in and explore how this culinary principle translates beautifully into the realm of machine learning.

In cooking, adjustability is not just preferable; it is essential. After all, who hasn't faced the jarring realization that your brand of flour acts like a rebellious toddler when you try to bake? Be it too dry, too wet, or just downright finicky, each ingredient has its own personality, much like team members in a workplace environment. Adjusting your recipe in response to the ingredients at hand might mean swapping out olive oil for avocado oil one day or deciding between fresh basil and the suspicious jar at the back of your pantry that's been there since before you discovered TikTok. Similarly, in machine learning, adjustability ensures that algorithms can learn from diverse datasets and refine their outputs based on the variables they encounter. If you rigidly adhere to one single input or dataset without flexibility, you're going to end up with algorithmic spaghetti that doesn't resemble anything remotely appetizing!

For instance, let's imagine we're endeavoring to bake a soufflé (or at least I am, having watched countless cooking shows, I'm feeling quite confident). When the cake rises and then surprisingly collapses, similar to my hopes of rising to the culinary elite, there's a key realization: I must adjust my method! Maybe it's a matter of beating the egg whites or learning from my past failures. Each adjustment contributes vital knowledge for the future. Just as that moment of hesitation causes you to rethink your pasta dish, "Was that an actual cup of Nutella I accidentally added to the fettuccine?", the same is true of machine learning algorithms. They require ongoing adjustments to remain effective, adaptable, and relevant in our rapidly changing worlds of data.

The same idea translates to tuning hyperparameters in algorithms. Just as altering the temperature mid-roast can mean the difference between a perfect meatball and an inedible hockey puck, changing the regularization strength or the learning rate in your model can drastically influence its performance. In the AI realm, it all boils down to that delicate balance of adjustments, shifts, learning, and re-evaluations, much like deciding whether to add another pinch of salt or a dash of paprika. If we blindly follow the original recipe, we may miss out on the potential surprise of bringing a new twist to the classic. Embracing adjustability provides the excitement of discovering flavors we didn't even know could harmonize on the palate!

Now, you might ask, "But how can I infuse this sense of adjustability into my algorithms?" Well, the key lies in the cyclical nature of machine learning processes, allowing systems to receive feedback and transform accordingly. Just like I would clutch an acceptance letter from a culinary school at the first whiff of cinnamon wafting through my kitchen, machine learning thrives on adaptation. Regular modeling practices require ongoing reshaping of features and responsiveness to input variations. The beauty of this lies in recognizing that growth doesn't happen in isolation; it flourishes in an environment that encourages feedback, experimentation, and the ability to pivot just as often as I find myself pivoting from one questionable ingredient to another!

Furthermore, adapting to customer preferences is crucial not just in cooking but also in building algorithms that cater to user preferences. The moment you notice Aunt Edna, notorious for her aversion to garlic, resume her grumbling complaints as you serve your new Italian dish, you know you must adjust. Similarly, when users exhibit preferences based on how they interact with your product, datasets must evolve to reflect those changes. An adaptable algorithm can ensure relevance in an environment filled with competing tastes and shifting behaviors, much like a good chef augments their culinary creations to satisfy the latest dining trends.

In conclusion, adjustability in recipes and algorithms isn't merely a virtue but a necessity, an essential ingredient in crafting delicious meals and effective AI. It's about allowing the flavors to mix, the textures to harmonize, and the results to be nothing short of extraordinary. Embrace the joy of tasting and evaluating, whether you're adding that crucial hint of nutmeg to your next dish or reconfiguring your machine learning parameters in real-time. After all, the hallmark of both good cooking and effective algorithms is the willingness to embrace change, adjust the plan, and embrace the unexpected, much like serving an irreplaceably jarring-but oddly delightful peanut butter and popcorn pasta to your friends. So take a culinary leap of faith, adjust on the fly, and remember, the magic truly happens when you allow flexibility into your creations!

Real-World Applications of Continuous Learning

Real-world applications of continuous learning in the realm of artificial intelligence might just delight you as much as finding a hidden stash of noodles in the back of your pantry. It's like when Aunt Maria shows up with her nonna's secret marinara sauce recipe, and you realize there's a world full of culinary gems just waiting to be uncovered. Continuous learning is the secret sauce of AI, enabling machines to adapt, evolve, and ultimately deliver results that could impress even the most discerning of

Italian grandmothers, or the most demanding of corporate CEOs. Let's delve into the delectable world of continuous learning and explore its real-world applications in a way that even your nonna might understand (albeit with a little less hand-gesturing).

One of the most riveting applications of continuous learning can be found in the field of recommendation systems, which are like a well-meaning friend who claims to know all your favorite pasta dishes. You know the type: they always suggest the risotto you've already sworn to avoid since your last ill-fated attempt left a hovering cloud of disappointment in its wake. Continuous learning allows these systems to analyze user preferences, new data, and trends, fine-tuning their recommendations with a deftness that can only be compared to turning the perfect tomato into a robust marinara. The more data they gather (think of it like your ever-expanding recipe book), the better they can predict and serve up options that genuinely resonate with users, avoiding those uncomfortable "meh" moments like a true culinary oracle.

Then there is the glorious world of self-driving cars, a field where continuous learning works overtime to ensure passengers are whisked away securely, much like how your transit-hating cousin never leaves the car unless absolutely necessary. These vehicles collect data from various sensors in real time, learning to navigate the complexities of traffic, weather, and road obstacles. Continuous learning enables the systems to adapt effectively, refining their driving behaviors and avoiding fender benders like a skilled chef avoids a bubbling pot that's about to overflow. With each trip, these vehicles gather insights that not only enhance their driving capabilities but also contribute to overall roadway safety. Consider it a delightful fusion of learning and road-sawy pasta perfection.

Healthcare also benefits immensely from continuous learning applications, akin to a doctor extending her culinary knowledge by adding a sprinkle of turmeric for its anti-inflammatory properties (or at least trying to after writing a hundred prescriptions). AI algorithms can analyze vast amounts of medical data, identify patterns in patient responses, and develop personalized treatment plans over time. Continuous learning enables these algorithms to adapt as new research emerges and patients' unique health conditions evolve. In essence, your friendly neighborhood AI system is learning how to make the best lasagna for its audience, ensuring that each patient receives appropriate and tailored care, no rubbery options involved!

The realm of customer service is another prime candidate for continuous learning applications. Just imagine those chatbots designed to assist you at your favorite online store; after all, it's not fun trying to explain what you want to an algorithm whose references date back to the late '90s! Continuous learning enables these bots to analyze conversations, better understand customer queries, and improve their responses over time. It's like having a loyal sous-chef who learns the secrets behind your family recipes, continuously adjusting their techniques to meet your specific desires, like learning that, no, it's not okay to put anchovies in the family pizza recipe!

Let's not forget the fascinating world of marketing analytics, where continuous learning drives improvements in campaigns and messaging, a bit like a potent blend of seasonings that transforms an average dish into pure magic. Brands can analyze consumer reactions, engagement levels, and purchasing behavior to refine their marketing strategies and discover what works best for their target audience. This adaptive approach allows businesses to pivot at a moment's notice and ensures they're always presenting the most delectable offers to their customers. Think of it as a chef constantly updating the menu to reflect the latest and greatest culinary trends.

In conclusion, continuous learning is a powerful force shaping real-world applications across diverse domains, from recommendation systems and healthcare to self-driving cars and marketing analytics. Each system thrives on the ability to update, adapt, and improve, just as any knowledgeable chef evolves their craft over time. Whether you're navigating the complexities of data or whipping up the perfect marinara sauce for Sunday dinner, the key takeaway is clear: integration of continuous learning offers invaluable insights that can lead to a world filled with better solutions and more sumptuous flavors. So, the next time you glance at algorithms or AI models in your life, remember: sometimes, all it takes is an understanding of continuous learning, a dash of patience, and perhaps a sprinkle of optimism to serve up something truly exceptional!

Chapter 12

Cooking for Everyone: Ethical AI

The Importance of Fairness in AI

The age-old adage: "Fairness is key," right? You might have heard it tossed around at family gatherings when it comes to dividing lasagna, or perhaps when your cousin Mario refused to share his imported tiramisu. But let's put aside the culinary battles of yore for a moment and focus on something that impacts all our lives in the 21st century: fairness in AI. Surprisingly, it's not just about ensuring everyone gets an equal slice of the digital pizza; it's about building trust, promoting justice, and ensuring that no one gets served a plate of unfair predictions or biased decisions.

In the world of artificial intelligence, fairness is akin to the unmistakable taste of a well-balanced tomato sauce. If you've ever tasted a sauce that has more garlic than tomatoes, or worse, one that has too much sugar, you'll understand the horror of imbalance. Just as you wouldn't want to drown your pasta in a misaligned flavor profile, we don't want AI systems spewing out biased results that ruin the recipe for equality. Imagine a world in which your toaster decides that whole-grain bread is too healthy for you while it serves your neighbor's white bread with extra butter and a side of judgment. Not only is that machine unqualified to make dietary choices, but its bias could lead to a whole generation of unhealthy toast-eaters who blame the toaster for their lack of whole grains, virtually toastless victims of discrimination.

Fairness in AI is not just a warm, fuzzy feeling; it has real-world implications. When algorithms unfairly favor one demographic over another, say, giving better loan terms to applicants with certain names or zip codes, it's like a chef consistently favoring one type of cheese over another in a pasta dish, leaving the dish lacking in flavor and depth. In the same way, chefs must choose ingredients that enhance the dish equally, AI must evaluate inputs without cultural, racial, or gender biases. Picture a world where your opportunities are dictated by an algorithm more concerned about your last name than your qualifications. Talk about a recipe for disaster! Such discriminatory algorithms don't just take the joy out of cooking; they serve a bitter dish of inequality that no one wants a bite of

Now let's sprinkle in some humor because, as they say, "laughter is the best seasoning." Picture a future where robots roam the earth, judging all your life choices. "Oh, you didn't opt for avocado toast? You get a 20% higher chance of your algorithm denying your mortgage!" You see, an unfair AI is like a rude waiter who spills your drink and then blames you. "You shouldn't have ordered that fancy cocktail!" Stereotypes and biases in AI are the unwanted garnishes we need to remove, the equivalent of parsley on a plate of spaghetti that no one asked for.

To achieve fairness, we need diverse datasets. Imagine preparing a colorful salad; the more ingredients you add, the tastier the result. Toss in a few ripe tomatoes, crunchy cucumbers, zesty olives, and maybe, dare I say, some anchovies for good measure? (I promise, the anchovies won't ruin the party!) In AI, including varied perspectives in our datasets creates a robust algorithm that understands the complexity of human situations. A well-rounded dataset represents all voices, preventing an algorithm from sounding like that uncle who insists that the "old ways are the best ways," while choking down his outdated spaghetti recipe. A harmonious mix is what we want to capture, ensuring that everyone gets a fair shot at the measurement of success.

Now, you might be wondering, "John, how do we ensure fairness in our AI?" Fortunately, the answer isn't to hire a sous chef to supervise the algorithms! Instead, it involves a multi-faceted approach. Implementing fairness audits is like tasting your dish at different stages of cooking; it allows us to catch biases and recalibrate before serving it to others. Integrating diverse teams brings us innovative perspectives, like inviting your Italian grandmother, a vegetarian cousin, and that one friend who swears they can never live without bacon, all to the same dinner table. Everyone brings their unique taste buds, allowing for a more balanced meal, and, more importantly, a fair AI.

To wrap this up, addressing fairness in AI is not just a suggestion; it's a necessity. Like a good Italian meal, fairness should be part of the recipe. If we fail to consider fairness, we risk serving up a toxic dish of biases that nobody wants to consume. So next time you consider the importance of fairness in AI, remember: it matters as much as ensuring enough cheese on your pizza. Happy cooking!

Catering to Diverse Palates: Inclusivity in AI

Inclusivity, like the olive oil drizzling gracefully over a well-prepared pasta dish or the cheeky addition of jalapenos in a classic Italian recipe that wasn't asking for it, but when you try it, you're suddenly questioning your life choices in the best way possible. Inclusivity in AI is akin to cooking with a pinch of imagination and a whole lot of openness to new flavors. It's not just about making sure everyone gets a seat at the table; it's about evolving the dish itself to create something delicious and harmonious, where every taste is considered, and every preference catered to.

Imagine you're hosting a dinner party, and amidst the bustle of pots clanging and the tantalizing aroma wafting through your home, your guest's dietary preferences pop up. Your vegan friend announces they've decided to go gluten-free just this week, while their counterpart insists on a strict regime of cheese-only dishes. Confused, you look at your options: a lonesome bowl of salad, some sad breadsticks, and a rogue wheel of parmesan. Now, how do you craft a feast that satisfies both the cheese lovers and the herbivores? You get creative! Think of lentil pasta smothered in fresh pesto, topped with a sprinkle of nutritional yeast as a cheeseless compromise. In the same vein, inclusivity with AI means creating adaptable systems that account for diverse needs and preferences rather than defaulting to the "traditional" approach, which often leaves out many appreciated flavors.

In AI, inclusivity isn't just a fancy word we slap on our mission statements to sound progressive; it's pivotal to how we build models and interpret results. Increasing representation in our datasets ensures that we're not only validating some narrow demographic but actually capturing the sweet essence of humanity in all its splendid diversity. Remember that one time you whipped up an exciting new dish but neglected to consider just how many people actually detest Brussels sprouts? Well, that recipe was bound to fail faster than you can say ''nonna's meatballs!"

Now, when it comes to AI, we have to recognize that if our training data reflects only certain populations, it risks creating algorithms that misinterpret or misrepresent the vast tapestry of human experiences. Imagine an AI judgmental oven that refuses to bake your apples because it thinks they're too "out of the box" for conventional pie-making. Now that's an oven that seriously needs an attitude adjustment! Inclusivity in AI ensures we don't allow bias to develop based on who is represented and who gets brushed under the carpet, like last week's leftover pasta. Nobody deserves to be ruthlessly ignored like a forgotten fruit bowl while the unyielding avocados and oranges bask in their prime.

One of the delightful parts of inclusivity is that it engenders creativity. The more diverse the voices you include in the AI conversation, the more likely you are to bake up something genuinely impactful. Include your spicy aunt, your gluten-sensitive neighbor, and the vegan boyfriend who brings nothing but kale to the potluck; they may surprise you with flavors you didn't even know could coexist! With AI, having a variety of perspectives means the algorithms can develop a more holistic understanding of human traits and preferences. Whether you're building systems for hiring, healthcare, or even automated pizza recommendation engines (so important!), inclusivity gives AI the right ingredients to deliver delightful outcomes.

Moreover, inclusivity isn't a solo endeavor. It requires collective action, like forming a kitchen brigade of sorts. When chefs collaborate, they share their expertise and form a crescendo of culinary artistry. In our AI kitchens, creating diverse teams that encompass different genders, ethnicities, ages, and experiences makes it possible to cook up more robust and responsible models. Not only do they bring different insights into the pot, but they also champion inclusivity at every step of the way, because who said artificial intelligence needed to be invented in isolation?

Let's be honest, folks, the future of AI is as much about flavors as it is about analytics. We can't just build algorithms the way we think we know best and then feed them to the public, like all those recipes that look amazing on Instagram but flop spectacularly in reality. Just like that infamous soufflé that takes down the dinner party, failing to embrace inclusivity in AI could lead to terrible results with dire consequences. If it isn't inclusive, it isn't learning, and if it isn't learning, it certainly isn't evolving.

So, let's roll up our sleeves and whip together an AI recipe that embraces diversity at every turn. After all, isn't life too short to serve bland pasta and uninspired algorithms? Let's make inclusivity our secret ingredient and transform the AI landscape into a spread of delectable options everybody can enjoy. Who's hungry?

Navigating Cultural Sensitivities

Cultural sensitivities aren't just about avoiding the awkward silence at the dinner table when you happen to serve lasagna dipped in ketchup (an unforgivable crime against Italian cuisine, I assure you); they're also about recognizing and respecting differences that shape our collective experiences. When discussing AI, cultural sensitivities become critical as we strive to ensure that our algorithms don't accidentally clobber someone's heritage like a misunderstanding at an Italian family reunion (''Wait! You're telling me that's not how we make fettuccine?!"). Just as cooking takes into account the various ingredients and methods stemming from countless cultures, AI must similarly navigate the intricate tapestry of human background and belief.

Picture a world where you're heading to a potluck, but your dish of spaghetti and meatballs is met with a glare from your friend who just came back from a month in Italy. Suddenly, your traditional recipe, which you intended to share lovingly, is on trial in the courtroom of international cuisine, making you feel as though your entire culinary existence is collapsing. Much like that moment, AI systems can dramatically misinterpret or misrepresent cultural norms if they aren't built with a robust understanding of diverse contexts. For instance, an algorithm aimed at recommending food might end up serving you a nice big plate of offense if it mistakenly pairs a halal dish with a wine recommendation. I mean, unless you're trying to make a new culinary trend, that's a massive fail!

To navigate cultural sensitivities in AI, one must start with active listening and a willingness to learn. Remember that infamous scene in *The Godfather* where they say, "Leave the gun, take the cannoli"? Think of it as "Leave the stereotypes, take the time to listen." Designers and engineers should embrace this foundational practice: engaging with various communities to glean insights that guide AI development. Imagine the flavor explosion when olive oil meets traditional Thai chili paste, what a combo! That's where the magic happens, and we need to bring this attitude into our algorithms.

It's crucial to understand these cultural nuances, especially when building models that might influence lives. For example, let's say we create an algorithm for mental health resources. If it doesn't focus on cultural differences, it's like offering a textbook "How to Fix Your Life" manual that conflicts with someone's deeply held beliefs. It risks pushing people away instead of pulling them toward valuable support, kind of like serving pizza to someone who's gluten-free. Misalignment can lead to disastrous outcomes, reinforcing barriers rather than breaking them down.

But how do we ensure AI doesn't end up as the culinary equivalent of a grumpy chef who refuses to accommodate anyone's tastes? The answer lies in extensive testing and a dash of humility. Just as you might taste-test various dishes for salt and spice levels before serving your guests, AI teams must continually evaluate algorithms within cultural contexts. This can prevent methodological mishaps that would make anyone cringe. External audits for such systems are essential. Imagine bringing in your 'Food Network' critic friend to give a thumbs-up before you spring your special creation on the family. Seek diversity within your team, not only as chefs but as storytellers; they, too, have rich experiences to contribute and can guide your AI model through the intricate dance of cultural sensitivity.

Furthermore, transparency is the big parmesan cheese here! Well-painted algorithms are like well-crafted dishes: they should reveal the layers of their complexity without resorting to secrets hidden under a heap of mashed potatoes, er, I mean, blind spots. When people know how decisions are being made, they are more likely to trust AI outputs. The more transparent we are about the underlying algorithms and datasets, the more likely we can avoid messy misinterpretations, like openly discussing your aunt's infamous lasagna recipe instead of pretending it's some top-secret culinary code.

Navigating cultural sensitivities in AJ isn't about tiptoeing hesitantly, nervously biting into the sacrilegious lasagna. It's about embracing connections, recognizing diversity, and ensuring all flavors are honored and represented. We must ask ourselves: Are the algorithms reflecting just the bland consensus or the true tapestry of humanity in all its colorful glory? That's where our triumph lies, in building AI that celebrates heritage and recognizes that a single recipe is never enough!

When we get this delicate balance of cultural sensitivity just right, we're offering up a buffet, not just a single dish. In turn, we create a world where AI doesn't just function but flourishes! Now, let's raise a toast (perhaps with some sparkling grape juice for the kids) to an inclusive future, one where our algorithms do more than serve, they celebrate! After all, life is too short for mediocre pasta, robotically bland AI, or forgetting to respect the richness of our cultural tapestries. Buon appetito!

The Role of Transparency in Ethical AI

Transparency is the secret sauce that turns a potentially murky AI stew into a nourishing broth of clarity. You see, just like a good marinara sauce isn't a mystery wrapped in layers of unidentifiable spices, transparency in AI means your algorithms shouldn't be served with a side of confusion and skepticism. We need to see what's cooking, especially when the outcomes can affect lives! This is the equivalent of making sure that when you invite friends over for dinner, you're not just serving them spaghetti with "surprise" meatballs and plenty of "mystery" sauce. No one wants that, believe me!

Transparency in ethical AI is about demystifying the decisions made by algorithms, making it clear how inputs are transformed into outputs. Think of it like a chef explaining the ingredients of a signature dish, no one wants to bite into a pizza just to discover that the "mozzarella" they're savouring was, in fact, a questionable cheese substitute. In a world increasingly driven by AI, a lack of transparency can sour public perception, raising the specter of doubt: "Is this AI my friend or my foe? Should I trust it with my bank details, or is it just waiting for me to slip up so it can take a bite out of my savings?"

We need to be upfront about AI because let's face it, scaring people away from new technology isn't the goal here, unless, of course, you're an overdramatic director aiming for an AI horror movie, which, by the way, I can totally see happening! For most of us, it's vital that AI works to serve the greater good rather than merely fiddling around behind our backs like some sneaky sous-chef trying to steal the last piece of dessert. By peeling back the curtain on how these algorithms function, we stand a better chance of fostering trust and confidence. After all, if my AI model were a pizza. I'd want folks to know I wasn't using expired toppings, or, worse, anchovies, if they were adamantly against them!

Another aspect of transparency in ethical AI is traceability. This refers to our ability to track how specific outputs result from particular inputs, much like tracing the origins of high-quality olive oil back to sun-kissed groves. If an algorithm makes a mistake, or worse, a discriminatory choice, can we pinpoint the source? This not only allows us to diagnose issues, but it also encourages accountability. Picture finding a single rogue spice in your bolognese that led to a culinary disaster; if we could trace it back, we could standardize our recipe and prevent future fiascos. By the same token, understanding why an AI makes particular decisions is crucial to preventing future blunders.

Of course, there's also the old saying that "what you don't know won't hurt you." This holds true in cooking: if you pretend that the burnt pan is still perfect, you will never learn how to cook better. Ignoring transparency in AI is analogous to believing that your burnt lasagna is still a five-star dish simply because nobody wants to question it. But trust me, everyone will notice when they taste it! People may not always articulate their concerns about AI, but rest assured, a sense of skepticism will simmer beneath the surface, leading to widespread mistrust and reluctance to engage with AI applications.

But let's not be all doom and gloom, I like to think that transparency can lead to empowerment! When people understand how AI systems work, they feel more in control. It's like watching a chef craft a delicately balanced risotto; you'll appreciate the effort and skill involved, making it all the more rewarding to dig in! By sharing how algorithms make choices, we can motivate users to engage with them, offering valuable feedback for continuous improvement while ensuring that the AI remains ethically aligned and community-focused.

However, transparency must be balanced with privacy considerations; it's not about divulging every pixel of an algorithm like airing out the family's cherished recipes for the whole world to inspect. Instead, we need to offer a comprehensive understanding without sacrificing sensitive information. If your AI were a family recipe, you'd want it shared across generations, while still holding on to that secret ingredient that makes it shine, fulfilling the promise of transparency while respecting the sanctity of privacy.

In conclusion, transparency in ethical AI isn't just about pulling back the curtain; it's about laying out the full spread, showing everyone what's being served. It's about building trust while avoiding the dreaded reputation of being the chef known for serving up dubious dishes. As we embrace transparency, we can foster a more informed and engaged society, a community where AI serves as a delicious feast of possibilities rather than a precarious gamble. So, let's raise a glass of Chianti to an ethical future where transparency reigns supreme, and may our algorithms never, ever run out of good Parmesan! Cheers!

Building a Diverse Team for Better AI Outcomes

When we talk about building a diverse team for better AI outcomes, it's like putting together an exceptional five-course meal. Every dish needs a unique flavor profile, and each ingredient contributes something vital to the overall experience. If you don't believe me, just imagine inviting your friends over for dinner and serving them eight different versions of spaghetti. Sure, it's Italian, but let's be real: that dinner party would go from gourmet to an unholy fiasco faster than you can say "tinned sauce." Similarly, if we only focus on a narrow range of perspectives in AI development, we're bound to end up with algorithms that lack depth, dimension, and, ultimately, the respect they deserve.

Diversity in the workplace isn't just a buzzword tossed around in corporate PowerPoint presentations as if it were the trendy new beetroot-infused bread at your local bakery. It's a crucial ingredient for innovation. When people from different backgrounds and experiences come together, they challenge each other's thinking, filling their algorithmic pots with various cultural ingredients that enrich the recipe for AI. Reflect for a moment: imagine if your team consists of individuals with wildly different backgrounds. Suddenly, you have someone from a tech-savvy upbringing, another from a humanities-loving family who speaks five languages, and, to round things out, perhaps that friend who insists on providing that secret sauce recipe passed down for generations. They'll put together an AI system as exquisite as crafted artisan pasta instead of bland, mass-produced noodles!

The dynamic shifts when everyone brings their own spice to the table, each person's lived experiences act as the salt that enhances the flavor. Consider the high-stakes world of fintech, where AI is rapidly reshaping how we handle money. If a team focuses solely on traditional perspectives, it risks missing the unique insights of marginalized communities that face financial barriers daily. A diverse team is equipped to recognize potential pitfalls that a homogeneous group might overlook, much like a potluck featuring a range of culinary talents. For instance, if the only input comes from tech-savvy experts, the resulting product might overlook accessibility and usability for people with different lived experiences. That's akin to focusing on perfecting a soufflé while ignoring the fact that some guests can't handle egg dishes!

So, how do we build these teams of culinary, oops, I mean technological, diversity? First on the menu is recruiting from a variety of channels. Let's think beyond the traditional "Ivy League or bust" mindset, we don't want to restrict ourselves to just one flavor of talent. Seek potential team members from different academic backgrounds, industries, and regions, and scoop fresh talent from universities, vocational schools, community colleges, and networks that highlight underrepresented individuals in tech. Just like a bountiful vegetable market, the more variety you pick, the richer your AI flavors will be!

Next, foster an inclusive workplace culture where every voice is encouraged to chime in like a chorus of kitchen helpers. Establishing an environment where team members feel safe expressing their ideas, concerns, and innovative suggestions is as important as reaching the right cooking temperature. If your team feels free to let loose, share ideas, and even point out when the dish is a little off, like using too much garlic in your sauce, they will collectively elevate the quality of the project to new heights. Don't be the chef with an oversized ego, convinced your way is the only way. Engage with your team's diverse perspectives to ensure your AI has the proper cultural seasoning.

Moreover, regular training and workshops on diversity and inclusion can help tame any lingering biases. These sessions serve as the culinary school for your team, similar to how aspiring chefs study the nuances of cuisines from around the world! It's not just about sprinkling in inclusivity for flavor; it's about mastering techniques that enhance everything. Nobody wants to serve a dish with stale or improperly understood elements. Equipping team members with the knowledge and skills to empathize with diverse users fosters an environment ripe for innovation instead of an algorithmic echo chamber.

When you build a diverse team, you're effectively setting up your AI system to be more ethically sound and grounded in a wider context. Algorithms designed by diverse teams not only serve a broader audience but also help to reduce biases by incorporating more perspectives. Just like cooking, it's about balance: taking in various influences and inspirations to craft something unique. A well-rounded, thoughtfully designed AI system is ethical, ready to embrace humanity's breadth and depth rather than reducing it to mere algorithms.

So, let's raise our metaphorical chef hats and embrace the richness of diversity in AI. After all, when we cultivate an environment where varied experiences and skills come together to create, we're not just making a little software, we're crafting a feast that will resonate with everyone. Remember, the secret to a successful AI outcome doesn't lie in the tech alone; it's built upon the diverse array of ingredients that make up the team, working in harmony to create something truly spectacular! Bon appetit!

Chapter 13

Kitchen Confidential: AI In The Workplace

The Rise of AI in the Culinary World

In recent years, the culinary world has embraced artificial intelligence like a long-lost cousin who suddenly shows up at Thanksgiving, bringing an awkward mix of charm and panic. AI is now slicing, dicing, and plating its way into our kitchens, revolutionizing how we cook, or, more accurately, how we examine food through the tech-fueled lens of data and algorithms. I mean, who would've thought that the secret ingredient to the perfect lasagna might actually be a complex algorithm rather than your nonna's annotated "passata" recipe?

Let's take a trip down this tech-infused culinary lane, shall we? Imagine an army of data-crunching robots donning chef hats, teleporting between kitchens as they analyze vast oceans of recipes to whip up new and exciting dining experiences. AI systems now have the culinary expertise of a thousand chefs, though they still can't taste the difference between basil and dust yet. They study thousands of recipes to predict what flavors harmonize best. It's like a dating app for ingredients, each ingredient swiping right on another based on compatibility, and AI matches them for dates in your pot. The old chefs are deemed irrelevant, standing in the background like actors in a Shakespearean tragedy, lamenting the loss of pure, messy culinary improvisation.

In a world where Michelin stars are increasingly sought after, AI comes to the rescue, acting as a sous-chef with a Ph.D. in flavor balancing and machine learning principles. A company called Foodpairing has made a name for itself by employing AI to unearth new flavor combinations, who knew that mango and rosemary could dance a tango in your mouth, right? As our palates demand ever more complex culinary experiences, the pressure on chefs to innovate is immense. So, while they're sweating over the stove and praying for inspiration, AI offers suggestions that are both spectacular and, let's be honest, downright bizarre at times. If your next culinary adventure involves sipping a blue cheese-and-pineapple smoothie, just know that AI might've had a hand in it, because apparently, it's the latest trend, and can't we all just feel the collective cringe?

But is there a downside to this gourmet robot uprising? Oh, absolutely! While chefs can now rely on AI to enhance their recipes, we also risk cooking becoming as soulless as a board meeting without a coffee break. We cherish our grandma's secret family recipes, which were lovingly crafted over time, with all the kitchen disasters and triumphs woven in. AI lacks that emotional intelligence, and it often misses the big picture, the love, laughter, and tears that come with stirring a pot of sauce made from ripe tomatoes and crushed dreams. While we let AI take the wheel, will we sacrifice the art of cooking on the altar of efficiency? Will we eventually wrap our pasta in a spreadsheet?

Indulge me for a second while I tell you about a recent episode in my life, an Al-meets-cooking soiree, which I mistakenly thought would be the culinary event of the season. I decided to give a tech-driven cooking class a whirl, where an AI assistant guided us through the process of making ravioli. It felt like the plot of a futuristic movie, with us, the unsuspecting chefs, armed with rolling pins while the AI chattered happily about pasta dilation. "More flour, John, or it will stick!" it squealed. I found myself rebelling against the chirpy little robot. I like the risk of over-flouring my dough! What if I wanted to embrace the chaos? That's the fun of cooking, the thrill of throwing caution to the wind!

You may wonder how these AI culinary adventures tie into your dining experience. Well, the rise of AI in cooking means the future of restaurants is less about Aunt Carmela's home-cooked charm and more about flashy innovations that could reduce wait times and improve consistency. Yet, beneath this shiny exterior, a twinge of irony remains. You might find yourself asking: "Am I dining on five-star food or algorithmic predictions?" Dining out might turn into a futuristic trip to a tech-savvy tasting room where, rather than a real chef, you have a gray box spewing out the latest food fads recommended by an algorithm, yummy, yet somewhat dystopian!

As AI continues to weave its way through our kitchens and restaurants, one thing is clear: it's not just about saving time or, dare I say, transforming how we eat. It's a blend of tech and tradition that might eventually create dishes we never thought possible, like a spaghetti-inspired data visualization, which, while delicious in theory, might just leave you scratching your head and reaching for the garlic bread. The rise of AI in the culinary world is a test that sits squarely on the kitchen counter: learn to balance flavors as well as flesh out what it means to cook with the heart and soul, before AI decides it's too busy to care. Who will triumph in this battle of the robots versus the chefs? Only time, and perhaps a well-cooked lasagna, will tell!

Automation vs. Human Touch in Cooking

In the grand cooking arena, a fierce battle is waging: automation versus the human touch. On one side, we have a shiny robotic army ready to dice, sauté, and plate with the precision of a world-class surgeon, delivering meals that look like they belong in a high-fashion magazine. On the other side lurks our messy, lovable human side, the one that improvises, tastes, and occasionally sets off smoke alarms in the name of culinary creativity. As someone who revels in the art of Italian cooking, I often ponder this existential question: will I someday hand over my beloved wooden spoon to a machine because it can do a better job? Spoiler alert: not on my watch!

Let's set the scene in your average kitchen. Picture it: pots bubbling, the aroma of garlic infiltrating the air, and the delightful chaos of spices flying about like confetti at a celebration. Now inject a sous-chef robot in there who doesn't feel pressure, doesn't have good days or bad days, and, shocker, has never burnt the garlic. This mechanized companion can whip up a carbonara with exacting measurements, ensuring that the ratios of yolk to pecorino are flawless. But dare I say: where's the soul in that?

Automated cooking appliances are designed to replicate human actions with unnerving accuracy. Take a look at those Instant Pot recipes, you follow step-by-step instructions, and in the end, you emerge with a dish that is undeniably edible but lacks that certain je ne sais quoi. Let me tell you, folks, recipes are merely guidelines, like GPS directing you on a road trip through Italy. Sure, it can take you to your destination, but who doesn't enjoy taking a detour for that hidden roadside trattoria? Cooking should be about exploration and gut instinct, not robotic efficiency.

Nevertheless, the automated culinary revolution is hard to ignore. AI algorithms analyze countless recipes and tell you the most popular combinations, great for big food companies trying to sustain a matrix of blandness, but what happens to the creative spirit? A chef's gut feeling is an invaluable resource that can turn a simple dish into an unforgettable one. I once had a masterclass on ragu, where the chef famously ignored the conventional recipe, stating, "The meat has to speak to you!" Well, robots don't have ears or emotions to understand that poetic call. They're busy crunching numbers while we're amidst an impassioned chef rant about the importance of time and love in every sauce. Who needs that kind of talking head in the kitchen, anyway?

And let's not forget the sheer joy of preparation! A crucial element of cooking is the experience itself, chopping onions while weepily listening to stand-up comedy, smushing garlic cloves with the heel of our palms, and slicing basil with love and a hint of madness. Automation takes away the tactile joy of that messy, hands-on process. For me, the kitchen is a symphony of sounds: sizzling, chopping, and the celebratory clang of a chef's knife on the cutting board. When a robot takes over, my kitchen becomes a silent, sterile laboratory. Where's the laughter? Where's the chaos? Where's the secret ingredient of unfiltered joy?

Moreover, one of the biggest misconceptions about automated cooking is the idea that it is flawless. Technology, as we know, can stumble spectacularly in the most jaw-dropping ways, much like my Aunt Rita's attempt to create an "exotic" Italian fusion dish involving sushi and spaghetti, an unholy nightmare of rice and tomato sauce! I fear a robotic revolution could lead us to a future where the dishes go haywire, leaving us to cringe as we unwrap "squid ink gelato" or "vanilla pizza" dreamed up by an AI gone rogue. It's bound to happen: we'll find ourselves gathering around the table, questioning who invited these unintended hybrids and mentally preparing to clog our arteries, just to be polite.

Ultimately, there lies a powerful, beautiful truth in manual cooking that can't be distilled into ones and zeros. A dish crafted with love is akin to a family heirloom, each meal tells a story, encapsulates memories, and cradles the spirit of its maker. Automation is a boon, but like a pinch of salt, too much can ruin the dish. In the kitchen of our lives, we must remember to embrace the human touch, its spillovers, flavor explorations, and joyful mishaps. When I gather loved ones over a steaming pot of ragu, I want them to taste the love, the laughter, and yes, even the occasional burnt garlic, because that is what makes a meal truly special.

So, my fellow culinary adventurers, let us rock the delicate balance between automation and human touch! May we always pair our precision with passion, and may our kitchens be vibrant arenas where creativity flourishes amidst the hum of machines. After all, no robot can ever replicate the sound of laughter shared over a bowl of pasta dripping with family history. And if that burns that garlic just once again, well, it's just another charming chapter in the story of a cook, and boy, do we have a lot of tales to tell!

Case Studies: When AI and Chefs Collaborate

In the ever-evolving landscape of cooking, we're seeing a curious fusion of wires and whiskers, a peculiar partnership is brewing between human chefs and artificial intelligence. It's like watching a scene from "Beauty and the Beast," where the grumpy chef reluctantly partners with the overly enthusiastic robot. If only AI had a teapot's knack for charming our socks off. But there's merit to this collaboration, too, as evidenced by some remarkable case studies where kitchen sorcery meets digital wizardry.

Take, for instance, the culinary experiments at The Grey Area in San Francisco, a restaurant where acclaimed chef Ryan Mcllwraith has teamed up with AI. The concept is simple yet daunting: teach a computer the intricacies of flavor to create new dishes that are both enchanting and palatable. This is no small feat, mind you. It's like teaching your dog to dance ballet; it can be done, but who knows what will happen during the performance? Mcllwraith wanted to merge the artistic flair of a chef with the rigor of AI, and together they've crafted dishes that challenge our taste buds and still make us chuckle at the sheer absurdity of it all.

One of their concoctions involved AI employing neural networks to analyze flavors and predict combinations. Their grand revelation was "pumpkin-spice pulled pork tacos." If that doesn't sound like an addiction waiting to happen, I don't know what does! Here's where the magic lies: the dish turned out to be a crowd favorite, thanks in part to the AI finding the harmony between southwestern flair and autumnal flavors. It's like when your friend pairs a loud Hawaiian shirt with plaid shorts you never thought could work, audacious, but against all odds, it actually does. So, you see, cuisine remains somewhat of an experiment, and it's great to have an AI on board that doesn't roll its digital eyes when the potatoes start talking!

Then we have restaurants like Creator in San Francisco, where they've taken the concept of an AI-powered kitchen to a futuristic extreme. This eatery specializes in gourmet, custom burgers, all made by robots. Now, you may be thinking about how this harmonizes with your sentimental love for your local grill, flips your nostalgia into high gear, and has you reminiscing about the crackle of sizzling beef. However, Creator introduces you to the burger of the future, custom-built by AI with inputs from you, the omnivorous consumer. Patrons place their orders via a delightful interface, and they watch in awe as their dream burger is brought to life by a well-oiled robot army! There's something strangely mesmerizing about watching robotic arms construct a cereal bowl-sized burger patty with the grace of a ballet dancer. You've got your precision, your perfect toppings, and your perfectly portioned sauces in an unforgettable way, though I admit I miss the human ability to add just a wee bit too much mayonnaise when nobody's looking.

However, not all stories between AI and chefs are smooth sailing in a culinary utopia. In fact, some fail spectacularly, leaving us chuckling while also shaking our heads. There was the infamous incident at a prominent New York restaurant where an AI program suggested "oysters with jellybeans" as a new dish. Unfortunately, the chef didn't exactly embrace the concept, leading to a near mutiny in the kitchen. The AI, being the naive little data processor it was, must've thought it was on a food journey to a surreal art exhibition rather than trying to create an appetizing meal. Sometimes, you just can't teach an AI about good taste, even if it knows how to make a mean guacamole dip!

And while we're on this shaky ground of food juxtapositions, we can't forget about the widely adored BeeTwo, an AI chatbot from Vietnam that literally helps users create their own recipes based on personal preferences. It often manages to produce some outlandish suggestions, like a "Spaghetti Bolognese Pudding," where the line between savory and sweet seems to vanish entirely. One can't help but marvel at the bravery of those who dare to embark upon these culinary quests suggested by an all-knowing digital oracle. I mean, it's amusing to consider your dinner parties featuring "Bolognese Pudding", a culinary mystery that leaves everyone guessing whether they need dessert plates or forklift kits.

So, there's comedy and camaraderie in collaboration; AI finds itself trembling in the warm radiance of human creativity. Sure, we might end up with some outlandish concoctions along the way, but that's what makes cooking an art form as diverse as our personalities. Therefore, from technicolor tacos to extravagant burgers, AI and chefs march together into the unknown, illuminating the kitchen with technology while leaving space for a sprinkle of humanity. With every glimmer of hope we find in these collaborations, we must remember that behind every mechanical whir is a human soul ready to evolve. As we embrace this union of flavor and innovation, we can rest assured that laughter, in all its messy glory, is still high on the menu!

Transforming Business Processes with AI

As we dive headfirst into the exciting world of artificial intelligence, one can't help but marvel at how it's reshaping businesses across the globe, like a seasoned chef jazzing up an old family recipe with unexpected ingredients. Gone are the days when mundane tasks dominated the corporate landscape. Now, AI is here to sprinkle a little magic (and a fair amount of confusion) into the mix, transforming everything from customer service to inventory management. The question remains: will it lead to culinary perfection, or are we just stirring the pot with a dash of chaos?

Let's talk about those old-school, mind-numbing business processes for a moment. You know, those monotonous tasks that make employees feel like they're trapped in a never-ending cycle of culinary purgatory, just waiting for the moment someone frees them from the shackles of spreadsheets and email chains. Enter AI, stage left, ready to trade in those dull days for a delicious future. Imagine cooking with tools like predictive analytics, akin to a crystal ball for business forecasts. Whether it's predicting customer trends or optimizing supply chains, AI can identify patterns faster than I can burn a pot of water. And trust me. I'm an expert in that field.

Take the food service industry, for example, a sector steeped in tradition. Many restaurants are now deploying AI to streamline their operations. Picture a restaurant that employs automated inventory management systems to keep track of stock levels while monitoring expiration dates and supply chain disruptions. It's like having a virtual sous-chef that ensures you

never run out of those essential truffle oils or cumin spices. No more diners lamenting the sad absence of risotto just because the chef forgot to order the arborio rice! Efficiency is the name of the game, and when restaurateurs shift their focus to creative cooking rather than inventory woes, the benefits are both flavorful and profound.

But brace yourselves, because AI's transformative prowess doesn't just stop at inventory management. Imagine placing an order for that perfectly cooked lasagna, one that's been meticulously crafted to meet your dietary needs. Many eateries now engage AI-driven systems that offer personalized recommendations based on your palate preferences, order history, and allergies. You could say it's like having a personal digital sommelier guiding you through the pasta course of life! Just when you thought you'd forever be relegated to the mundane task of asking your waiter to recommend something, AI swoops in with probabilities and logic, making dining adventures more exciting.

And let's not overlook the challenges that come along with the rapid adoption of AI. Sure, on one hand, you have an elegant new solution to streamline workflows and reduce costs, but on the other, you might find employees feeling like they're playing a bad round of "Musical Chairs" in a tech-savvy dystopia. When menial tasks become the domain of AI, what happens to the human element in the workplace? We risk losing that spark, like a chef forgetting to add salt, if we become overly dependent on algorithms. The world is already filled with enough anxiety; we really don't need machines deciding who gets the last piece of tiramisu at the corporate potluck!

To illustrate this sentiment, imagine a corporate office where a robot is now in charge of customer service interactions. It's programmed with a database of FAQs, but when someone asks, "Is the garlic bread gluten-free?" the bot responds with an overly literal answer: "Garlic is a vegetable, and vegetables are gluten-free." Hilarity ensues, but the charm of the personal touch is lost amidst the pixelated chatter. Never underestimate the power of human curiosity or the sense of warmth that comes when we share stories in the kitchen, something a metal contraption simply cannot replicate.

Yet, there's hope! Businesses investing in AI don't have to abandon the personal connection entirely. By balancing automation with authenticity, companies can deliver superb customer experiences without sacrificing the human element. Perhaps we could imagine a world where AI handles mundane tasks like scheduling meetings, allowing employees to engage more deeply with each other, and making conference calls a little less torturous and a lot more enjoyable. Who wouldn't want a workplace teeming with personality while inundated with delightful coffee breaks?

Ultimately, the transformation of business processes with AI promises a tantalizing feast of opportunity. We can envision a future where our culinary delights blend seamlessly with innovation if we choose to navigate the challenges with humor and creativity. AI isn't here to replace us; it's here to elevate our journeys, freeing us from the tedious while allowing us to focus on the artistry at hand. In a world where the machines hum and whir, let's continue to savor our creations, infuse our meals with meaning, and remember the importance of balancing the flavors of efficiency with the zest of human connection. Bon appetit to our Al-enhanced adventures ahead!

The Future of Cooking and 7U* Integration

As we stir the pot of innovation bubbling away in the kitchen, it's time to discuss what the future of cooking and AI integration holds for us. Picture this: a world where your culinary decisions aren't just based on a hasty glance in the pantry but guided by a hyper-intelligent AI that knows your deepest, darkest cravings and assists you in crafting meals fit for a royal banquet, all while you recline on the couch, binge-watching your favorite reality shows about competitive cooking. The forecast? A delightful mix of efficiency and culinary creativity, with a quirky sprinkle of laughter for good measure.

In this brave new cooking world, the boundaries of flavor will be pushed beyond what we ever imagined. Imagine bionic sous-chefs whipping up dishes at breathtaking speeds, perfectly timing each step of the recipe like a pitch-perfect conductor leading the Berlin Philharmonic. With gee-whiz technology, AI will master not just the science of cooking but will enhance the nostalgic experience of it, urging chefs to interpret classic dishes through a new lens. It's equal parts science fiction and culinary fairy tale, where your grandmother's famous stuffed peppers might get a twist of AI-generated flavor from the mysterious depths of a database filled with the culinary secrets of every culture known to humanity. Who knew stuffed peppers could take a detour to Bangkok?

Moreover, we'll see a rise in personalized meal-planning tools powered by machine learning. In this idyllic world, your meal suggestions will be tailored not only to your health goals but also to your food preferences and mood swings, yes. I'm talking about those evenings when a bowl of mac and cheese is truly a top contender for "Meal of the Year." Imagine your AI telling you, "John, since you mournfully scrolled through your collection of dessert recipes last night while lamenting the loss of your diet, I suggest you indulge in a chocolate avocado mousse. It's the perfect balance of decadence and health!" Talk about a relationship that understands you!

Of course, any discussion about cooking would be incomplete without mentioning sustainability. The future of AI integration is ripe with the opportunity for environmentally conscious cooking practices. By supplying chefs with data about local ingredients, AI can encourage seasonal eating while reducing carbon footprints. Ever wondered about that little "Farm-to-Table" concept? AI can turn that into an effortlessly manageable, mouthwatering reality. With a little help from tech magic, we can say goodbye to those sad tomatoes shipped halfway around the world and embrace locally sourced produce with a story attached, flourishing under the sun of our beautiful communities. And really, who could resist hearing a tomato's epic tale of adversity?

But as we dip our toes into this futuristic reality, we must also recognize the challenges that accompany these tantalizing advancements. The kitchen of the future might come with its own brand of comedic chaos. Imagine a dinner party where your hyper-intelligent cooking assistant misinterprets that last-minute request for "gluten-free" to mean "aloof avant-garde." Suddenly, you're serving guests an extravagant gluten-free dish that resembles something plucked straight from an abstract art gallery rather than a delectable meal! Yes, technology is fantastic, but we'll have to keep an eye on it to prevent those small disasters, like when your kitchen assistant tries to roast a Brussels sprout using sensitive marshmallows as the main ingredient.

Speaking of social interactions, there's a challenge yet to be embraced: how will we maintain a sense of camaraderie with our fellow cooks in an AI-driven kitchen? The future must balance technology with the laughter and chaos we cherish in the culinary experience. We cannot allow ourselves to be boxed in by machines that create perfectly assembled dishes while we sit in silence, nodding solemnly at precisely crafted aesthetics. Cooking must still ignite moments of shared storytelling, playful experimentation, and glorious, heartwarming mistakes, the kind that aroma wafting from the oven unleashes family tales with every bite.

So, welcome to the kitchen of tomorrow, and prepare your taste buds for the flavorful ride of the century! With artificial intelligence and human creativity teaming up, we can expect a plethora of culinary conundrums, gourmet innovations, and delicious collaborations, ensuring that cooking remains a chaotic, fun adventure rather than a sterile process dictated by circuitry. Embrace the future with open arms and maybe a spatula or two. Our beloved dishes will evolve more rapidly than ever as we face each new challenge, all while sharing laughter and stories around the proverbial kitchen table. And let's remember: in a world of advanced AI, it's not just what's on your plate that matters, but the memories created along the way that make every bite worthwhile!

* 7U AI Server Infrastructure is built for intensive AI workloads, deep learning, cloud virtualization, and high-performance computing (HPC).

Chapter 14

The 7 Cooking Principles: Fundamental AI Concepts

The Essential Ingredients of AI

The essential ingredients of AI, akin to that ever-elusive tomato in the perfect marinara sauce. You know the one I'm talking about, the kind of tomato that not only knows it's a tomato, but also dreams of becoming the next superstar in a Michelin-rated Italian restaurant. In the world of artificial intelligence, just as in cooking, having the right ingredients can make or break the dish-, or, in our case, the algorithm. So let's explore what you need to whip up a successful AI recipe without ending up in a technicolor disaster.

First and foremost, we need to talk about data. Imagine preparing a rich spaghetti bolognese with nothing but a tin can of stale tomato sauce. Not appealing, right? Similarly, AI thrives on good quality data. It's the lifeblood that nourishes our algorithms, and if you skimp on quality, you're likely to end up with something resembling a poorly constructed lasagna, heavy, soggy, and utterly unappetizing. That's like feeding your AI system a diet of junk data; you're just asking for trouble. Quality data is like a perfectly ripe tomato, bursting with flavor. It comes fresh, clean, and rich in nutrients, all of which are essential to our AI dish coming to life. Without adequate data preparation, you're setting yourself up for a pasta primavera where nothing holds together, and your algorithms are left floundering in a pool of confusion.

Next up, we have algorithms, the secret sauce that ties everything together! Just as no two chefs make carbonara the same way, there are myriad approaches to building algorithms. Think of algorithms as flavor profiles. The classic ones, like linear regression, are the garlic and olive oil of the AI world, dependable and always in style. However, if you're feeling daring, you might lean into neural networks or deep learning, think of it as adding truffles and saffron to your mediocre pasta dish. Sure, it sounds extravagant, but if done right, it can elevate your dish to legendary status. Just don't forget, even the fanciest sauces can be ruined by careless execution. Too much heat, and you risk scorching the roux; too much tweaking with your algorithm, and you might overfit your model, turning it into an overcomplicated mess that's as appetizing as a bowl of rubbery spaghetti.

Ah, but wait! Our recipe doesn't end there. What about the human touch? If data is the raw material and algorithms are the gourmet inspiration, then the chefs, yes, that's us, are the key ingredient that can make or break the entire setup. I mean, you wouldn't want a robot doing the cooking, would you? Well, maybe a robot that can actually make a proper risotto, but let's not wander off into fantasy land here. The human touch in AI lies in its interpretation and the decision-making processes that follow. It's about making decisions when your AI returns an output that looks more like a soufflé that flopped rather than the light and airy dish you envisioned. We need to be part chef, part sommelier, and part psychic to foresee the possible mishaps and course-correct in real time.

And speaking of the unpredictability inherent in both cooking and AI, let us now celebrate the role of creativity. No dish is worth its salt without a sprinkle of imagination! AI development often comes with decisions made on pure intuition. Have you ever found yourself adding too much salt to a dish just because you thought, "Hey, that's what the recipe calls for!" Well, welcome to the realm of hyperparameters in machine learning! Tuning them is a precarious art, much like making sure your cheese-to-noodle ratio in lasagna is just right. It's a balancing act, a little creativity here, a pinch of calculated risk there, and voila! You might just concoct the next big thing in the AI kitchen.

As we meld these crucial ingredients together, it's important to keep our eyes on the prize, the final dish. Just like any Italian feast, the way you present your dish matters. You could whip up the best tomato sauce known to humanity, but if you serve it like a 5-year-old's finger painting, nobody's going to want a taste. In AI, presenting the outcomes effectively is just as important. We need to communicate our findings to stakeholders in a way that makes them drool over our results, not leave them scratching their heads and wondering what the heck they just saw.

In conclusion, the essential ingredients of AI are diverse and yet intricately interwoven, much like a delicious plate of pasta. By focusing on high-quality data, flavorfully tuned algorithms, creative human insight, and thoughtful presentation, we can create something truly magnificent. So the next time you sit down to launch an AI project, remember: it's not just about the technology; it's about creating a harmonious balance, like that perfect pairing of spaghetti and meatballs that pairs effortlessly with your grandmother's secret wisdom. Now, let's get to cooking up some virtual magic!

The Alchemy of Data: Penne alla Data Preparation

Data preparation, ah, the unsung hero of the AI world, much like the wise Italian nonna who secretly adds a pinch of love to every dish she makes. You see, data preparation is where the magic happens, where the raw ingredients transform into something spectacular, or, in the worst-case scenario, something that resembles a culinary catastrophe. Think of data preparation as making a glorious penne alla vodka; it takes a slew of ingredients, a little time, and a whole lot of care to create a masterpiece, rather than a sticky, stringy mess that nobody wants to eat.

Just as one wouldn't toss a bunch of unwashed vegetables into a pot and hope for the best, you can't throw unprocessed, messy data into your AI models and expect them to perform miracles. First things first, cleaning the data. This step is akin to washing your veggies in cool, clear water, getting rid of dirt and pesticides before you start cooking. Similarly, in data preparation, you'll need to scrub away the inconsistencies, errors, and duplicate entries that act like unwanted guests at your dinner party. You uncover the gold hidden beneath layers of grime, basic entries like the missing values are like a sad tomato that rolled under your refrigerator: it's a foul inconvenience and won't turn into a gourmet dish on its own. Without handling that effectively, you'll end up with a recipe where the base note of flavor is straight-up confusion.

Next comes transformation, my friends! You're not looking to create just any pasta dish; you want to create a unique penne alla vodka experience that beckons diners from miles away. You might need to convert categorical data into numerical data, like transforming a few too many ingredients in your refrigerator into flavorful sauces and toppings. Using one-hot encoding, label encoding, or any other lovely culinary tricks you have in your repertoire is key to providing your AI model with delicious flavors and ensuring it understands the nuances of your data. Think of each transformation like crafting a signature sauce; some chefs opt for a spicy kick with crushed red pepper, while others prefer a mellow embrace of sweetness with a dash of sugar. Your choice of transformation affects how your AI learns and proceeds.

Now, let's not overlook the importance of feature selection, deciding which aspects of our dish will shine the brightest and which will fade into the background like that leftover limb of broccoli you never bothered to serve. Choosing the right features is like picking the freshest basil from your garden, the one that'll elevate your penne alla vodka from mundane to "mamma mia!" without throwing in every herb and spice within a five-mile radius. You want to strike the right balance between what to keep in the spotlight while avoiding feature overload, because, let's face it, no one wants a pasta dish that looks like it's wearing a clown suit; it simply becomes hard to digest. In the world of AI, define your key attributes wisely, or risk ruining the harmony of the entire meal.

Then comes the modeling stage, which is akin to the cooking of your penne. You've prepped and preened your ingredients, and now it's time for them to play nicely together in that bubbling pot of delight. This is where you should be on high alert, watching every second and adjusting the heat as needed, just like stirring your sauce along the way to avoid burning. Don't you dare walk away and let the data simmer unattended! If you find your model is overcooking, it's your culinary duty to step in, add a splash of cream here, a dash of salt there, and adjust the hyperparameters, much as adding extra sauce to soften a dry dish.

But wait, we're not done yet! Once you've dished up that sumptuous penne alia vodka (or, in our case, our formatted dataset), you'll want to validate your creation. As any self-respecting Italian chef will tell you, you must taste your dish before serving it to guests. This is where cross-validation enters. Just as you wouldn't hesitate to nibble on a forkful of pasta to check your seasoning, you must evaluate your model's performance to ensure it meets expectations. Is your AI serving up insights as well as it should be, or is it delivering confusion akin to mismatched meatball recipes? This step is essential; otherwise, your grand feast could easily turn into an embarrassing gathering of disgruntled diners.

As we finish this delightful journey of data preparation, our much-needed culinary foreplay, remember that the way you treat your ingredients reflects in the final dish. Proper data preparation is the glue that holds it all together, ensuring that when your AI reaches the table, it dazzles more than a perfectly al dente penne tossed in the richest tomato sauce. After all, the process of preparing our data doesn't just ensure a sumptuous meal but creates an experience that delights, surprises, and satiates our hunger for knowledge. So, as you prepare your next AI project, be the master chef, wield your data with confidence, and let the alchemy of transformation unfold!

Sauce or Algorithms: The Role of Optimization

Optimization in the world of artificial intelligence is fundamentally like finding that perfect blend of ingredients that turns a simple tomato sauce into a culinary masterpiece. You see, just as every chef strives to refine their recipes, tweaking the amount of garlic here, the pinch of salt there, and perhaps adding a splash of red wine for that rich depth of flavor, AI practitioners optimize algorithms in pursuit of a model that hits all the right notes. If you've ever wondered how the chef manages to create that sauce that makes your taste buds perform a little happy jig, it's not by leaving things to chance; they optimize their craft. And just like a pot of simmering marinara, optimization is an ongoing, iterative process that demands an expert palate and a bit of experimentation.

Let's hop into the kitchen, shall we? When you start cooking up an AI algorithm, it's akin to throwing a saucepan on the heat without fully knowing the recipe. Sure, it'll begin bubbling away, but without optimization, you risk heading straight for a soupy disaster. The first step is to understand that your algorithm isn't just a static form; it's more like a living organism that necessitates constant maintenance and adjustment, much like how a good tomato sauce requires regular stirring to prevent burning at the bottom. The goal of optimization is to ensure that our algorithm reaches its peak performance, think of it as coaxing flavors from a reluctant tomato. You've got to coax and swindle the best into the sauce until it thickens and brightens.

Now, let's talk about hyperparameters, those little devils that oftentimes masquerade as the essential seasonings of our AI dish. Just as you wouldn't throw in an entire jar of oregano or cumin into your sauce (unless you're aiming for a new kind of creative disaster), hyperparameters require precise tweaking to deliver a balanced outcome. These parameters, which govern the behavior of our algorithms, are not one-size-fits-all. Adjusting a hyperparameter can influence learning speed, accuracy, and everything in between. In certain cases, it's like hitting the "just right" spot of your favorite alfredo, you know, not too creamy, not too starchy, but that divine middle ground that wraps itself around your pasta like a warm Italian hug.

To further spice things up, we have different optimization techniques that resemble the various sauce options available to any good pasta dish. Gradient descent, for instance, is often the go-to method, much like a classic marinara sauce, simple yet foundational. Imagine following a perfectly laid-out path through a vineyard, where you gradually move closer to the best grapes (or the lowest error in your algorithm). This method updates your model iteratively, calculating the steepest slope to guide your optimization. Meanwhile, we also have the more intricate optimization strategies like Adam or RMSprop that remind us of those flavorful sauce recipes we only pull out when we really want to impress dinner guests, think of a rich, herb-infused pesto that surprises with every taste.

But here's where things get entertaining. In the quest for that coveted, optimally trained model, we often find ourselves facing a dilemma, as if we were at a buffet of sauces, trying to decide which dish to indulge in while all our favorites stare back at us. Do we favor a quick optimization shortcut to achieve faster results, but risk ending up with a bland, one-dimensional sauce? Or do we take our time, letting flavors develop naturally, ensuring we hit every culinary milestone, albeit at a slower pace? In AI, the challenge is akin to balancing underfitting (when our algorithm is not complex enough to capture the intricacies) against overfitting (where it tries to memorize the training data rather than generalize).

Let's not forget about performance evaluation; it's the tasting that ensures we don't serve up duds to our guests, who'll demand an explanation if the sauce tastes too oily or the algorithm produces nonsensical results. Evaluating our model's performance metrics is akin to having a trusted confidante (preferably one with a discerning palate) judge our creation.

It guides us into recognizing whether we need to simmer the flavors longer, tweak the balance of our hyperparameters, or even toss the whole concoction altogether and start anew. After all, no one wants to end an evening with a poorly optimized algorithm that feels like a plate of limp, watery spaghetti.

In conclusion, the role of optimization in AI is every bit as critical as perfecting that luscious tomato sauce. From properly understanding hyperparameters to deciding on the right optimization techniques, each choice we make can elevate our AI models from the mundane to the marvelous. As you embark on your culinary AI adventure, keep in mind that, like great Italian cooking, great optimization requires patience, experimentation, and a willingness to adjust your seasonings. And remember, just as no two chefs approach their sauces the same way, no two AI practitioners will optimize their algorithms in exactly the same fashion. With a bit of creativity and a whole lot of tasting along the way, you'll soon have an optimized model that's the piece de resistance of your AI feast! Mangia!

Simmering Ideas: Iteration in Cooking and AI

Iteration, ah, that beautiful dance of refining, adjusting, and perfecting a recipe until it's finally worthy of a spot on the family table. In both cooking and AI, iteration is the secret process that separates a good dish from a truly great one. Think about your average lazy Saturday afternoon; you toss some ingredients into a pot, confident in your prowess as a home chef, only to discover that what started as a promising idea slowly devolves into a somewhat questionable stew. That, my friends, is where iteration steps in, much like the wise grandmother who gently nudges you to taste and adjust before serving.

When we think about cooking, consider a classic lasagna, layered with pasta, ricotta, marinara, and sprinkled with cheese. You might kick things off with a bold vision, "This masterpiece will have the perfect balance of creamy and tangy!" But unless you're testing it layer by layer, tasting, adjusting, and fine-tuning, there's a high probability that what emerges from the oven might be more akin to a gooey mess than a delectable dish. In the world of AI, the parallel is striking: models need iteration to improve performance, just as lasagna needs subtle tweaks to achieve culinary harmony.

This brings us to the heart of the concept. In cooking, we're often found simmering ideas, letting flavors meld and evolve over time. Simmering resembles a steady flame under a pot, allowing your dish to gradually transform. Similarly, in the AI space, iterative training enables our algorithms to gradually learn, adjust, and sneak up on that elusive optimal performance over time. AI models are like errant chefs who need direction; through iterations, we teach them the ropes, unwrapping complex neural connections to find that perfect balance that makes our outputs dazzle, not leave us screaming in terror like that unfortunate burnt lasagna.

And just as there are different ways to simmer a sauce, some chefs prefer high heat for a quick reduction, while others lean toward slow and steady, there's no definitive approach to iteration in AI. You might use batch training, where models digest smaller portions of data, a bit like feeding a picky eater small bites of lasagna, rather than overwhelming them with a giant slice that sends their taste buds into shock. Using iterative feedback loops allows AI to adjust its parameters based on results from previous iterations. What's more, it helps avoid cases where your algorithm learns the wrong lesson, overfitting to specific data qualities and flavorings, causing it to sputter under any challenge outside that "safe" zone.

Now let's not be too hasty. Tender care is also paramount. When a dish is on the burner, there's no point in stirring every two seconds; you create chaos in your sauce and inevitably turn it into a splattered nightmare. Like waiting patiently for a slow-cooked ragu to develop its flavors, AI algorithms also require designated checkpoints throughout iterations. These check-ins allow you to evaluate performance, tweak hyperparameters, and refine features, ensuring we don't abandon the simmering pot of creativity because we're overly eager for results. If you forget this vital detail, you're leaving your lasagna with little time to meld its flavors, a horrendous betrayal!

Furthermore, the beauty of iteration lies in its feedback mechanisms. As chefs, we frequently ask ourselves, "What's missing? Should I add more salt? A sprinkle of crushed red pepper?" Similarly, in AI, we rely on metrics to tell us if our iterations are on track. Performance metrics provide critical insight, allowing us to adjust our ingredients (or features) based on what resonates and what doesn't, guiding our culinary and algorithmic journeys into the blissful realms of satisfaction. Is your AI model producing results that resemble gourmet meals or more of a toddler's art project? Adjusting based on the feedback we garner is crucial, lest we unleash a model onto the world that not even our most sympathetic friends would eat.

In summation, think of iteration as the culinary compass guiding us through the turbulent waters of cooking and AI development. It's the methodical process, the ongoing simmering that can transform potential disaster into delightful creations, be it a rich bowl of pasta or an AI model capable of incredible insights. So the next time you embark on preparing your next AI project, or perhaps tackle a new gastronomic endeavor, embrace the power of iteration. With patience, careful adjustments, and a flair for creativity, you'll soon find that the magic lies not only in what you're cooking but also in the glorious process of refining your ideas along the way. Mangia bene, and build better AI!

The Family Recipe: Collaboration in AI Development

Collaboration in AI development is the unsung joy of bringing together diverse talents to create a magnificent feast for the intellect! Just as the most cherished family recipes emerge from the combined wisdom of several generations, the most effective AI solutions are born of collaboration. Picture this: you're at a big Italian family gathering, surrounded by a chorus of voices all enthusiastically adding their secret ingredients to the sauce. That's the beauty of teamwork in AI; it's a blend of various skills and perspectives that results in a dish, or in this case, a model, that all can savor together.

At its core, collaboration in AI resembles a family gathering where every member, from the toddler who just mastered the art of tossing spaghetti to the stern Nonna who insists her marinara is the only correct version, is invited to contribute. No one is too small or unqualified to craft a delicious dish or an innovative algorithm. Each individual's knowledge, be it raw data handling or advanced machine learning techniques, adds depth and flavor to the overall concoction. Often, a data scientist might be tunnel-visioned on their 'beautiful' model, without appreciating the insights from a department that understands business objectives, the equivalent of forgetting the garlic in a pasta sauce. Without that pungent flavor, the dish is just... meh.

Collaboration also ensures that no step in the cooking process or development cycle, is overlooked. When crafting an AI model, having a person dedicated to data validation is crucial, akin to the family member who steps in to chop vegetables to perfection while you hover over the stove, fretting about burning the sauce. In a collaborative atmosphere, ideas are shared, pitfalls are highlighted, and suggestions for improvement are presented. Everyone has a proverbial potholder in hand while stirring the pot, ensuring the AI is robust and functional, much more reliable than if one lone chef tried to do it all while simultaneously juggling the pasta and sauce.

Let's not forget the roles that define this culinary ensemble. Just as you might have family members who excel at different aspects of cooking, some are exceptional at sauces, while others are pasta connoisseurs, in AI development, different team members bring their unique talents to the table. Programmers, data analysts, project managers, and domain experts each represent the various spices and herbs that enhance the overall flavor. A good chef knows when to blend those ingredients thoughtfully; similarly, a successful AI project manager ensures team dynamics work harmoniously. If your project manager isn't channeling each individual's skills, it's like trying to make rich risotto without realizing the broth needs to be stirred in slowly!

But let's address the elephant in the room: the dreaded miscommunication! Oh, how "al dente" can lead to drama in the kitchen and in the boardroom! There's always that "that guy" who insists on the importance of their secret sauce, using industry jargon that flies way over others' heads. This leads to confusion and frustration akin to the family bickering over whether the appropriate amount of salt is needed. Everyone must be on the same page, speaking a common language about goals, deliverables, and the glorious vision of what the final dish, er, model, should accomplish.

Let's take a moment to appreciate the serendipity that occurs when collaboration invites unexpected sparks of creativity. Just think about it: an AI expert brainstorming with a marketing whiz can lead to insights that neither of them would uncover alone, just as a dash of unexpected nutmeg can elevate your beloved family pumpkin pie to uncharted greatness. Often, true innovation arises when disparate minds come together. As they whip up ideas and blend perspectives, they create something that resonates universally, like pizza's ability to please even the pickiest eater at the dinner table!

Finally, nurturing a collaborative spirit fosters a sense of community and belonging that can prove invaluable during the challenges of AI development. All great chefs know that cooking is about more than feeding the hungry; it's about bringing people together and celebrating life.

Likewise, when team members feel supported, inspired, and connected, they are more likely to invest in their work, leading to richer enhancements to their algorithms! When you enjoy the making of a dish as much as the meal itself, it transforms the entire experience, leading to innovative solutions that effectively meet users' needs.

In conclusion, collaboration in AI development mirrors the warm, inclusive fervor of creating a family recipe. Embracing the talents of each individual, effectively communicating, overcoming conflicts, and nurturing a sense of community culminate in a project that succeeds at a greater scale. So next time you embark on an AI project, gather your proverbial family around the kitchen counter, mix in diverse ideas, and stir the pot until you concoct something that not just meets expectations but leaves everyone clamoring for seconds, all before the meal turns cold! Buon appetito to teamwork, because together, the possibilities are endless!

Chapter 15

The Family Table: Collaborating Across Disciplines

The Power of Collaborative Cooking

The magic of collaborative cooking! Let me take you back to a time when I stood in a bustling kitchen, not unlike a tech startup on caffeine overload, surrounded by my trusty sous-chefs, my family. Picture this: pots bubbling, utensils clanging, and a whole lot of shouting about who forgot to pick up the basil. It's like a fine-tuned orchestra, but instead of music, we're creating culinary dishes. This chaotic energy parallels what I see in the world of machine learning and AI, a symphony of collaboration that can lead to remarkable results.

When I think about collaborative cooking, I reminisce about the beauty of making homemade lasagna on a Sunday afternoon. It's a family affair; everyone has a role. My eight-year-old nephew is rolling the pasta dough while trying his best not to make a mess that looks like a sauce explosion, and my mother is lamenting the fact that nobody in the family can slice onions without crying. Meanwhile, I am in charge of the meat sauce, and let's just say that "perfect" is relative when you're mixing in just enough wine to warrant a personal cheer from the glass in front of me. But amidst the chaos, ideas and flavors meld together as we debate the merits of oregano versus thyme, precarious discussions that often devolve into laughter, highlighting the importance of different perspectives.

In a kitchen, every individual brings unique skills to the table, much like a diverse team working on a complex AI project. You wouldn't want a room full of pasta rollers; that would just be a disaster laden with gluten and flour, not to mention an abundance of overcooked penne. In AI, just as in cooking, it's the amalgamation of skills, the data scientists, software engineers, and the project managers (yes, they deserve some love too!), that transforms raw ingredients into a refined product. Each contribution adds a unique flavor that parallels the specific tasks required in the machine-learning pipeline.

And speaking of ingredients, have you ever tried a dish made by a single cook who insists on handling everything alone? It's often a flavorless mess resembling something that should have been left in a corner to atone for its culinary sins. The same can be said for attempting to build an AI model without collaboration. If a developer treats their algorithm like a lone wolf, they may just end up with a model that suffers from overfitting, the neural network equivalent of trying to serve a six-course meal with just spaghetti. That's not a culinary triumph; that's a block party gone wrong.

Collaboration in cooking means sharing ideas, feedback, and even the occasional awkward silence when someone realizes they don't know how to separate eggs properly. It's the feedback loop that matters. Just like tasting your stew as you go, refining the flavors, adjusting the seasoning, and responding charitably to your nephew's critique of overcooked pasta (though that's more emotional pain than culinary), teams in AI benefit from constant iteration. Each cycle of feedback allows us to pivot, ensuring that our "dish" remains palatable, or in AI speak, ensuring our model is accurate.

The kitchen becomes a melting pot of strategy and spontaneity, a space where innovation is nurtured because everyone has the freedom to share their wild ideas, like adding pineapple to pizza (don't worry, I'll be addressing that controversy later). Ideas and adjustments may seem ridiculous at first, but you never know which one will lead to the next culinary breakthrough. Well, most of the time. Sometimes you end up with a sauce that could double as home security glue, but hey, it's the risk we're willing to embrace in the spirit of collaboration.

So, the next time you're in the kitchen, whether with family or as part of a project team in AI, remember that the power lies not in working alone like a hermit crab, but in blending different abilities to create something that delights the senses, or in the case of AI, unlocks new opportunities. Collaboration, for me, is akin to stirring a pot of sauce; it takes time, patience, and often some heated debates, but the result is transformative. Just don't forget to taste as you go; nobody wants bland pasta, just like nobody wants a mediocre model. In the world of flavor and data, variety truly is the spice of life.

Breaking Down Silos: Cooking with Diverse Ingredients

Breaking down silos: it's not just a corporate buzzword thrown around during quarterly meetings; it's a necessary philosophy for both cooking and machine learning. Imagine if our beloved spaghetti and meatballs were confined to their "respective departments." Spaghetti would stay in a pot on the stove, while meatballs would languish on a baking sheet, never having the chance to mingle. The horror! We'd be deprived of experiencing that glorious amalgamation! And honestly, what kind of culinary world would that be? A tragic one, akin to a world where pineapple is a free agent playing for both teams without ever committing to a true pizza partnership.

When it comes to cooking, removing these"silos" is essential. Diverse ingredients bring balance to meals and elevate flavors. A successful dish is like your group project in school, everyone must contribute, even that one person who insists on adding too much salt. Think of a salsa that calls for only tomatoes, without the zesty onion or lively cilantro. What are you left with? A bland concoction that might as well be a sad, unseasoned vegetable medley. Embracing the flavors of diversity helps avoid the pitfall of mediocrity, just as applying different perspectives enriches AI model development and breaks down the walls of siloed thinking.

Take, for instance, the concept of "rainbow salad." The dish emerges as a delightful explosion of colors that visually invites you before you even sink a fork into it. Just as we should embrace bright bell peppers, purple cabbage, and carrots, machine learning models should shoulder the weight of diverse data sources. Data is the lifeblood of an algorithm! But while we're at it, think of each ingredient as a team member. We need them all, from sweet to savory, to build robust models that aren't afraid to take on challenging predictions. Imagine relying solely on dull, gray data; it's like attempting to create a masterpiece using nothing but beige paint, exciting, right?

In a kitchen, many cultural influences come together, creating dishes that tell stories. The iconic Italian risotto, for example, whispers tales from Northern Italy, while the vibrant curry hails from the rich spices of India. Each culinary culture offers a diversity of flavor profiles, which lend themselves to greater innovation. It's quite like creating a new AI model, drawing upon the wisdom and experiences of various fields can lead to astonishing discoveries. You'll find creativity in combining what seem to be disparate elements; think of a taco with spaghetti nestled inside, because why not? It might sound absurd (and a little revolting), but if it can yield a surprising burst of taste, why shy away from exploring it?

Plus, let's face it, nobody likes a one-note dish. A meal that lacks diversity is like a song stuck on repeat: monotonous and played out. The same can be said for approaches in machine learning. Models that refuse to use mixed methodologies risk becoming stale and underperforming. Who wants that? It's critical to embrace different strategies, data techniques, and workflows, like introducing more nuanced seasoning to your simmering pot of marinara. A pinch of this, a sprinkle of that, and suddenly you have a cultural feast that engages the taste buds and celebrates variety.

Now, let's not forget that breaking down silos in cooking can lead to unexpected culinary disasters. Like my infamous attempt at a "fusion" dish: I once thought I could blend lasagna with sushi. Spoiler alert: the melted mozzarella did not harmonize well with the seaweed. The results left my family bedridden, not from enjoyment but from the sheer shock of what I dared to put on a plate. But just as in innovation, these setbacks are simply learning experiences. When crossing cultural boundaries, we might land a flop or two, but they often spark even greater ideas.

Ultimately, whether it's a frittata that stems from an ode to a breakfast buffet or an AI model leveraging multiple approaches to optimize accuracy, breaking down silos is integral to success in both arenas. Embracing the diverse ingredients of life, culinary and intellectual, leads to a richer experience where ideas breathe and flavors flourish. So, the next time you find yourself in the kitchen or at a brainstorming session, remember that amalgamation can lead to delightful discoveries, and may your culinary adventures always be spiced with new perspectives. Because, after all, who wouldn't want to taste the world?

The Role of Communication in the Kitchen and Beyond

Communication in the kitchen is akin to the secret sauce we all wish we had the recipe for; it connects the diverse ingredients and enhances the overall flavor of the culinary experience. Imagine a scenario where every cook is communicating like a bunch of clams in a bubbling pot, lots of noise and agitation, but no real understanding. Now, imagine how that would affect your dinner party. Picture my mother shouting, "Where's the garlic?" while I'm frantically trying to figure out if "diced" means "fashionably chopped" or just "bring out the chainsaw." Without effective communication, chaos would rule the kitchen, and a simple marinara could quickly turn into an Italian horror film titled ''The Day of the Undercooked Pasta."

Effective communication keeps kitchens running smoothly, much like a well-oiled AI system. In both realms, clarity is key. When preparing a dish, you need to know not just what to add, but when and how. For example, if someone thinks ''add the salt" means hurling it into the pot from across the room, we're not just risking a culinary disaster; we're talking about a potential tidal wave of flavor that could drown even the most resilient of sauce recipes. In an AI context, correct input is paramount. If we miscommunicate our data requirements or expected outcomes, we might just train a model that predicts spaghetti will start teaching cooking classes, a notion that's fun to ponder but rather impractical.

In my kitchen, there's always a mad rush, ingredients flying around like confetti on New Year's. With so much bustling energy, communication takes on various forms: half-sentences, hand signals, and those delightful grunts that we tend to share with one another as if we were part of a primitive cooking tribe. Let's face it, when you're liberally sweating over a hot stove, clear words may be replaced by exaggerated gestures or frantic eyebrow movements to signal to my brother that, no, chopping onions does not require a butcher's cleaver. To add a humorous spin, I often imagine if we had a co-chef from the future equipped with a smart AI assistant. "Siri, remind him that he doesn't need to play 'chop-a-thon' with his finger."

Expanding this communication theme into the broader world of AI, we see a similar need for clear expression among team members. Teams comprised of data scientists, developers, and project managers often speak different languages. It's like the Tower of Babel, but without the divine intervention that led to a successful building. "I'll just push my code," says one developer confidently. Meanwhile, the data scientist is frantically waving their hands, confused as to whether "push" refers to coding or just general frustration stemming from endless debugging. That's a recipe for collaboration disaster. Understanding each other's jargon and styles, along with humility to ask questions or admit misunderstanding, is critical in both the kitchen and tech ecosystems.

Moreover, let's not overlook the importance of feedback loops. In the kitchen, if someone tells you the casserole needs more cheese, they're not trying to insult your culinary skills; they're trying to salvage the dish! Similarly, in AI development, feedback is essential for refining algorithms. When team members share their critiques openly, models can adapt and improve, as long as no one suggests we throw in banana peels for good measure (that's the culinary equivalent of throwing in random data). Iteration and communication foster a symbiotic environment, one where both cooking and data science thrive on collaboration, adapting to mistakes, and making each new offering more delightful than the last.

And let me pivot for a moment to the disastrous side of miscommunication. Picture this: my illustrious attempt at preparing carbonara, where, due to a misunderstanding, I substituted the pancetta with cereal, yes, you heard that right. I'll spare you the details, but let's just say early reports indicated it was breakfast at dinnertime, and dinner at the hospital. This hilarious hiccup reminded me that the lack of communication and failing to clarify expectations can result in unpredictable, in this case, highly regrettable, outcomes.

So, as we whisk, saute, and likely overheat our culinary ambitions or dive into the world of machine learning, we must recognize the inherent value of communication. It's not just a means to an end; it's the "extra virgin olive oil" that enriches our work and gives life to our dishes or models. Embrace clarity, engage in constructive feedback, and let laughter fill the gaps. After all, in both the kitchen and AI, effective communication is what transforms a chaotic fiasco into a delicious masterpiece.

Learning from Each Other: Knowledge Sharing in Teams

Imagine a world where every chef operated in isolation, hoarding their recipes like precious jewels, guarding the secrets of their grandmother's marinara sauce with the ferocity of a dragon protecting a pot of gold. In this realm, culinary innovation would be stifled, and we'd still be peeling potatoes with knives made from stone. Thankfully, this is simply a dramatic exaggeration of how knowledge sharing works! Just like in a kitchen, sharing knowledge is what makes teams productive, creative, and surprisingly edible, without the awkwardness of dinner guests politely chewing on bland spaghetti.

In my experience, cooking is a team sport, just ask my family, who has often been forced into culinary teamwork under the guise of how it's "fun." When the flames rise, and the pressure cooker hisses with foreboding intent, mere mortals become culinary ninjas, each chef tossing in their unique ingredients and techniques. I can't tell you how many times my sister's bold addition of her secret smoky paprika has turned a basic soup of despair into a palatable feast. In our little kitchen, the goal is never to outshine one another, but rather to illuminate everyone's strengths and concoct a gastronomic delight worthy of applause, or at least enough to drown out my niece's incessant banter about unicorns.

Let's pivot that to the world of AI and machine learning. Here, collaboration and knowledge sharing can lead to groundbreaking breakthroughs that rival any unexpected culinary triumph. Just as I leech valuable cooking techniques from my family members (seriously, my aunt's tiramisu recipe should be backed up in several culinary databases), team members, whether they're data scientists or software engineers, should share their expertise to refine models, enhance processing, and respond to technical challenges. It's through this sharing that we cultivate a culture of learning that enhances our collective knowledge. If you have "input," let's consider sharing it! Otherwise, we risk discovering that the input we're using is a half-baked idea.

I remember a moment in our kitchen when my brother waltzed in, an air of false bravado surrounding him, and declared he was preparing his family's "world-famous" mac and cheese. As we crowded around, eager to see this so-called culinary miracle, we quickly learned it involved far too much cheese and not nearly enough thought. However, instead of humoring him with our safety concerns, we jumped in, offering tips and suggestions. "What if we added some breadcrumbs? Or toss in a few herbs?" Before we knew it, the dish was transformed into something respectable, signaling the power of pooling ideas. In the AI realm, we face dilemmas daily that could benefit from peer collaboration. A simulation solution here, a modeling method there, and suddenly we're not just engineers; we've become culinary artisans of model perfection.

But here's the twist: just as we share our culinary successes, we must also share our glorious flops. I often tell friends that my kitchen disasters are as important as my successes. From the time I forgot to put the lid on the blender and ended up decorating the kitchen ceiling with a beetroot smoothie, to the infamous time I raged against the spaghetti sauce that tastes like disappointment, it's crucial to learn from the messes. In the tech world, we experience our share of "cooking disasters." Perhaps an algorithm failed due to missing data, or team members went down a rabbit hole of convoluted ideas until they forgot the original problem entirely. It's in admitting these failings and reflecting on what went awry that we learn and grow, not unlike assuring your future cooking prowess by looking back on the times you've accidentally created culinary weaponry.

Similarly, I've found that cross-pollination of ideas between different disciplines can yield fascinating results. It's akin to creating a pizza topped with blue cheese and pears, an unexpected but delightful surprise! In teams, individuals from various backgrounds, be it physics, biology, or engineering, bring unique perspectives that can illuminate unseen possibilities for our projects. Each different layer of knowledge is a bit like adding more spice to a dish; just when you think you've nailed it, a gust of rosemary or a hint of smoked paprika pulls everything together and kicks it into high gear.

When these different perspectives combine, it creates an environment ripe for innovation and creativity. That's when the true magic happens: flavors, ideas, and insights blend seamlessly, culminating in something extraordinary. "Ah-ha!" moments abound as spontaneity fuels collaboration, similar to how a struggling risotto morphs into a luxurious, creamy dish through teamwork. So, just as my niece's unicorn musings continually surprise us, so too can the exchange of ideas unlock magnificent possibilities in the world of machine learning and beyond.

In conclusion, never underestimate the importance of knowledge sharing in a team, whether in a bustling kitchen or the data-driven world of AI. It's about creating an ecosystem where we uplift one another, lean on our peers' expertise, and foster a sense of humor about our inevitable misadventures. Every laugh, every tip, and every misfire leads us closer to amazing concoctions, both delicious and intellectually enriching. So, let's roll up our sleeves and stir the pot of collaboration, let's learn together and cook like there's no tomorrow!

From the Kitchen to the Boardroom: Interdisciplinary Success Stories

From the kitchen to the boardroom, a phrase that bridges the worlds of culinary finesse and corporate enterprise! You might wonder how known kitchen disasters and haphazard spaghetti-slapping can somehow parallel the high-stakes atmosphere of a corporate meeting. But believe me, interdisciplinary success stories frequently find their roots in this here connection. Just as an expert chef can transform a hodgepodge of ingredients into a Michelin-starred meal, skilled professionals from diverse backgrounds can create incredible, multi-faceted solutions that transcend the ordinary.

Take my family's Sunday dinner as a perfect example. As customary, each of us had our special role: my sister was in charge of the salad, using her background as an environmental scientist to insist on locally sourced kale and recycling the leftover carrot peels. Meanwhile, my cousin, an engineer, ensured our pasta was timed to perfection (because God forbid we serve al dente only once!). Each unique skill set came together to create a harmonious dining experience. This recipe for interdisciplinary collaboration can be transferred to the boardroom, where cross-functional teams are the secret ingredient for unleashing greatness. Those meetings, filled with product managers, analysts, designers, and developers, are not so dissimilar from my chaotic kitchen: everyone is a key ingredient, adding their flavor to the pot.

Just like a chef must leverage the strengths of each ingredient to compose their masterpiece, a team must tap into the varied expertise of its members. When I once managed a project to revolutionize our lending processes at the credit union using AI, I had members from marketing, compliance, engineering, and operations. Each team member brought a unique spice to the table, marketing pushed for user-friendly interfaces, compliance ensured legislative compliance, and engineering worked to turn dreams into code. We blended these perspectives, much like tossing together ingredients for a salad, and suddenly the outcome was a refreshing salad of productivity! The result? A product that didn't just serve our needs but empowered our members, granting everyone the satisfying crunch of collaboration.

However, let's not forget that kitchens often produce a blend of successes and, shall we say, culinary "opportunities." I once led a project that brought together data scientists and business strategists to create a decision-making model. The idea was brilliant; however, it turned out to be like throwing meatballs into the blender without checking if the lid was on. The model became a hot mess express! But just like some failed recipes can lead to happy accidents, like scented air fresheners or glue substitutes in an emergency, this debacle ended up teaching us the value of iterative feedback. It reminded us that success doesn't typically come from a vacuum but rather from valuing missteps as part of the learning process.

As it turns out, interdisciplinary work mimics the chaos of the kitchen. When chefs blunder, they don't throw in the towel; they make adjustments, adapt their approach, and ensure they have the right flavors up their sleeves next time. Similarly, when boardroom discussions draw on diverse knowledge pools, innovation flourishes. Suddenly, we weren't just combating the proverbial meatball explosion; we were discovering new ways to leverage data across departments to positively shape outcomes for our members.

Outside of my work life, I often participate in local community cooking classes that mix together chefs with diverse cooking philosophies. It's always a recipe for success (pun intended!) when food cultures collide. During my last class, a vegan chef teamed up with a butcher, a match made in culinary comedy heaven! They collaborated on a dish that satisfied both vegans and meat-lovers alike, creating stuffed peppers that transcended kitchen boundaries. This collaboration exuded a sense of unity that extends far beyond food: it sparked conversation and shifted perspectives, proving that combining talents and viewpoints can yield delicious results in any setting, whether the kitchen or the conference room.

As I glide between my culinary exploits and meetings filled with dry-erase boards, scribbled notes, and charts, one thing remains constant: the magic lies in the intersectionality of diverse experiences, perspectives, and skills. Whether whipping up a traditional risotto with a science-based twist to ensure no undercooked rice grains disturb our culinary universe, or collaborating across departments to enhance our business processes, I find the flavors of collaboration sweeten that success. So here's to the next time you pick up your chef's knife or your keyboard; remember that every dish and every project is an opportunity, including all the potential messes that can lead to spectacular breakthroughs! Let's savor the conversations and outcomes that emerge when we tap into the richness of interdisciplinary collaboration and sprinkle the world with a dash of creativity.

Chapter 16

Simplicity is Key: Avoiding Overcomplication

The Beauty of Simplicity in Italian Cooking

Italian cooking! The very mention of it conjures images of pasta swirling in rich sauces, the aroma of garlic wafting through the air, and a table overflowing with friends and family, all sharing a meal that's much more than just food; it's a celebration of life. But what strikes me most, as I navigate both the kitchen and the bewildering world of machine learning, is the unassailable beauty of simplicity embedded in each Italian dish. If you think about it, Italian cuisine is like that one friend who doesn't need flashy clothes to steal the spotlight; it shines brightly with its authenticity and elegance.

Take spaghetti aglio e olio, for instance, just spaghetti, garlic, olive oil, and perhaps a sprinkling of parsley if we're feeling fancy. There's no three-hour simmering sauce, no elaborate preparation; it's as straightforward as it gets. Yet, it's a dish that has captivated hearts across the globe. You might think,

"What's so great about that?" Oh, dear friend, therein lies the charm! The beauty of simplicity is that it allows the ingredients to shine; it elevates the essential flavors rather than drowning them in a sea of complicated sauces. And if you're anything like me, you know that sometimes a little garlic and oil can make all the difference between a mediocre dinner and a culinary revelry.

This mirrors the concept of simplicity in machine learning models. In a world where we're tempted to stack layer upon layer of complex algorithms like overzealous lasagna makers, it's crucial to remember that simpler models often yield better results. Think of it as cooking with just a handful of quality ingredients instead of a grocery-store explosion in your pantry. Machine learning can easily devolve into a labyrinth of hyperparameters and intricate tweaks, much like an overly ambitious chef who decides to add just one more ingredient because, you know, why not? The result can often be disastrous: a relationship breakup over the state of the kitchen, a ruined dish you just can't bring yourself to serve your guests.

Let's pause for a moment to talk about what happens when we overcomplicate things. Imagine a classic cacio e pepe. Just three ingredients: pasta, Pecorino Romano cheese, and black pepper. Yet, misstep that combination with overcooked pasta, clumpy cheese, or some misguided attempt to introduce truffle oil (which, for the record, should never be within fifty feet of this dish), and you've not only ruined a classic, but you also risk inciting a culinary riot among purists. Similarly, when we load our models with unnecessary features, those million-dollar variables that sound impressive but contribute little, we create chaos, leading to overfitting and making our models less effective in real-world applications.

In Italian cuisine, respect for the ingredients is paramount. When you cook with simplicity, you learn to appreciate the quality of each ingredient and how it interacts with the others. This is an essential lesson in both cooking and machine learning. Maintaining a balance in our models requires recognizing the importance of each variable. The best chefs understand that the magic lies not in bombarding the dish with flavors but rather in harmonizing the few key components to create something extraordinary.

As I reflect on the principles of simplicity in both cooking and machine learning, I find myself nodding in agreement with my nonna, who always said, "Less is more." It's the culinary equivalent of the KISS principle (Keep It Simple, Stupid). In a world bogged down by technological complexities, embracing simplicity can be refreshing, like a glass of homemade limoncello that cuts through the monotony of life.

Ultimately, the beauty of simplicity in Italian cooking serves as a profound reminder of the elegance in both the kitchen and the realm of machine learning. It teaches us to savor the essence of what we create while ensuring that both our pasta and our algorithms remain pleasingly straightforward. Whether I'm stirring a pot of marinara sauce or tuning hyperparameters in a complicated AI model, I endeavor to honor simplicity, the secret ingredient that makes all the difference. So, let's raise a glass of Chianti to simplicity, may it forever guide us in both culinary and computational endeavors, and may we never drown our spaghetti in a sea of confusion!

Why Overcomplication Leads to Confusion

Overcomplication, the dreaded beast that lurks in the shadows of both our kitchens and our machine learning models. It's like that overly ambitious uncle at a wedding who insists on showing off his dance moves, ultimately causing more embarrassment than entertainment. Yes, we've all been there: a beautifully simple dish ruined by unnecessary embellishments or an elegant algorithm derailed by a thousand irrelevant features. When it comes to both cooking and AI, more isn't always merrier; in fact, it often leads to confusion faster than a toddler wandering into a buffet without supervision.

Let's start with a classic example from the kitchen. The other night, I decided to make a risotto, you know, that creamy Italian comfort food that begs to be appreciated for its balance of texture and flavor. As I approached the cooking, I found myself tempted to add more ingredients than necessary. "Maybe some saffron?" I thought. "What if I threw in asparagus, mushrooms, and perhaps a handful of pine nuts for good measure?" The risotto turned out to be a chaotic, confusing mess that resembled a dish from a culinary showdown gone wrong. In my effort to impress, I created something that looked more like a food fight than a delightful meal. The lesson was clear; overcomplication had turned a simple comfort dish into an indecipherable mess.

It's amusing how easy it is to slide into this trap when designing machine learning models, as well. There's a certain thrill in the data's complexity, a siren's song that beckons us to keep layering on features, each seemingly more dazzling than the last. Before you know it, we end up in a labyrinth of hyperparameters, feeling like a punter in a pasta aisle with too many choices.

It's like entering a pizza restaurant that offers every topping imaginable. Sure, it might sound fun, but you'll find yourself questioning your life choices as you stare at a Hawaiian petri dish. Simplicity gets lost amid the fray, and suddenly you're stuck with a model that's more complicated than a soap opera plot.

I can't help but ponder how confusion has a way of sneaking up on us, like a well-cooked piece of eggplant. It lures you in with its smooth surface, and just when you think you've figured it out, you bite down only to find it overly mushy, thank you, overcooked disaster! In the realm of machine learning, when models become convoluted, interpreting results can feel an awful lot like deciphering a bad translation of a famous Italian novel. Suddenly, you're left scratching your head, wondering if those accuracy metrics are speaking gibberish or if it's simply your brain trying to make sense of a Rube Goldberg machine disguised as a predictive model.

Think about it: just as clear and concise instructions can make or break a recipe, clarity in model design can inform actionable insights or spiral us into a data-based abyss. Not to mention the poor souls trying to comprehend your complicated concoctions. Have you ever tried to explain a convoluted dish to a friend? Their eyes glaze over, and you're left with nothing but a vague nod of understanding. I can't help but feel that the same happens in data-heavy discussions, where everyone's pretending to get it while silently plotting to flee from the conversation.

So how do we combat this overwhelming tendency toward confusion? Much like a perfect bowl of spaghetti, it's about finding that delicate balance. Start with the essentials: get comfortable with your ingredients, whether culinary or data-related. Simplify the process, take a step back, and regularly ask, "Is this really necessary?" The mantra should ring in our ears like a culinary siren: "If it ain't broke, don't fix it!" Knowledge, like pasta, is best served al dente, not mushy with overcomplication.

In short, overcomplication leads to confusion, and confusion breeds disaster in the kitchen and beyond. Let's all commit to stripping away the layers that don't serve us, embracing elegance instead of chaos, and proudly serving our hypotheses with a side of clarity. With a sprinkle of humor and a hearty dose of restraint, we can navigate our culinary and computational quests without losing our minds or our friends. So the next time you find yourself knee-deep in a bloated dataset or a recipe gone rogue, just remember: sometimes, less truly is more!

Analogies Between Simple Dishes and Simple Models

When I think about Italian cooking, I'm reminded of how certain dishes manage to capture the essence of simplicity in the most delightful way. Just a handful of ingredients, combined with the right technique, can create culinary magic. This got me thinking: isn't it awfully similar to crafting a machine learning model? The parallels are so striking that I can't help but share them, even if a few cooking enthusiasts and data scientists cringe simultaneously at the thought of me mixing metaphors like I mix pasta dough.

Take, for instance, the humble marinara sauce. There it is, a medley of tomatoes, garlic, olive oil, and a few herbs, simmered to perfection. It doesn't require complex techniques or obscure ingredients. You won't find truffle oil sneaking in to steal the spotlight here; the tomatoes stand confidently in their red glory. Similarly, in machine learning, the most effective models often rely on the simplest features, those few golden nuggets of data that truly matter. Just like your grandma's marinara, powerful and elegant, all it needs is a splash of creativity and a healthy pinching of common sense to shine.

Now, picture, for a moment, a sophisticated-sounding dish like duck à l'orange. It sounds fancy and all, but if you look closely, it's a complex dance between quite a few flavors, science, and art on one plate, resulting in a delightful explosion that might require a degree in molecular gastronomy just to replicate. You see, much like a convoluted machine learning model that tries to accommodate every possible feature, this dish can quickly become a chaotic mishmash of flavors if we're not careful. The result? Confusion on the palate and a dataset that looks less like "insights" and more like a bewildering carnival of data noise.

On the flip side, let's revisit our simple cacio e pepe. This delightful dish consists of just pasta, Pecorino cheese, and black pepper. Yet, it remains one of the most celebrated Italian dishes around! The ingredients meld beautifully, creating something that feels luxurious despite the unpretentious nature of its components. This is directly akin to crafting a straight-line regression model in machine learning; fewer variables, a straightforward equation, and you have a pathway to insight without overcomplication.

It's amusing to consider that both culinary and data practices share a thread of simplicity: a few good ingredients lead to stunning outcomes. I mean, who needs an exotic blend of twelve spices when a perfect bruschetta can steal the show with just tomatoes, basil, garlic, and some good extra virgin olive oil? In the same breath, one can argue that who requires a complex neural network when a simple decision tree could effectively slice through the chaos of a problem? It's like putting a thousand toppings on pizza versus celebrating the harmony of a Margherita pie; sometimes, simplicity wins the foodie and modeling awards!

Take pizza again, but let's look at a variation that overshoots the mark, like a "pizza of the month club" that throws every available topping on a single crust. I mean, a pineapple-shrimp-jalapeno-pesto extravaganza sounds adventurous until you take a bite and realize you're wrestling with more flavors than a reality show about a cooking competition. Conversely, a well-made Neapolitan pizza, bubbly crust, fresh mozzarella, and a sprinkle of basil, proves that sometimes, less is indeed more. The same goes for our datasets; while it may be tempting to slam every conceivable new feature into your model, stick with the essentials to keep your insights as effective and true as that pizza's delicate flavor balance.

Ultimately, both simple dishes and simple models illuminate a universal truth: complexity is tempting, but it doesn't always lead to beauty or clarity. The elegance of a handful of genuine ingredients is mirrored in choosing the essential features in our models. So, as we twirl spaghetti around our forks or analyze the robustness of our algorithms, let's hold our culinary and computational choices to the same high bar: keep it simple, let the ingredients shine, and let us not drown our delightful discoveries in unnecessary embellishments. After all, there's an entire world of flavors and data out there, and sometimes the simplest expressions are the ones that resonate the most, whether on our plates or in our predictions!

The Dangers of Feature Bloat

Feature bloat! That slippery slope where the thrill of countless variables lures us in like a flashy buffet with all-you-can-eat intentions. As I survey both my well-stocked kitchen and the convoluted datasets scattered across my computer screen, I realize that feature bloat is akin to adding unnecessary ingredients to a simple recipe that was already perfect. It's like someone thought, "You know what this perfect tomato sauce needs?" and then proceeded to dump a gallon of ranch dressing into the pot. Spoiler alert: nobody asked for that, and that's likely the moment dinner goes south faster than a rogue carrot in a soup pot.

Let's break it down. Picture an ambitious new chef entering the kitchen, eyes sparkling with dreams of grandeur. They scan the shelves and see the exotic spices, rich sauces, and a plethora of funky vegetables. Instead of mastering the basics of flavor, they throw everything in and hope for the best. The result? A kitchen disaster that smells suspiciously like desperation. Similarly, in the realm of machine learning, the excitement of an abundance of features can lead to models that are more confused than a cat at a dog show.

Now, I'll share a story from my own culinary follies. I once attempted to create what I fancied would be the "ultimate" tiramisu. I thought it would be whimsical to toss in everything from caramel sauce to chocolate sprinkles and the obligatory coffee liqueur. Never mind that the classic recipe is already a symphony of sweetened mascarpone, coffee-soaked ladyfingers (or, Pavesini), and cocoa. The outcome was, shall we say, a cacophony of conflicting flavors, a disjointed dessert that made even the bravest tasters take a step back. And just like that, I was reminded that complexity does not equal creativity.

In the world of data science, feature bloat manifests in a similar fashion, clouding our models with excessive, redundant variables. Perhaps you're feeling brave and want to include every possible feature in your dataset, convinced that more will translate to better. Here's a truth bomb: it often leads to overfitting, where your model is as eager to please as a puppy with too many treats. It remembers the training data, perhaps too much, over-generalizes, and loses its grip on the real-world scenarios you want it to predict. It's like having a dinner guest who aces trivia about your favorite food but can't taste the piquant nuances of your homemade ragu. They may seem knowledgeable, but they miss the crucial flavors that matter most.

At this point, I can't help but tip my hat to the elegant Italian saying, "La dolce vita", the sweet life. In the context of cooking and modeling, it reminds us that simplistically designed dishes and straightforward models are often the pathways to perfection. Just as I'd prefer a well-balanced caprese salad with only the freshest mozzarella, basil, and tomatoes, I, too, will embrace models that focus on essential features without excessive fluff.

So, how do we avoid the perils of feature bloat? By practicing restraint and learning to say "no" when tempted by data overload. Identify the critical variables that directly impact the outcomes you seek to predict.

Cultivate a discerning eye, much like a master chef who chooses only the finest ingredients for a dish rather than drowning it in a sea of mediocrity. This process isn't about throwing away data; it's about emphasizing quality over quantity.

Ultimately, as we navigate both the culinary and technical realms, let's embrace simplicity as our guiding principle. Let's curate our data the way we would our pantry: carefully, judiciously, and with a clear vision of the deliciousness we wish to create. When we strip away the distractions of feature bloat, we make way for something phenomenal, something genuinely delicious, whether that's a flawless dish or a trustworthy model that can withstand the test of time. So, the next time you find yourself enticed by the siren call of unnecessary variables or overzealous recipe elements, just remember: less really is more, unless, of course, you're talking about dessert, but let's save that conversation for another chapter!

Finding Joy in the Basics

Finding joy in the basics is a philosophy that echoes through both my journey as a cook and my work as a risk manager in the tech realm. You see, in both worlds, there's an elegance to simplicity, much like discovering that a perfectly roasted garlic clove can elevate a dish without fighting for attention. This concept speaks volumes; in a society that's always pushing for the next big thing, there's something so reassuring about returning to the fundamentals, whether it's crafting pasta from scratch or developing a straightforward machine learning model.

Let's take a moment to explore the art of making pasta, an Italian staple that embodies the joy of basics. Picture this: flour, eggs, and a sprinkle of salt. That's it! No need for robotic contraptions or test tubes filled with exotic flours (unless you're aiming for a noodle that resembles a fashionable bioengineered creation). With just these simple ingredients, kneading the dough becomes a meditative act, almost like a workout designed for a food lover's soul. The rhythm of rolling out the dough is soothing, like the gentle lapping of waves against the shore. In that simplicity lies the heart of Italian cooking, and one could argue it's where I find some of the most profound joys.

Now, fast forward a few hours to the dining table. I've served my beautiful, homemade fettuccine, glistening with a dash of olive oil and sprinkled with black pepper. But you know what's delightful? It's not just the taste; it's the sense of accomplishment that fills the room. This isn't a dish overshadowed by complexities or gimmicks; it's a testament to the beauty of craftsmanship that one can admire, the art of being comfortably uncomplicated. This resonates so well with the simplicity inherent in machine learning as well, where we often overlook the significance of basic algorithms that are reliable, repeatable, and effective.

In the realm of machine learning, it's all too tempting to get swept up in the allure of cutting-edge techniques and grandiose theories. But at heart, we have some terrific, time-tested algorithms, linear regression, decision trees, clustering methods, that deliver reliable results without requiring the intellectual equivalent of an entry exam to the "Convoluted Machine Learning University." These models are our foundations, and much like a solid marinara, they can stand the test of time. There's a profound joy in getting past the buzzwords and jargon, focusing instead on building meaningful models with the simple tools we have at our disposal.

Moreover, the beauty of embracing basics lies in accessibility. When I whip up a classic caprese salad, I revel not just in the flavors but also in the understanding that anyone can replicate it. Fresh mozzarella, ripe tomatoes, basil leaves, a pinch of salt, and there you have it! It's a joyous celebration of ingredients that transcends culinary prowess. This spirit carries over into the world of machine learning, where equipping those new to the field with the right tools to build their own models can empower them to forge their paths, joyfully experimenting without the intimidation of advanced coding languages leading them astray.

Finding joy in the basics also teaches resilience. There's something wonderfully satisfying about catching a mistake in a recipe or a bug in a code and realizing that with just a few adjustments, things can be salvaged. When I faced an unexpected sauce that turned out too watery (because who knew too much wine isn't always a good thing?), I learned to embrace that mishap, adjusting and enhancing rather than abandoning ship. It's a small victory to transform the mundane into the remarkable; this similarly holds true when your algorithm offers limited accuracy, teaching us that refining the fundamentals can lead to unexpected brilliance.

Ultimately, finding joy in the basics connects every aspect of life, whether in the kitchen or in the world of algorithms. So let us gather around the table, celebrating those simple, wholesome ingredients, be they tomatoes or features, and recognizing the importance they hold in our culinary creations and models alike. Making pasta, mixing it with love, or adjusting a few features in our dataset orchestrates a beautiful symphony of possibilities, reminding us that amidst life's complexities, simplicity can always reign supreme. Embrace those basics, folks, because when you indulge in simplicity, you discover joy that's as hearty as a well-cooked risotto and as satisfying as a successful prediction!

Chapter 17

Lost in Translation: Overcoming AI Misconceptions

Common AI Myths: The Pasta Illusion

When it comes to artificial intelligence (AI), a veritable spaghetti bowl of myths and misconceptions gets served up faster than a chef can say "al dente." If AI were a dish, we might be tempted to label it "Pasta Illusion," because, much like an overcooked noodle, it's become limp and lost its shape amidst the heat of public discourse. It often seems that the more we talk about AI, the further we stray from the truth, and the more ridiculous things become. So, let's untangle this pasta plate of AI myths together, shall we?

First and foremost, let's address the grand champion of all myths: the belief that AI possesses consciousness. Yes, I know, it's more tantalizing than a steaming plate of lasagna, but the truth is, AI doesn't have feelings, desires, or a penchant for joining book clubs. It's essentially a highly sophisticated blender, programmed to whip up impressive analysis, but it won't be discussing the merits of classic Italian literature anytime soon.

This misunderstanding often leads people to regard AI like the sentient robots in movies. News flash: AI isn't secretly plotting to take over the world while humming the theme to ''The Godfather." It simply lacks the cognitive seasoning.

Next, we need to ponder the myth that AI can do anything and everything. It's kind of like assuming that just because you know how to boil water, you can suddenly become a Michelin-star chef. We've all seen those incredibly impressive videos of AI playing chess or composing symphonies, quite the culinary spectacle! But let's not forget that these are specific tasks with specific data. My AI doesn't suddenly know how to make my Nonna's marinara sauce just because it can beat a grandmaster at chess. This leap of faith would be akin to believing that throwing a bunch of ingredients into a pot will somehow yield a delicious Risotto alla Milanese without a talented hand to stir the pot. AI excels at specialized tasks, but don't count on it whipping up a gourmet feast of diverse abilities.

Now, let's take a moment to contemplate the notion that more data always leads to better outcomes. Think of this myth as the overzealous diner who thinks that ordering ten different pasta dishes is a sign of sophistication. In reality, it just creates a whole lot of confusion and a serious risk of indigestion. In the world of AI, too much poor-quality data can actually hinder the results. Having a ton of data is like having a mountain of expired ingredients in your pantry; no matter how much you shovel in, your dish will still taste like disappointment. The key here is quality, folks! A handful of fresh, vibrant tomatoes is far more valuable than a decade-old can of mush.

Furthermore, let's dive into the frequently misinterpreted idea that AI can be entirely objective. Picture this: a bowl of spaghetti with a generous helping of red sauce versus an unseasoned corkscrew noodle. The choice is often subjective, inherently influenced by personal tastes. Similarly, AI systems are only as good as the data fed into them. Many times, biases sneak in like unexpected guests who just happen to bring their own judgmental opinions. If the data is flawed or biased, believe me, the results will reflect that. It's crucial to season your AI with fairness and transparency, lest it ends up refusing to serve you anything that strays from its preconceived notions.

As we explore the kitchen of AI misconceptions, let's not forget the misunderstanding that AI is meant to replace humans. It's almost as ludicrous as believing that the grocery store cashier will someday declare their retirement because a single scanner is taking over. Far from it! AI is more of a sous-chef, working alongside human creativity and insight to whip up satisfying solutions. By collaborating with AI, we can elevate our game in the kitchen and beyond, translating the hidden genius of traditional recipes into modern masterpieces of machine learning.

In the end, the key takeaway is this: much like with Italian pasta, knowing how to appreciate AI is all about the right ingredients, preparation, and context. Embracing the humor in the absurdity of these myths helps us glean insight into the true potential of AI. So next time someone tries to tell you that AI isn't just a glorified kitchen gadget or that it's got ''deep thoughts" about our culinary future, remember that even the finest bolognese is still just meat sauce if you don't know how to pair it with quality ingredients, effective management, and a pinch of humor. Bon appetit... or should I say, "A.I. mix-it!"

How Cooking Techniques Parallel AI Misconceptions

There's a delightful irony in the fact that cooking, an art form revered and practiced across the globe, shares many parallels with artificial intelligence. Yup, you heard that right! Venture into the kitchen as an AI enthusiast, and you'll find that the cooking techniques we're so fond of can explain (with a hefty dollop of humor) many of the misconceptions surrounding AI. It's like being handed a wooden spoon of knowledge while dodging a paring knife of confusion. So, roll up your sleeves, because we're ready to chop through the myths, one misguided food analogy at a time.

Let's begin with the myth of the "perfect recipe." If I had a euro for every time someone asked for a foolproof way to make lasagna, I'd have enough dough to open a pizzeria in Naples. Here's the kicker: there is no perfect recipe, just as there is no singular ideal AI model. Cooking involves adjustments for taste, texture, and the particular quirks of the ingredients at hand, much like how machine learning algorithms must be tweaked to suit specific data sets. If someone claims they know a magical recipe that works every single time, either they're lying, or they're about to throw a poorly constructed dish in the oven that resembles a sad, flat soufflé. In short, understanding that discrepancies exist in both cooking and AI is fundamental to avoiding culinary and computational catastrophes.

Moving on, let's talk about the importance of preparation. In cooking, we all know the significance of mise en place, the concept of having everything in its place before you start. Imagine embarking on a pasta-making adventure without first measuring the flour and cracking the eggs. Chaos would ensue! Similarly, in the realm of AI, failing to prepare your data properly can lead to disastrous results. The internet may call it ''data wrangling," but it's really just a fancy term for ensuring you've got the ingredients sorted before you start mixing. It's like trying to bake a cake with expired baking powder. Don't blame the recipe when it collapses; blame the cook!

Yet another parallel can be drawn from seasoning (and yes, this is a genuine culinary inquiry). Picture it: you've followed the recipe to the letter, and your dish looks immaculate. But one taste reveals a tragic flaw, it's bland! The same can be said for AI's interpretability and the requirement for adequate evaluation. Just as you have to season a dish thoughtfully to enhance its flavors, AI models must be tested against real-world situations to ensure they deliver results that satisfy our appetites for accuracy and fairness. Without this peppy kick of seasoning, AI can turn into a bland "serve and forget" process; satisfying only if our goal was to replicate the dull taste of cardboard.

And let's not overlook the concept of "time." Ah, the age-old kitchen adage: "good things come to those who wait." Whether we're simmering a rich sauce or waiting for the dough to rise, patience is indeed a virtue. Unfortunately, the belief that AI can generate results at lightning speed is akin to expecting spaghetti to boil itself just by staring at it long enough. I've seen folks excitedly demand instantaneous solutions, only to be confronted with the reality that high-quality learning demands patience and time, like letting that tantalizing marinara sauce simmer to perfection. So, next time someone complains about the time it takes to train a model, tell them about the virtues of a soufflé; fleeting beauty requires patience and a touch of finesse!

Now, let's take a moment to discuss innovation in the kitchen. When food scientists developed sous vide cooking, suddenly a whole new world of culinary delights opened up; they took traditional cooking techniques and gave them a shiny upgrade! AI operates under similar principles of enhancement through innovation. However, this doesn't mean we should throw out grandma's recipes just because a new Swiss Army knife gadget is available. Innovations should complement existing practices. Unfortunately, the myth persists that AI will render everything "old-school" obsolete, even the cherished family recipes. But in reality, it's like replacing grandma's wooden spoon with an AI chef that can't taste; innovation should enhance, not replace.

Lastly, my friends, there's the delightful expectation that cooking is merely about following instructions. If only it were that simple! The culinary world thrives on intuition, exploration, and the occasional messy mistake. Meanwhile, people often view AI as a rigid set of instructions that produces a flawless outcome every time. Just as a cook learns from blending flavors, discovering that too much salt could result in an overflowing salt lick, AI practitioners must embrace experimentation to understand what works and what doesn't. Overcoming hiccups is often how we refine our skills, both in the kitchen and in the world of AI development.

So, there you have it! The myths surrounding AI are as misguided as assuming you can make a gourmet meal by merely heating frozen chicken nuggets in the microwave. Just like cooking, mastering AI requires time, practice, and the willingness to learn from those charred edges. Embrace the kitchen chaos, throw some garlic in the pan, and dig deep into the world of AI misconceptions. Trust me, it'll be a savory journey sprinkled with laughter and plenty of "Whoops! Did I really just do that?" moments. After all, we're all just chefs trying to create the perfect blend of ingredients to serve up our deliciously intricate AI world. Buon appetito!

Difficult Ingredients: The Complexity of Machine Learning

When I think of machine learning, my mind often wanders to the metaphorical kitchen, a place where the finest ingredients must be carefully selected, measured, and mixed in just the right way to craft the culinary equivalent of a masterpiece. But, dear reader, let's not sugarcoat it: machine learning can sometimes feel like you've been tasked with preparing a high-stakes soufflé with nothing but tricky ingredients and a recipe written in a foreign language. Just like in a kitchen battle, the complexities can overwhelm you faster than an undercooked egg sliding off a plate. So, pull up a chair, because it's time to explore the challenging ingredients of machine learning and laugh at the chaos along the way.

Let's start with our primary ingredient: data. If you've ever tried to bake a cake without flour, you know precisely how unfortunate that can be, similarly, machine learning models can flounder without good data. The tricky part? Not all data is created equal! Some data is fresh and bursting with flavor, while other bits may be stale and lack nutritional value. It's the difference between pulling ripe tomatoes from the vine and using the sad, shriveled specimens from the back of your fridge that you've been too afraid to toss out. In machine learning, dirty or poorly chosen data can lead to disastrous results. A model trained on subpar data is as useless as a day-old slice of pizza on a Saturday night when everyone is craving a fresh pie. You wouldn't serve guests melted cheese on soggy crust while claiming it's gourmet, and similarly, you can't present an AI model with unsound data and expect it to shine.

Then, there's the mysterious world of feature selection, arguably one of the most significant complexities in machine learning. Choosing the right features is akin to picking the perfect spices for your signature dish. Too much coriander, and your guests might think they're being punished for a previous life; too little, and they might leave with bland, uninspired experiences. In machine learning, irrelevant or redundant features can confuse the model, leading to what we lovingly refer to as "overfitting." This is the moment when your model performs spectacularly on training data but downright abysmally on real-world inputs. It's like a cook who only knows how to prepare the exact dish they've been training for, rather than adapting to the diverse flavors of the world. If the model can't generalize, it's as if you've spent hours preparing an elaborate feast, only to realize your guests are expecting spaghetti but you've made sushi. Bon appetit, right?

Now, let's not forget about those hyperparameters, the sneaky little seasoning variables that can make or break your machine learning model. Adjusting hyperparameters feels like trying to achieve the perfect dough consistency without ever having made it before. Every cook has been there: too much water, and you've got soup; too little, and it's like attempting to mold a brick. In machine learning, finding the right balance of learning rates, batch sizes, and regularization can either propel your model to stardom or push it right into the dumpster behind a greasy diner. It's that precarious tightrope walk between trial and error that often leaves the unprepared in a puddle of flour and angst.

Speaking of trials, we all know that cooking often involves a healthy dose of experimentation. You may be thinking, "Why can't I just follow the darn recipe?" Well, in the deliciously chaotic world of machine learning, following the recipe precisely might not yield the desired results. With so many variables at play, equal parts data, algorithms, computation resources, and luck, cooking up a successful machine learning model can feel much like hosting an all-you-can-eat buffet while blindfolded. You just have to hope you end up serving something edible while trying not to step on any toes in the process.

And comes the final piece de resistance: model evaluation. It's here that we taste our creation to see if it has matured into a culinary masterpiece or whether it's about to join the ranks of infamous kitchen disasters. Think of it like presenting your finest dish to a panel of kitchen elders who will lament your life choices while critiquing your seasoning decisions. In the world of machine learning, validating the model against a test set is the moment of truth. After all those hours of experimentation, you hold your breath, hoping that your creation won't flop and become the laughter of the AI community.

As you can see, the complexities of machine learning are daunting and often resemble the nuanced challenge of preparing a gourmet meal, a glorious endeavor filled with thrills, spills, and yes, sometimes burnt offerings. Still, it's the very struggle of mastering these difficult ingredients that leads us to the joys of learning. So, embrace the culinary chaos of machine learning, after all, every cooking mishap is merely another ingredient in your journey towards mastery! With a pinch of humor and a dash of patience, we can tackle any AI dilemma and serve up something that's as tasty as a well-cooked pasta. Buon appetito!

Mistakes in the Kitchen: Learning from AI Errors

The kitchen, a realm of culinary dreams and horrifying disasters! You've been there; we all have. You attempt to whip up what you envision as a 5-Star gastronomic delight, only to end up serving your guests a charred brick disguised as a meatloaf. Mistakes happen, often more frequently than we'd like to admit, and these kitchen disasters are a perfect metaphor for the errors we encounter in the world of artificial intelligence. So, grab your apron, tighten those shoelaces, and let's dig into the spicy, yet sometimes pungent, relationship between mistakes in the kitchen and the world of AI.

Let's start with the fundamental truth: mistakes are a natural part of life, especially in cooking. Remember when you tried to flambe a dish but accidentally set off the smoke alarm? Yes, that fragrant mango chicken could've been a crowd-pleaser, but what it turned into was an impromptu fire drill. Similarly, in machine learning, when we make an error, often a doozy, we might trigger alarms in our carefully constructed models. The infamous "overfitting" error, where an algorithm memorizes training data but fails miserably at new data, can feel like that unfortunate recipe gone wrong. You see, just as every burned pot roast teaches you a new lesson about temperature control, every AI hiccup teaches us to refine our models to adapt better. If we can learn to tolerate the occasional flambe, we can certainly learn to embrace our AI screw-ups!

Speaking of learning, let's discuss one of the more comically relatable kitchen experiences: measuring ingredients. You might think you've got it all figured out, grabbing a "generous handful" of salt like a seasoned pro. If you've ever taken a bite of your creation only to feel like you've just licked the ocean floor, you know precisely how wrong this can go. In the AI realm, misjudging our model parameters can lead to detrimental results as well, an algorithm straying wildly from what you intended. It's like believing that a judicious dash of cayenne will transform a bland sauce into a masterpiece, only to accidentally unleash a volcano of spice. In both cooking and AI, learning to measure correctly is crucial. Not quite understanding how much data a model needs can leave you with a disappointing result, like eating a rubbery soufflé that never rises.

The art (or lack thereof) of timing is another mistake so familiar to home chefs. You can't just throw a lasagna together and leave it in the oven forever, hoping it will miraculously change into culinary perfection. Similarly, in machine learning, if we don't allocate appropriate time to train our models or tune our hyperparameters, we may end up with something that tries but ultimately stumbles. Imagine serving a slightly raw chicken because you were too eager to eat! That same impatience can haunt us when we rush to deploy an AI model that hasn't been properly evaluated. We all know what happens when we take shortcuts in cooking, it's seldom pretty, and no one leaves the table happy. Learning to respect the process, whether cultivating flavors or fine-tuning algorithms, can make all the difference in ensuring that our AI dishes aren't just edible, but downright sensational.

And how about those days when you forget a crucial ingredient? The scenario where you stand there, horrified, realizing that you've committed the ultimate betrayal to your epic cookie recipe by neglecting the butter. It's a culinary nightmare that leaves even the best home chefs questioning their worth. In the same vein, this mirrors the moments in AI development where critical features or data are overlooked, leading to results that are akin to baked cardboard. Ignoring vital inputs can leave an algorithm performing bafflingly poorly. Learning from our mistakes, just like sheepishly adding butter moments before the cookies go in the oven, is what helps refine our approach.

Finally, let's explore the power of feedback. After a dinner party, there's always a hint of discomfort in asking your guests how the food tasted, but doing so is invaluable for future cooking endeavors. "Oh, you meant you wanted a hint of garlic, not an avalanche?" This same philosophy applies to machine learning: model evaluation is key! When we receive feedback from our AI systems, it's akin to hearing that the risotto was too creamy (who knew that was possible, right?). Every critique helps refine the model, molding it into something more robust and appealing over time. Embracing this feedback, instead of throwing our hands up in frustration, is the crucial ingredient for both culinary and computational success.

In closing, my friends, mistakes in the kitchen and errors in AI bear striking similarities. Both offer monumental opportunities for growth, learning, and humor. Whether you've septic tanked a soufflé or deployed a model that couldn't classify a tomato if it was standing on its own, it's imperative to embrace the chaos and learn from it. With a smirk and a sprinkle of salt, we can elevate our culinary and computational escapades to new heights. So, let's celebrate our kitchen catastrophes, our AI foibles, and the lessons learned along the way, after all, every burnt lasagna and miscalibrated model teaches us to craft something even better the next time around. Buon Appetito and Happy Learning!

Humor in Mistakes: Finding Joy in Misunderstanding

Let's face it: mistakes are as inherent to cooking as flour is to pasta. You may have perfected the art of boiling water (a notable feat, needless to say), but the moment you leave your sauce unattended on the stovetop, you're greeted with the lovely aroma of disappointment wafting through the kitchen, an olfactory reminder that even the best chefs don't always hit the mark. This delightful rigidity of reality brings us to the heart of our discussion today: humor in mistakes and the sweet joy of misunderstanding. Because, let's be honest, what's more amusing than a culinary misadventure paired with a splash of creativity?

The kitchen is akin to a stage for comedic performances, where mishaps spark spontaneous laughter and the regret of charred edges becomes the stuff of grand stories. Ever had one of those "masterchef" moments where you attempt to flambe a dish, only to set off the fire alarm instead? There's something simultaneously horrifying and hilarious about the spectacle of burnt garlic and smoke as you crack open a window and ponder both your cooking skills and life choices. Frankly, it's a moment that captures the essence of understanding in the culinary realm, evidence that mistakes paint our experiences with delightful strokes of absurdity. In a flourishing culinary journey, it's the blunders that often steal the spotlight, inspiring us to whip up fresh creativity in the midst of chaos.

Now translate that joy of kitchen mishaps to the world of artificial intelligence. Here's the truth: AI has a knack for making mistakes too, and sometimes the outcomes can be more entertaining than a slapstick comedy. Every so often, our cherished algorithms churn out outputs that leave us scratching our heads in utter disbelief. Picture this: an AI model that wrongly deduces the classic spaghetti pomodoro recipe involves a generous dollop of jelly (trust me, it has happened!). The absurdity of serving up pasta with grape jelly is something that would make even the most brave-hearted of taste-testers run for the hills. But rather than burying our faces in our palms, we should learn to chuckle, using these blunders as a catalyst for improvement and growth.

The beauty of mistakes lies in their educational value. Just as in cooking, these errors offer the opportunity to explore new flavors and learn new techniques. Think of the embarrassment of presenting currant-invaded spaghetti as a metaphor for the joys of "learning from AI fails." If these models lovingly decide to add jelly while you hoped for umami, let's treat that misalignment as a chance to regroup and reevaluate our approach. Why did the model think jelly was an essential ingredient? Was there data from a quirky recipe blog influencing its decision the same way a misguided guest at a potluck might bring caviar on toast, thinking it's a hit? These realizations only help in crafting better algorithms, allowing us to address the confounding data points that lead us astray.

Moreover, laughter is a powerful remedy, especially when something awry happens in the kitchen (or the virtual world of AI). Amidst the chaos of scorching a pan or deploying an AI model that gives bizarre predictions, there's a liberating sense of joy in finding humor in the predicament. In both cases, it seems our culinary adventures (or data analytics jobs) bring us existential lessons that transform the fumbled mishaps into moments we can share and commiserate over later, perhaps over a plate of perfectly cooked pasta, free of jelly this time!

Let's not forget that humor acts as a healing balm. The culinary world has its share of frenetic chaos that can leave even the most balanced chef feeling flustered, defeated, and questioning their life choices. Releasing laughter amid the stress of kitchen mishaps or validating AI outputs helps us grasp the absurdity of the situation. When you can find humor in the burnt edges of a cake or a misguided recommendation for spaghetti with jam, you acknowledge that it's simply part of the beautiful mess of life. This acceptance reminds us that our affinity for cooking (or coding) is inherently attached to trial and error, and mistakes are just as important as successes when it comes to flavor or technical prowess.

In conclusion, the beauty of mistakes, whether in the kitchen or the labyrinthine world of AI, lies in how we can embrace humor, share joyful tales, and transform ugliness into opportunities for creativity. The next time you find yourself standing over a concoction that appears to be little more than a culinary betrayal, take a step back, laugh it off, and remember that mistakes are what spice life up. With humor as our guiding light, we can tackle AI's enigmatic deliveries, sprinkle them with a dash of introspection, and serve them up alongside an extra helping of laughter at the dinner table of life. Buon appetito, and may your kitchen blunders be just as flavorful!

Chapter 18

The Taste Test: Evaluating AI Models

The Culinary Analogy: Tasting vs. Evaluating AI Models

In the world of unpredictable culinary adventures, tasting can often feel a bit like the art of evaluating AI models. Picture this: you've just whipped up a beautiful batch of spaghetti with your secret sauce, tangy tomatoes, fragrant basil, and just the right touch of chili flakes to kick things up a notch. Before serving it up to your family or maybe that snobby friend who always claims to know more about Italian cuisine than you do, you take a moment to taste it. This is not just any moment; it's the vital test that distinguishes great chefs from those who think a can of store-bought marinara suffices. Similarly, in AI, before you unleash your model into the wild, you must taste it, I mean, evaluate it carefully.

Now, let's dive into the differences between tasting a dish and evaluating an AI model. When we taste food, we engage all our senses: the aroma wafting through the air, the texture of the sauce on our tongues, and the delightful symphony of flavors playing a melody in our mouths. Each of these elements creates an experience that is both subjective and deeply personal. Evaluation in AI, while somewhat less delicious, is similarly nuanced. The metrics we employ, accuracy, precision, recall, are merely the numbers on a scale. They don't account for the entire experience. Did the model actually understand the nuances? Did it go rogue and decide to recommend pineapple pizza instead of your traditional margherita? These are some of the existential questions one faces when dealing with AI.

Just like a chef may incorrectly balance the sugar and salt in a dish, we can also create models that go off the rails. Sometimes, it's as if they've taken a sun-soaked vacation in the jackfruit aisle without any direction. So, whether you're tasting a dish or evaluating an AI model, balance is crucial. Too much salt or too many false positives can ruin an otherwise perfectly good creation. Remember that scene from every Italian kitchen where Nonna looks at you sternly, releasing that iconic sigh and saying, "Non e cosi che si fa, bambino!" (That's not how you do it, kid!) It's the same response you might expect from an angry dataset that chokes on a poorly trained model. The art of evaluation, much like cooking, is all about moderation.

Now, here's where it gets interesting: tolerance levels. As a technology risk manager, I occasionally find myself in meetings discussing acceptable error rates in models. It's unlike the discussions over how much chili powder to put in your arrabbiata sauce. Trust me; no one goes to a restaurant cup-in-hand to comment on the "acceptable hotness" of their meal. "I'm sorry, chef, but this is more of a level-four spice when I requested a level-six!" Yet, in the AI realm, we painstakingly debate those acceptable error margins as if we're negotiating with the Department of Motor Vehicles over a questionable parking fine.

Furthermore, just as you might choose to rehearse a formal tasting menu during a family gathering, choosing when and how often to evaluate your AI model is equally critical. Do you swoop in just once after initial deployment, or do you do it regularly for continuous improvement? A chef doesn't just prepare a dish and forget about it; they revisit the recipe, tweak here, adjust there, much like how we need to keep an eye on our models post-deployment. After all, leftover spaghetti can taste fantastic the next day if you reheat it correctly, but ignore it long enough, and who knows what you'll find lurking at the bottom of your fridge.

In conclusion, the relationship between tasting in culinary arts and evaluating AI models is nuanced, laden with personal preferences, and outrageously critical for success. If you don't know how your spaghetti tastes, how can you expect your model to make the right decisions? So, next time you're at the stove or in front of your computer running evaluations, remember that both processes demand respect, nuance, and a pinch of humor. Like an uninvited relative crashing dinner who insists on bringing expired wine, poorly evaluated AI models can also ruin your gathering. And remember, there's no harm in tossing your old secrets and coding practices into the bin, just like that questionable jar of tomato sauce at the back of your pantry!

Consistency in Flavor: The Importance of Model Validation

Consistency in flavor! It's the holy grail of cooking, especially when it comes to Italian cuisine. Imagine you open a family restaurant offering the best carbonara in town. The first time a customer savors that creamy, pancetta-infused delight, they are transported to culinary heaven. However, if they return next week only to find a dish that resembles a sad shadow of its former self, watery sauce, and floppy noodles, they may well rethink their dining choices. This inconsistency not only tarnishes your once-storied reputation but also risks having old friends and relatives openly question what the hell happened to your cooking. Voila! Welcome to the parallel world of AI: model validation, where consistency is just as vital, yet far less delicious... or crumbly, for that matter.

Model validation in machine learning is like ensuring every batch of your famous meatballs is as mouthwatering as the last. Just as you must meticulously mix the right amount of breadcrumbs, egg, herbs, and spices to whip up those ideal orbs of deliciousness, validating your model's performance is equally critical to its success. Here's where things often get comically messy, much like when you accidentally add a cup too much of oregano, turning your family recipe into an Italian herb smoothie. This is where validation steps in like the steadfast Nonna, ensuring your blending ratios are spot-on. Think of it as an AI culinary guide yelling "More garlic! Less oregano!" while you aren't even looking.

In the tech world, if we skip model validation, like skipping salt in a pasta dish, it leads to a mediocre meal, a subpar, uninspired model peddling forth erroneous predictions like an ex-boyfriend trying to win you back with empty promises. The validation stage, dear reader, is what helps us ensure that our precious model works not only on our training data but also on new, unseen data. Why? Because AI models can be sneaky little gremlins. They often learn all the peculiarities of the training dataset, just as some people intrude into your kitchen without asking for permission, proudly proclaiming their 'experience' while they hover too close for comfort. Think of this data overfitting as charming yet confusing dinner guests who just keep talking about their ''expert" opinions instead of asking you for the recipe.

Just like the difference between rubbery pasta and perfectly al dente strands hinges on careful timing, model validation requires us to set the right parameters to avoid pitfalls. It's essential to establish metrics and validate our models across various datasets to avoid ending up with a soupy mess that doesn't hold together, much like that disastrous attempt at homemade gnocchi made without any potatoes. You don't want to become that person who takes a bite and desperately tries to remember the last time they served something noteworthy.

Moreover, let's not forget the agony of finding yourself on the receiving end of a bad rehash. Consumers can be volatile, much like fickle food critics who can turn on you faster than your last oven timer dinged ominously. Consistency in flavor, or rather model validation, keeps the complaints at bay. A validated model has been rigorously tested and gloriously refined to ensure it's all together; it's the high road to avoiding serving spaghetti with an inexplicable sunflower oil sauce. The beauty of diligent model validation rests in its ability to prevent every algorithmic wannabe from impersonating gourmet masterpieces.

So, what's the takeaway? An unyielding commitment to consistency is vital in both the kitchen and the data science realm. While a killer marinara sauce might take time to master, validation isn't an optional condiment. In the realm of machine learning, consistency in flavor, be it from your spaghetti carbonara or predictive modeling, is often the difference between delighting your diners or shocking them into a state of culinary confusion. Next time you're grappling with metrics instead of dough, remember: countless generations of chefs have lived and died by the flavor of their dishes. Keep that in mind while you juggle hyperparameters like an overcaffeinated circus performer. Cheers to consistent flavors and validated models; both make for a happily-ever-after... or at least until the next batch!

A Pinch of Humor: Common Pitfalls in AI Assessment

The world of AI assessment! It's a magical land where numbers and algorithms tango their way into the hearts of data scientists everywhere. Yet, like that time you confidently added chili flakes to your nonna's famous bolognese, only to find out that "a pinch" meant just a whisper of heat, AI assessment is rife with common pitfalls that can absolutely derail an otherwise promising model. Let's meander through some of these missteps with a generous pinch of humor, because if we can't laugh at our blunders, what's the point? The culinary world would be a lot less fun if we took ourselves too seriously!

First up on our comical journey is the dreadfully classic pitfall of overfitting. It's much like making a lavish feast for a room full of friends, only to realize halfway through that you've created an elaborate banquet, five different pasta shapes, three sauces, and a tower of tiramisu, all crafted precisely to appease the whims of a single, very picky eater. Sure, it looks beautiful, but guess what? You've effectively ignored the tastes of everyone else at the table, and now you've trapped yourself in a culinary quagmire. Overfitting in AI is remarkably similar; you create a model that performs exceptionally well on your training data but fails spectacularly when faced with any new data. Talk about a table full of disappointed guests!

Next on our list of pitfalls is the "set-it-and-forget-it" mindset, which I know can feel tempting, like that juicy steak resting on a grill while you wander off to check Instagram. The problem is that, unlike steak, which benefits from a bit of attention (and perhaps a smidge of garlic butter), your AI model demands you keep it in check. Leaving a model unattended to run unchecked is like walking away from your fermenting tomatoes. Before you know it, they've turned into a science project instead of a savory sauce. Validation is key; we need to keep overlaying our models with new data, much like a chef who constantly tastes their concoction rather than letting it boil into oblivion.

Ah, then there's the infamous metric obsession. You've heard of it: the race to chase the trendiest metrics like a chef sniffing around for the newest culinary craze. I've seen it way too often, teams becoming overly enamored with accuracy, precision, and recall as if they're the culinary Holy Grail. But just like adding saffron to every dish doesn't guarantee success, a model showcasing high accuracy doesn't necessarily mean it's effective or meaningful. It's essential to have a balanced palate, or in our case, metrics. Nothing ruins the dining experience quite like that friend who talks only about "gluten-free" desserts when what your heart really craves is a good tiramisu! The balance between evaluating multiple metrics ensures that our models serve their intended purpose, not merely serve as pretty faces on a presentation slide.

Speaking of presentation slides, let's talk about the pitfall of data quality, or as I like to call it, the 'junk in, junk out' syndrome. Imagine painstakingly preparing a lush layered lasagna with the most mediocre, soggy, pre-packaged noodles. My friends, your lasagna may look enticing, but the moment someone takes a bite, it's game over! AI models are no different. Feeding them low-quality data is like seasoning your dish with expired herbs. Your model might taste great (you know, in theory) in your head, but when the moment of exposure arrives, it unravels like an ill-fated soufflé, gone in an instant with a loud crack. Hence, procuring top-notch data is paramount for any serious chef in the AI kitchen.

Another amusing yet critical folly is avoiding bias. Much as you would select the freshest tomatoes for your sauce, we must strive to avoid developing models that are wobbly or skewed by biased data. It's like cooking a risotto with miscalibrated salt levels that may ruin perfectly cooked rice. When our AI learns from screwball biases, whether intentional or incidental, our entire creation risks falling woefully short of its design goals. Nothing prevents the joy of culinary genius like a dish that inadvertently offends half of my Italian family, right? When we allow biases to seep into our AI assessments, we could serve up a recipe for disaster.

In summary, the pitfalls in AI assessment are as varied as the potential pasta shapes. From overfitting and neglect to obsession with metrics, junk data, and bias, it's a humorous but real rollercoaster ride! It is crucial to learn from our funny, messy missteps as we cook up innovative solutions. So grab your apron, adjust your algorithms, and remember: a pinch of humor will go a long way in both the ethical kitchen and the unpredictable realm of AI. Buon appetito, and may your assessments always yield delicious results!

Flavor Profiles: Understanding Your Model's Strengths and Weaknesses

Flavor profiles! Ah, the essential essence of any delightful dish. Just as a well-crafted sauce can be both zingy and savory, a robust AI model has its unique strengths and weaknesses. Imagine holding a dinner party where each dish paints a vivid picture of its flavor profile, the rich umami of a mushroom risotto, the invigorating zest of a lemon chicken, or perhaps the unexpected punch of a chili-infused gelato. When we talk about culinary creations, understanding these flavors is paramount, and the same holds true for our AI models. Today, let's traverse the savory landscape of algorithms, exploring their strengths and weaknesses as though we were creating a delightful Italian feast.

Every good dish begins with an understanding of its ingredients, and likewise, every effective model emerges from a clear grasp of its data, its base flavors. In the kitchen, a dash of salt enhances the taste of a tomato sauce, elevating the entire dish from mundane to magnificent. In the AI realm, knowing the type of data you're serving up can be equally transformative. Is your data clean, rich, and well-prepped like freshly harvested basil? Or is it more akin to that limp parsley lost at the bottom of the fridge? It's essential to analyze the strengths of your model, its propensity to identify patterns, make predictions, and adapt to new situations, and to ensure that the data acts as the perfect ingredient rather than a culinary catastrophe waiting to unfold.

Now let's consider the weaknesses, that stubborn piece of caper that seems to linger in your dish. Perhaps your model performs brilliantly on specific tasks but falters dramatically under pressure. This is akin to a lasagna that seems perfect in the kitchen but, upon arriving at the dinner table, collapses like an unsteady Jenga tower. Predictive power can be as fickle as the moods of a family gathering. Understanding when and under what conditions your model handles itself best is crucial. This is why modeling without a clear awareness of the boundaries can lead to disastrous results, resulting in your algorithms shaping predictions as tragic as a poorly constructed tiramisu.

Flavor profiles in cuisine also require balance. A successful dish isn't just about the presence of strong ingredients; it's about creating a harmonious combination. Similarly, a well-tuned model leverages strengths to mitigate its weaknesses, just as a properly seasoned sauce balances acidity and sweetness. In AI, ensemble methods can be your great design allies, combining the predictions of various models into one mighty concoction. Think robust training models working together like a family of chefs: one focusing on pasta, another on meat, and the enthusiastic grandchild in the corner who insists on sprinkling everything with the 'secret ingredient', a metaphorical pinch of sentimentality. Together, they create masterpieces, while individually, they may not hold up quite as well.

Alas, we cannot forget the ever-important tastes that come with our flavor profiles: biases! Sometimes, we create algorithms that only cater to specific datasets, akin to that friend who insists on serving anchovies at every dinner party despite the grumblings of the rest of the crowd. If we fail to identify these biases, our models might be effective for one audience yet horrendously incompatible with another. Just like a dish that doesn't account for dietary preferences can leave guests in a state of disillusionment, undetected biases in your model can lead your predictions wildly astray. Understanding the full spectrum of tastes, be it sweet, spicy, or unforgivingly bland, is as crucial for our AI assessments as it is for our culinary endeavors.

Furthermore, it's worth analyzing our beloved flavor profiles, those strengths and weaknesses, to locate where improvements can be made. Just as chefs do not shy away from experimenting with dishes after receiving feedback, the AI community thrives on refining and iterating models. It may take a few rounds of "taste tests" before you arrive at a balanced and satisfying outcome, a spaghetti carbonara that even the most discerning critics would rave about! Regularly revisiting your assessments helps you diagnose the flavor of your model and anticipate any surprises lurking in its depths.

In summary, understanding your model's flavor profile is akin to mastering the art of Italian cooking. It requires an analysis of strengths, a keen awareness of weaknesses, and a commitment to ongoing refinement. So, whether building a neural network or whipping up homemade fettuccine, relish in the journey and don't forget to evaluate your creations, lest you find your algorithm teetering on the edge of disaster like a plate of overcooked ravioli slipping from your hands. Let's embrace the full symphony of flavors in both our culinary and computational adventures, and savor the joy of discovering how robust our results can be! Bon Appetit and buon lavoro!

Serving Up Feedback: The Role of User Input in Model Evaluation

User feedback! The secret ingredient in the ever-evolving recipe is model evaluation. Think of it as your Italian grandmother hovering over you in the kitchen, snatching the spoon from your hand and insisting that a little more salt will take your dish from"meh" to"magnifico." Just as you'd want your family to taste your culinary creations and provide some honest feedback, even if it stings a little, AI models crave that critique to thrive and improve. After all, nothing screams "I trust you" louder than a relative daring to critique your lasagna, even if it results in emotional tears and a fragile family truce!

When it comes to developing AI models, understanding the user experience and their feedback is like mining for truffles beneath the surface of your average mushroom risotto. You might think you have an impeccable dish, ready to impress the world, but it's only through diligent user testing that you learn whether your fabulous creation is truly a crowd-pleaser or merely a lukewarm appetizer. It's as if you hosted a dinner party, and while you confidently believe you've served the best spaghetti carbonara ever, your guests are quietly slipping pieces of fusilli into their bags to take home as a subtle PC reminder of their experience. In much the same way, your AI model may not land with end users as smoothly as you envision.

Gathering user input is crucial for several reasons. First and foremost, users bring diverse perspectives to the table, much like that family reunion where you discover Aunt Judie and Cousin Leo have passionately different opinions about whether pineapple belongs on pizza. Those varied opinions can help illuminate aspects you might have overlooked during development. Imagine trying to make something as exquisite as risotto without realizing that your "secret" starch was, in fact, a gnocchi recipe. By engaging with users, you riff on their insights, crafting a more palatable model with unique flavor inflections that resonate with end users who enjoy the dish.

Next, let's talk about the hilarious situations that can arise when you ignore user feedback. Picture this: you're proudly presenting your "next-level" AI-based recipe suggestion tool, convinced you've outdone yourself. However, as users interact with your tool, they find themselves confused because it keeps suggesting the same (stale) recipes over and over again. Like a one-trick pony, your model is stuck in a culinary rut, much like a chef who insists on serving yesterday's soggy frittata to every diner. User input is your saving grace here! Without it, you may be blissfully unaware that your model is about as useful as a can of expired pasta sauce. Feedback will throw you the lifeline you need to steer your culinary (or computational) ship in the right direction.

Of course, analyzing this feedback can sometimes feel like trying to sieve the shells out of your perfectly cooked spaghetti, but it's essential! What appears as straightforward input can be richer than a four-cheese pizza. User comments often harbor gems of wisdom, offering clues about model performance, identifying acute problems, and unveiling opportunities for improvement! Is your model misclassifying inputs? Users are the lifeblood of understanding these nuances! Their experiences expose weaknesses you might have thought were solid as a parmigiana. Besides, nothing lightens the mood quite like users joking about a model suggesting "lasagna" in response to requests for "gluten-free" options!

Additionally, pride can pose a serious conundrum when it comes to incorporating user feedback. Occasionally, you might find yourself holding on too tightly to that tantalizing, innovative recipe you've developed. Maybe this one-hour tomato sauce recipe was your baby, and parting with it is akin to tossing a prized heirloom vase off a cliff. Still, allowing yourself to lean into feedback opens up worlds of new possibilities. Users can push you to reevaluate your cherished recipes, resulting in extraordinary mashups, a combination of two traditional cultures that might lead you to biryani-flavored pappardelle, perhaps?

In conclusion, user feedback is both salt and sugar that elevates your model evaluation process to new heights. Whether it's a direct critique of your culinary endeavor or critical insight into your model's performance, it's essential to embrace the voices of those you seek to serve! So as you cook and code, remember the value of honest conversations that arise when you show your guests and users the respect they deserve. Cheers to being open to the many flavors of feedback and understanding that sometimes, just like Aunt Judie's infamous tiramisu, the only way to improve is to let others help refine the recipe! Buon appetito and happy coding, my fellow culinary data scientists!

Chapter 19

The Quantum Factor: The Future of AI and Beyond

The Basics of Quantum Computing: A Pasta Primer

Quantum computing, a subject so complex it makes deciphering the many layers of a lasagna seem like child's play. If you thought that the only way two things could be ''entangled" was in the context of pasta and sauce, well, prepare yourself for a reality check. Quantum computing is like a fresh plate of fettuccine alfredo, smooth, creamy, and with a whole lot of intricate ingredients that, when put together properly, create something truly remarkable. But let's not get too ahead of ourselves, let's start with the basics.

Think of the smallest unit of data in our conventional computing world as a bit, represented as either a 0 or a 1, much like deciding whether to add cheese to your pasta, either you do, or you don't. On the other hand, quantum bits, or qubits, bring a delightful twist to the table. They are akin to a ravioli that you can't quite decide if it's cheese or meat stuffed; it's both until you take a bite! In simplest terms, qubits can be o, i, or both at the same time, thanks to a wonderful phenomenon called superposition. This property allows quantum computers to process a massive amount of information simultaneously, which would take conventional computers an eternity, akin to waiting for the pasta water to boil while your niece insists on rigorously testing the spaghetti for doneness by slapping it against the wall.

Now, we must address entanglement, which sounds suspiciously like something you might encounter during a family meal involving too much wine. In the quantum realm, entangled qubits are interconnected in such a way that the state of one instantly influences the state of another, regardless of the distance separating them. Imagine you're at a family dinner, and every time you taste the marinara sauce, your cousin in another city also tastes it at the same exact time. Now that's some serious kitchen magic! This entangled connection can lead to a new form of communications and computations that traditional computers could only dream of. Talk about needing a bigger kitchen to handle those kinds of orders!

So, how do quantum computers handle the cooking? They utilize quantum algorithms to process data in ways that are wildly different from classical computations. It's almost like following a recipe that not only tells you the ingredients but also provides magical shortcuts! For instance. Shot's Algorithm can factor large numbers exponentially faster than classical algorithms, which, in culinary terms, means I can whip up a thousand noodle dishes while still having time to perfect my tiramisu.

But hold onto your chef's hat, because it's not all al dente and perfect sauces, quantum computing is still in its infancy. It's like having the finest ingredients and a beautiful recipe only to find that your oven refuses to preheat. We are facing challenges with qubit stability (or, as the tech wizards like to call it, decoherence) and error rates, which are enough to send any chef into a panic reminiscent of undercooked pasta at an important dinner party. You could have a thousand chefs in the kitchen, but if they can't agree on the cooking time, well, you're left with a mushy mess that definitely won't impress the critics.

Just as I meticulously wash each piece of produce before I start cooking, quantum computing must also focus on ''cleaning" its operations to facilitate reliable results. This means that researchers are scrambling like headless chickens to find ways to stabilize qubits so they can achieve reliable results over prolonged periods. With a dash of patience and a sprinkle of innovation, who knows what could emerge from this quirky culinary experiment on the quantum scale?

In the end, quantum computing is like pasta, though initially daunting, it reveals an infinite array of possibilities once you embrace its complexities. Imagine a world where AI and quantum computing erode the limitations of our current technology, that's a hearty plate of spaghetti with extra sauce! So the next time you twirl your fork around your spaghetti, ponder the wonders happening in the quantum realm. And who knows, maybe one day your pasta will be cooked via quantum entanglement, allowing it to taste good across the entire globe simultaneously! But until then. I'll rely heavily on my conventional cooking techniques while savoring the hope that quantum lasagna might one day be on our dinner tables.

Quantum Superposition: A Seasoned Approach

Quantum superposition, a delightful concept that serves as the backbone of quantum computing and, much like a chef's secret spice mix, can be the difference between a mundane dish and a culinary masterpiece. Imagine, if you will, the delicate art of making a perfect risotto. At first glance, it seems straightforward: add rice to simmering broth, stir, season, and voila! But it's not just about throwing ingredients into the pot, it's about knowing which ones go in and when, just like managing qubits in superposition.

To understand superposition, picture your favorite pasta shape: let's say, the far more sophisticated farfalle. In the world of classical computing, we can think of a bit as a piece of farfalle that must lie flat on your plate, in either an upright position representing i or a sideways position representing o. However, in the quirky universe of quantum mechanics, a qubit doesn't merely sit there; it somersaults, twists, and pirouettes in the air until it decides to land. This means that while it's in a state of superposition, it can represent both o and i at the same time, kind of like if you asked the farfalle whether it wanted to be a bow tie or a bow ruffle at your next family dinner. ''Why not both?" it responds, twirling elegantly in mid-air.

You see, this state of being in two places at once is much like me trying to decide what to make for dinner. On one hand, I could serve a classic spaghetti with marinara, and on the other, a rich seafood linguine bursting with flavor. But thanks to the wonders of superposition, I can practically serve both! With quantum superposition, we tap into the tantalizing prospect of parallelism. As each qubit can work on multiple calculations at once, it's like having an entire kitchen staff of sous chefs making sure every aspect of your meal is perfect without stepping on each other's toes. The ultimate kitchen symphony!

When we delve deeper into the implications of superposition, it becomes evident how it elevates the potential of quantum computing. Imagine trying to find a specific noodle recipe in a sprawling cookbook collection, each cookbook representing a qubit. In the classical world, you could comb through each book one by one, flipping pages like it's an act of exercise. But with superposition, the qubits can flick through all the cookbooks simultaneously, arriving at the golden recipe in record time! This delicious concept doesn't merely speed things up; it leaves you gasping at the table in awe, "How did you manage to make this exquisite dinner so quickly?"

But wait; there's more! If you think superposition is simply a matter of spinning qubits like they're at a cha-cha class, hold on to your chef's knife. The delicate dance of probabilities comes into play here, too. Each time a qubit is observed or measured, it collapses from its electrifying state of superposition to a definitive position, like a beautiful tiramisu slowly settling into its layers. Now, if the qubit were a bold and fancy tortellini, altering its flavor upon observation, wouldn't that throw a wrench into your culinary plans? Instead of achieving your desired flavor, you end up with something far less appealing! One moment you're basking in the glory of a perfectly seasoned dish, and the next, it's reduced to a sad pile of mush because you accidentally peeked at the risotto too soon.

As with all great things in life and cooking, there comes a caveat. Operating in superposition means that one must also contend with the inherent uncertainty of the quantum realm. Think of it like creating a quirky new pasta shape that may or may not hold its form in boiling water, exhilarating yet nerve-wracking! Until qubits are measured, we can only estimate the likelihood of arriving at a particular outcome, akin to wondering whether your nonna's lasagna will come out perfectly layered or puddled into an unrecognizable heap.

In our gastronomic world of quantum computing, embracing superposition is akin to celebrating the imaginative spirit of cooking. It's about exploration, creativity, and intrigue. As we engage with these processes, we become the daring culinary pioneers of the quantum realm. So, let's toss that pasta, embrace the chaos, and savor the uncertainty! Who knows? The next time I'm wrestling with an overabundance of ingredients in my kitchen, I might just tap into quantum superposition for the ultimate multi-dish dinner. After all, if you're trying to impress your guests, wouldn't it be spectacular to serve them an entire menu of dishes, all coming together in perfect harmony as you spin in the joy of existential culinary possibilities?

Entanglement: Connecting Flavors

Entanglement! Often regarded as one of the most delightful and paradoxical concepts in quantum mechanics, entanglement is akin to the unbreakable bond between a mother and her beloved pasta recipe. Imagine, if you will, that every time you make your signature marinara sauce, it results in an explosive reunion of flavors that transcends distance, time, and even the pesky notion of personal space. Yes, that's right! Entanglement connects particles in a way that they can influence each other instantaneously, irrespective of the distance separating them. It's like having a secret family recipe that magically connects all spaghetti dishes across the globe.

To illustrate this wonder, let's delve into the world of Italian cuisine. Picture this: you make a delectable plate of spaghetti aglio e olio, and somewhere across town, your friend Sarah, who has never stepped foot in your kitchen, suddenly experiences a craving for the very same dish. Coincidence? I think not! Entangled qubits share this mystical synergy, communicating with one another as if they've been lifelong culinary partners despite being light-years apart. If one qubit decides to take a dip in a savory marinara sauce, the other qubit, regardless of its location, will react as if it somehow knows the pasta pot was bubbling; it's almost like they've shared a spoonful of the creation!

Of course, while I would love to think of it as a playful game of tag with culinary flair, the truth is entanglement defies our everyday logic, much like that family member who insists that pineapple belongs on pizza. It's not visible to the naked eye, nor can you taste it, but it's there, delighting in its sheer weirdness. You see, when two qubits become entangled, they essentially share a kind of "quantum friendship." When you change the state of one qubit, the other qubit responds, regardless of how far apart they are, like a synchronized swimming team with a telepathic connection, ready to dazzle the crowd whenever you drop the sauce!

Now, I know what you're thinking: "John, how does this relate to my next dinner gathering?" Well, dear reader, this magical phenomenon of entanglement holds exciting implications for the world of quantum computing! Just as chefs often experiment with innovative ingredients to enhance their dishes, quantum entangled qubits can collaborate to solve complex problems that classical computers would take forever to unravel, like untangling that mess of spaghetti from last week's leftovers! By leveraging their interconnectedness, quantum computers can process information far more efficiently and effectively. It's like having a team of top-notch sous chefs who not only share recipes but also communicate seamlessly as they whizz around the kitchen, churning out food with flair.

However, for all its gastronomical grandeur, entanglement also comes with its quirks and challenges. The tiniest disturbance, like a rogue garlic clove joining the party without an invitation, can wreak havoc, causing the relationship between the two qubits to break down or "decohere." This idea can be likened to the intricate balance of flavors in a well-prepared ragu; if it's disrupted, too much salt, not enough basil, the entire dish can end up tasting like an unfortunate culinary mistake. In the world of quantum computing, maintaining entangled states requires a harnessing of precision, so researchers have to be as meticulous as chefs when creating their dishes.

To further complicate ideas, the concept of entanglement leads to some fascinating (and often humorous) implications in understanding our universe. As I ponder over my bowl of pasta, I can't help but imagine a world where quantum mechanics affects our daily culinary decisions! Perhaps our taste buds, when entangled with the ever-elusive quantum particles, would allow us to savor new dishes before we even taste them. What if our love for garlic-infused pasta could transcend space and time, somehow influencing others' taste preferences in entirely different continents? Imagine that we could share the flavors of a rich pesto beyond the borders of our kitchens!

In the end, entanglement is a whimsical celebration of connection and harmony, reminding us that flavors, just like particles, can interlink in ways we might not fully grasp. So, as we stroll through life, let's not forget to savor those moments of bonding, be it over a plate of spaghetti with friends, the richness of shared laughter, or the seemingly inexplicable connections we forge along the way. After all, whether it's through pasta or qubits, the world is a far more flavorful place when we embrace the beauty of entanglement, and each dish served can create ripples of joy that travel well beyond our dining table. Now, if only I could entangle my lasagna so that it cooks itself, talk about a culinary breakthrough!

Quantum Algorithms: Cooking with a New Recipe

Welcome to the wild and wonderful world of quantum algorithms, where the rules of cooking have changed significantly, and the recipes only get stranger, yet far more delicious! Just like how Grandma's classic lasagna takes on delightful twists with ingredients from global kitchens, quantum algorithms add their own quirky flare to the realms of computation. Essentially, they're like the "secret sauce" that turns a traditional dish into something out of this world! So let's roll up our sleeves, dust off the culinary apron, and dive into the exciting recipe book of quantum algorithms.

Now, the beauty of quantum algorithms lies in their ability to harness the unique properties of qubits, those wonderfully entangled little nuggets of data we talked about earlier. Unlike those parsimonious classical algorithms that are like a strict "no sauce for you" rule at a pasta bar, quantum algorithms bust down the kitchen door, pantry open wide, and say, "Throw in everything you've got!" They use superposition, entanglement, and interference patterns to make computation not just faster but also, dare I say, a bit more flavorful. It's like that rich, comforting bowl of minestrone soup where every ingredient, vegetables, beans, and herbs, works in harmony to produce an explosion of taste.

One of the most famous quantum algorithms is Shor's algorithm, which is revered in the quantum realm like my Aunt Patrizia's Sunday pot roast. Why? Because it can factor large numbers exponentially faster than any classical algorithm. It's as if you could whip up a complex five-course meal in the time it takes your neighbor to boil water for their tortellini. Can you imagine? The implications for fields like cryptography are mind-boggling. It's like finding out that your beloved tomato sauce recipe has the power to unlock the secrets of a treasure chest! With quantum algorithms at the helm, we can potentially render classical encryption methods obsolete. Thanks, Aunt Teresa, but I think I'll keep that recipe under lock and key from now on!

Let's not stop there! Another gem in the quantum algorithm cookbook is Grover's algorithm, that friend at the dinner party who not only knows where the best cheese is hidden but can practically teleport you there. Grover's algorithm accelerates unstructured database searches and does so in a fashion that has classical algorithms green with envy. If traditional algorithms are like rifling through a sea of fettuccine searching for that one elusive strand, Grover's takes a culinary shortcut and finds it in half the time. You're left wondering whether he's got a magical pasta radar or if he miraculously exhibits a sixth sense for finding the hidden ingredients. Either way, you're just happy to have it on your side!

Of course, just as cooking requires precision, timing, and a sprinkle of intuition, so do quantum algorithms. You've got to measure your probabilities just right and remember those pesky decoherence challenges lurking like a burnt garlic clove waiting to ruin your dish. Every time you implement a quantum algorithm, you're essentially dancing on the edge of a knife, balancing flavor and technique like a professional chef. In the world of quantum computation, a slight miscalculation could lead to burnt edges instead of delightfully crispy crusts. It's a real nail-biter, folks!

What's more, as we embrace these quantum recipes, we have to consider their compatibility with classical computing methods. It's like combining the culinary techniques of traditional Italian cuisine with modern molecular gastronomy, an exciting blend that could create culinary wonders but comes with its own set of challenges. Efficiently harnessing the power of quantum algorithms while ensuring they work harmoniously with existing technology is no small feat! In short, think of it as trying to pair a sumptuous ragu with a fine wine: you really want to get it right or risk ruining the whole meal.

The real magic of quantum algorithms lies not just in their technical prowess, but in what they signify for the future of cooking, oh, pardon me, I mean computing. Just as each chef brings their own spin to an age-old recipe, so too do quantum algorithms promise to reshape our approach to problem-solving and decision-making. They invite us to think beyond the conventional and embrace the deliciously strange and unknown. Who knows what mouthwatering innovations await us?

So, as we gear up to embrace this culinary evolution, let's remember that quantum algorithms are not merely a set of complex computations. They are a renaissance of flavors, a daring invitation to push the boundaries of what we thought was possible in the kitchen of life. So whether you're an aspiring quantum chef or just a pasta enthusiast hoping for a taste of the future, remember: the secret to delicious culinary experiences, and groundbreaking computation, lies in how we blend ingredients, embark on new recipes, and savor every moment along the way. Bon appetit and quantum bonanza!

The Future of Quantum Lasagna: Layers of Potential

The future of Quantum Lasagna, what a tantalizing dish to sink our teeth into! A metaphor that fundamentally captures the complexity, nuances, and rich potential of quantum technology. Picture several delectable layers of pasta, cheese, sauce, and filling, each representing distinct advancements in quantum computing, artificial intelligence, and their applications. Just like in a well-prepared lasagna, every layer contributes to a harmonious whole, a beautiful interplay of flavors waiting to dazzle even the most discerning of palates. So, let's pull on our culinary gloves and explore how Quantum Lasagna could revolutionize not only our tables but also the very fabric of technology!

At the heart of this quantum lasagna lie the concepts of superposition and entanglement, which we've discussed and which lend themselves to sweet and savory reinvention. The layers of this lasagna symbolize the infinite possibilities for qubits to be in multiple states simultaneously. Imagine stirring your sauce and uncovering new flavors with each ingredient you add, mushrooms, roasted garlic, and a hint of nutmeg, that's the essence of superposition in action! Each layer of pasta we stack represents data points waiting to be observed, and with each interaction, we analyze new outcomes. It's as if we're cooking with yesterday's leftovers, discovering new recipes every day.

Now imagine that your layers are a bit wild and unpredictable; they're not just pasta and cheese, but they're infused with a sprinkle of quantum magic. While traditional dishes offer consistency, the future of Quantum Lasagna could unveil surprises that keep even the familiar pasta aficionado on their toes. Consider the delicious implications of a quantum lasagna that can adapt and respond to different dining experiences based on guests' preferences, dietary needs, and even the ambiance of the evening. Can you picture a dish that embodies every whim and fancy of those gathered around the table? It's a tantalizing thought, much like a chef navigating every curveball thrown at them in a busy restaurant.

But let's not kid ourselves, while the vision of Quantum Lasagna seems delectable, there are hurdles to overcome in this culinary adventure. Spoiler alert: creating this masterpiece involves understanding the intertwining layers of technology, where quantum computers still face challenges that would make even the most seasoned chefs weep. Just as we must ensure our pasta is perfectly al dente before stacking the lasagna layers, we must also ensure the stability of qubits before delving into practical applications. The decoherence in the quantum realm can be as disruptive as overcooked noodles, threatening to unravel the entire beautifully layered dish!

As we contemplate the future, we must also consider the ethical aspects of quantum technology. Preparing our Quantum Lasagna means crafting it with intelligence and mindfulness. Imagine serving a dish meant for societal progress, one that can optimize resources, minimize environmental impact, and ensure flavor (and opportunity) isn't lost amidst complexities. Just as every ingredient carries a consequence, so too does advancing quantum M.. We must consider how these revolutionary technologies can elevate our culinary experiences while safeguarding against inequities in access and benefit.

Moreover, the metaphor of Quantum Lasagna sparks the idea of interdisciplinary collaboration; the kitchen could be seen as a microcosm of such teamwork. Chefs, farmers, artists, and scientists all fuse their creativity to birth a truly remarkable dish. Quantum computing similarly thrives on collaboration. Its tapestry weaves through areas such as healthcare, finance, and energy, creating fusion meals that are far more than the sum of their parts. How deliciously delightful to envision scientists and chefs brainstorming together, discussing how quantum computing could minimize food waste or enhance food safety processes!

Now, let's indulge and envision the absolute miracle, a Quantum Lasagna that can model every conceivable option based on flavor pairings, dietary preferences, and cultural inspirations before we even set our forks to the table. Imagine whipping up such a dish in mere moments, transitioning effortlessly from an Italian classic to an avant-garde fusion, all while maintaining an exquisite taste that leaves guests clamoring for the recipe. Here's where the potential lies: the interplay between classical and quantum methods igniting an unimaginable culinary journey, a feast of exploration, innovation, and creativity.

In conclusion, while the future of Quantum Lasagna may be filled with uncertainties and challenges, every hosted dinner reminds us that delicious meals and bright ideas often start with a sprinkle of innovation. As we plunge into the depths of this new culinary frontier, let us embrace both the layers of complexity and the joys of discovery. The future is waiting for its culinary artists to plate their visions. Quantum Lasagna could beckon a new age not just of dining but of revolutionizing the experience for generations to come.

So grab your spatula, toss in a bit of anticipation, and let's enjoy the ride! Bon appetit!

Chapter 20

Pasta, AI, and Life: The Final Serving

Embracing Imperfection in Cooking and AI

Embracing Imperfection in Cooking and AI is like realizing that your favorite pasta might come out slightly overcooked, or that your AI model prefers to serve up spaghetti instead of lasagna. Trust me; I've been there. The secret here is that while we all aim for perfection in our culinary creations and machine-learning algorithms, it's the delightful quirks and occasional catastrophes that make both the pizza and the programming world so captivating (and often, far more entertaining).

In cooking, as in AI, it's essential to remember that things will inevitably go awry. This is where the real magic happens. Picture this: you've carefully crafted a traditional marinara sauce, those tomatoes diced just-so, herbs added with the precision of a neurosurgeon, only to discover that your 'al dente' spaghetti has morphed into a gooey mass of regret. Instead of throwing your hands up in despair (or your pasta against the wall), you could dive into the glorious world of creativity and adjust your dish to unearth unexpected flavors. In this culinary crisis, you might find that a hidden ingredient, hello, chili flakes!, offers a kick that elevates your 'severely overcooked' pasta to something akin to a contemporary art installation.

This same mentality applies to our beloved AI endeavors. When you train a machine-learning model, the expectation is that it will develop an understanding of the patterns in your data and churn out skyscraping predictions. However, we all know that sometimes, it'll throw you a curveball that leaves you exasperated. Maybe it's classifying your cat photos as 'Pasta' or mistaking your startup's annual report for a recipe for tiramisu. Embracing those imperfections is crucial; after all, a spaghetti-obsessed model might just make for one heck of a dinner party conversation! Think about it: "Have you tried the new Cat-Pasta search algorithm? It's totally bonkers, yet oddly delightful!" Now that's a niche market ripe for exploration.

Humorously, the culinary world teaches us that the greatest chefs often become legends for their blunders, think of the 29-burners-on-a-stove debacle or the day someone mistook salt for sugar. When they were faced with those moments of'cooking despair,' they didn't crumble (pun quite intended). Instead, they harnessed those mishaps, turning them into something innovative, like a delightful new twist on gelato that no one saw coming, a lemon-basil epic that somehow became the highlight of the summer festival. In the realm of AI, those eyebrow-raising errors can serve as the ever-important learning opportunities for refining your models. Instead of sweeping those faults under the rug (or dumpster), embrace them like an old friend who brings baked goods, albeit slightly undercooked.

Now, while it's easy to dive into a pool of humor in these moments of so-called 'failure,' remember that execution is key. As a so-called expert in both the AI field and the kitchen, I've learned that how you handle those mistakes could make all the difference. When a model performs poorly, resist the urge to send it packing like a soggy soufflé. Instead, observe closely, like a seasoned chef watching their risotto reach that perfect creamy consistency. With attention and mindfulness, you can diagnose whether the problem lies in data quality, architectural missteps, or a completely misguided choice of hyperparameters (Yes, there is such a thing as AI hyperparameter culinary disasters).

At the end of the day, the art of cooking and the science of AI are about experimenting, tasting, and refining. Embracing imperfection in both disciplines opens pathways to unforeseen creativity and insight. So the next time you find yourself drowning in a swirling vortex of cognitive dissonance over that oddly-curating algorithm or that dry batch of gnocchi, take a deep breath. It's time to add your own dash of humor, a sprinkle of inspiration, and maybe even a splash of red wine to both your cooking pot and your algorithmic tendencies. After all, who knows what culinary and computational masterpieces await on the other side of imperfection?

Lessons from the Kitchen: Patience and Resilience

Lessons from the Kitchen: Patience and Resilience are two essential ingredients that everyone, from the greenest cook to the most seasoned data scientist, could benefit from. If you've ever attempted to make a soufflé while juggling your to-do list, you know that impatience is the enemy of culinary achievement, much like trying to force an AI model to learn faster than a toddler learning to color outside the lines (spoiler: it won't end well!).

Picture yourself in the kitchen, apron donned and a spatula in hand, preparing to make the perfect risotto. You've gathered all the ingredients: Arborio rice, broth, and perhaps a cheeky glass of white wine (for you, not the risotto). You stir and stir, pouring in the broth ladle by ladle, waiting for that creamy consistency to emerge like a phoenix from the ashes of unyielding grains of rice. But, in your eagerness to get to the glorious end, the siren song of instant gratification tempts you. You decide to dump in the entire pot of broth. Before you know it, your risotto has morphed into a soupy disaster reminiscent of the time your AI model confidently identified a ferret as an exotic Italian dish. The lesson here is simple: Patience, dear cook! Too much haste will lead to something you'd rather leave in the depths of the oven than serve at Sunday dinner.

Resilience comes into play when your culinary aspiration takes a nosedive, but you refuse to let it ground you. Let's say that instead of velvety pasta, your dinner guest is served an uninspired bowl of mush. It's tempting to throw in the towel or toss your pasta against the wall (but please, not literally, you don't want to risk another broken dish). Instead, it's time to channel your inner Italian Nonna, who has likely faced far worse over the years while managing to raise a family and keep the family cat away from the sauce pot. You pick yourself up, dust off your apron, and remember the mantra of all chefs: "Every meal is a lesson, not a failure." Ah, yes, the tried-and-true approach that involves a healthy dose of humility alongside your olive oil.

Now, let's transition to our beloved world of artificial intelligence. Just as cooking requires patience, so does tuning an AI model, a process that often feels like watching molasses overflow while waiting for a pot to boil. When your algorithm flops, showing less promise than a flat soufflé, doesn't it sometimes feel like all of your hard work is for naught? The key is resilience! Iterate on your model with a willingness to learn from your previous missteps, even if those missteps involve mistaking a steep learning curve for a rollercoaster of chaos.

Patience and resilience aren't optional; they're like the salt in your pasta water, key to bringing everything to life. For instance, when faced with poor predictive accuracy, you may feel like crying over your datasets (and not just because they won't fit into your training set). Instead, embrace the discomfort and pivot. Like the cook furiously kneading dough, you need to infuse your process with some elbow grease and a resolve that can withstand the toughest challenges. Push through, iterate over your nodes, and remember that tweaks and changes can lead to breakthrough moments like a chef discovering how saffron can elevate an otherwise mundane dish.

And just as in cooking, the most exciting discoveries often arise from the unexpected. Perhaps your latest model doesn't quite hit the mark, but in navigating those uncharted waters, you may stumble upon a previously undiscovered feature, like lemon zest brightening a dish in ways you never expected. Resilience demands that you stay mentally agile, navigating setbacks as gracefully as a chef flipping a crepe, so you can adapt and adjust your approach as needed.

So, the next time you find yourself confronted by a kitchen or AI catastrophe, channel your inner chef warrior. Approach the stove (or your code) with patience, honoring the process. Cook with resilience, thriving on those lessons learned from the soupy mess that once was your risotto, because failure is merely the first step towards culinary enlightenment. And who knows? You might just whip up the next big AI innovation or culinary masterpiece from those very imperfections, just remember to savor every moment along the way (and have a glass of wine in hand, for good measure!).

The Joy of Experimentation: Iteration and Adaptation

The Joy of Experimentation: Iteration and Adaptation is a delightful dance performed in both the kitchen and the realm of artificial intelligence. The beauty here is that both pursuits are more related than you might think, innovative, often messy, and characterized by a fair amount of "well, that didn't work" moments. You see, whether you're trying to create a culinary masterpiece or a model that predicts if your cat will sit on your keyboard, the thrill lies in the process of trying, failing, adjusting, and trying again (and again, and again, because who's counting, right?).

Let's begin this journey with a kitchen scenario that I'm sure resonates with many of you. Imagine it's a quiet weekend afternoon, and you've decided to whip up a batch of homemade pizza. You gather the freshest ingredients, visualize how that glorious golden crust will look, and, oh, wait! It's time to add a pinch of creativity to that classic Margherita. Instead of just mozzarella, you manage to convince yourself that goat cheese would give it a sophisticated twist. Fast forward an hour, and you've got a pizza that resembles a Picasso painting more than a culinary creation. The flavors clash; it's a bold experiment that could have an audience at an avant-garde art show but leave dinner guests scratching their heads. Instead of wallowing in shame, you embrace the lesson. Some flavors dance beautifully together, and others, well, not so much. You return to the drawing board (or should I say, the dough board) not with defeat, but with newfound knowledge about achieving that perfect harmony of toppings.

In the world of AI, experimentation is equally essential, albeit with fewer tears over burnt crusts. It's all about that delightful cycle of iteration. When you build a model, you start with a hypothesis, wrangle with your data, and hope to emerge victorious. Sometimes, there's a moment of triumph, like when your neural network classifies cats and dogs with uncanny accuracy. Other times, though, you stare blankly at the screen as your model predicts that every image of a corgi is actually a cabbage, prompting you to reconsider both your data preprocessing and your life choices! The key is to embrace these moments; they aren't failures, they're signs that your AI journey is evolving, just like your culinary skills.

Iteration builds resilience, and that's where the real joy lies. Each failure teaches you not only how to adjust your recipe or model but also helps to refine your palate for experimentation. As you revisit the kitchen or your code, armed with data and notes from your previous escapades, you begin to craft a masterpiece, a process akin to mixing traditional Italian cooking with modern gastronomy, creating a fusion dish that would make even the toughest food critics crack a smile (or at least raise an eyebrow). The next pizza you create might be a simple Margherita, perfectly balanced, but now with the confidence to mix in adventurous herbs like fresh basil or a subtle drizzle of balsamic glaze. Who knew pizza could turn into a canvas of your culinary creativity?

In AI, that iteration translates to tweaking hyperparameters like you're adjusting the seasoning in your grandmother's secret tomato sauce. Toss in a little more Regularization here and see if that helps reduce overfitting. Try adjusting your learning rate there; who knows, maybe a pinch less will yield that desired crispy golden harmonic balance! Where experimentation shines is in the unexpected joys that arise from these iterations. A small adjustment can lead to breakthroughs. It's the difference between serving a dish that looks like it belongs in a Michelin-star restaurant versus one that leaves your guests contemplating the lifelong mystery of whether it's actual food.

Adaptation is equally important. As data scientists, we sometimes find ourselves trapped within the narrow confines of a planned trajectory. But life, much like a dinner party, has its surprises. What if, against all odds, your AI model starts to overfit? It could be just like that time I tried to make homemade gnocchi, a once-easy task morphing into a stickier mess than I anticipated. So, I adapted! I added more flour and reset my expectations, recognizing that, like gnocchi, we all need a little room to breathe.

So, whether you're in the kitchen or the office, revel in the joy of experimentation, actively fail, adjust, and celebrate your newfound wisdom! As with any culinary adventure or deep dive into machine learning, the road may be long with far greater challenges than expected, but it's also lined with moments of creativity, laughter, and a few delicious or groundbreaking surprises. Celebrate each experiment as though it were the perfect sauce or the game-changing feature in your AI model, create, iterate, adapt, and keep stirring the pot of creativity! After all, the world is your kitchen (or codebase), and who knows what delightful flavors or insights you'll uncover along the way.

Culinary Philosophy: Feeding the Mind and Soul

Culinary Philosophy: Feeding the Mind and Soul is a deliciously rich subject that stretches far beyond mere sustenance. It dives deep into the essence of what it means to create and savor, whether stirring a pot of vibrant minestrone or wrangling the complexities of machine learning algorithms. Food and technology might seem like an unlikely pairing, but the philosophy behind both can nurture not just the body, but our very spirit and intellect.

As we dissect this relationship, imagine yourself indulging in a plate of pasta while decoding the mysteries of AI, talk about a dinner date for the ages!

At the heart of culinary philosophy lies the appreciation of what food represents. It transcends simple nutrition; it evokes memories, emotions, and sometimes questionable choices. Perhaps each bite transports you back to Grandma's kitchen, where the tomato sauce simmered for hours, high-stakes debates over garlic levels erupted, and the barbecue personal stakes were raised over who made the best tiramisu. Cooking is about cultivating joy, mischief, and community around the table, it's a ritual that stitches together relationships as closely as the ingredients in a well-made risotto. This connection extends to AI, too, through algorithms, we create solutions that enhance our lives and forge connections, often imbuing every piece of code with a bit of our essence.

Much like cooking, the journey of AI can be full of trial and error, unexpected flavors, and surprises. When an individual engages in either craft, they cultivate a space for creativity to flourish. Think of it as an act of radical self-expression. Whether you're braising a brisket or fine-tuning a neural network to recognize corgis, you're making decisions that reflect your experiences, dreams, and, sometimes, ambitions. Culinary philosophy teaches us to embrace that creativity, which, admittedly, may lead to the curious combination of pesto and peanut butter (an experiment best conducted in the comfort of your own kitchen). It's about daring to be different, learning from the culinary giants while patching together your unique contributions and flavors!

Now, let's address the elephant in the room: cooking and coding are both fraught with complications. Every dish requires a dash of patience and a healthy dose of resilience, much like the path of becoming proficient in algorithms. A burnt soufflé or a convoluted regression model often ignites the flames of despair. However, these experiences feed our souls, coaxing us to laugh at our failures and inspire us to tackle future creations with a fearless zest. Every grand meal is rooted not only in innovative ingredients but in a process honed from experience, cultivating a blend of knowledge that allows for new culinary discoveries and coding revelations.

Moreover, feeding our minds in both kitchens and data labs means engaging critically with the world. Cooking is, at its core, an intersection of art and science, offering sensibility with invention. It invites us to explore diverse cultures, tastes, and philosophies with curiosity and openness. Similarly, AI invites us into the realm of analysis, challenging assumptions, encouraging ethical considerations, and paving the way for innovation. By engaging in the interplay between AI and culinary adventures, we create worldviews that celebrate diversity while seeking deeper understandings of human experience.

At this crossroads of culinary and technological endeavors, we must remember that sharing our creations, ideas, and experiences is a fundamental aspect of nurturing ourselves and those around us. Whether inviting friends over for a homemade feast or discussing AI advancements over a glass of Chianti, sharing catalyzes growth and connection, much like precise measurements in a pastry recipe. Creative minds discuss, collaborate, and enhance one another's journeys, transforming their collective experiences into something greater and tastier than any one individual could produce.

Ultimately, the ability to impact those we encounter through culinary endeavors and innovative technologies rests within us all. Whether we're simmering spices in a bubbling sauce or fine-tuning a machine-learning model to predict pizza satisfaction, we aren't just creating; we're nourishing and inspiring minds and souls so that they flourish beyond the dinner table, or, in this case, the codebase. So, as we dive into the essence of culinary philosophy, embrace the mission to feed not just your stomach, but your heart, mind, and your very essence as well. Together, let's raise a spatula and a laptop in triumph, celebrating creativity that nourishes and enriches every corner of our lives!

References

1 Zeko R. (2025). Connecting the dots: through trash to the future. SVAR Enterprises, NY. ISBN 979-8-9986661-2-4

2 Giordani J. (2025). Machine Learning: The game show. SenAnSys Publishing. ISBN 97988312879902

3 Giordani, J. (2024). Mitigating Chatbots AI Data Privacy Violations in the Banking Sector: A Qualitative Grounded Theory Study. European Journal of Applied Science, Engineering and Technology, 2(4), 14–65. https://doi.org/10.59324/ejaset.2024.2(4).02

4 Giordani, J. (2024). Advancing Mitigation Strategies for AI-Driven Chatbots: Building Resilience Against Data Privacy Violations. A Follow-up Study. European Journal of Applied Science, Engineering and Technology, 2(6), 163–167. https://doi.org/10.59324/ejaset.2024.2(6).15

5 Giordani, J., & Zeko, R. (2024). An Empirical Study on Enterprise-Wide Governance Practices for Artificial Intelligence and Machine Learning. European Journal of Applied Science, Engineering and Technology, 2(6), 168–177. https://doi.org/10.59324/ejaset.2024.2(6).16

6 Giordani J. (2024). Implications of GPT-5 on Business Operations and Societal Structures: A Comprehensive Analysis. Journal Article. academia.edu

7 https://www.academia.edu/117835853/Implications_of_GPT_5_on_Business_Operations_and_Societal_Structures_A_Comprehensive_Analysis

8 Dick, S. (2019). Artificial Intelligence. Harvard Data Science Review, 1(1). https://doi.org/10.1162/99608f92.92fe150c

9 Bonasso, P. (2018). CASE: A HAL 9000 for 2021. Science Robotics, 3(24). https://doi.org/10.1126/scirobotics.aav6610

10 Charniak, E. (2024). AI & I: An Intellectual History of Artificial Intelligence. The MIT Press. https://doi.org/10.7551/mitpress/15482.001.0001

11 Copeland, J. (2020). Alan Turing 1912–1954. In B. J. Copeland (Ed.), The Essential Turing (Online ed.). Oxford Academic. https://doi.org/10.1093/oso/9780198250791.002.0003

12 Proudfoot, D. (2020). The Turing test - from every angle. In The Turing Guide (Online ed.). Oxford Academic. https://doi.org/10.1093/oso/9780198747826.003.0037

13 Neural Networks. (2014). Neural Networks, 49, v-x. https://doi.org/10.1016/S0893-6080(13)00287-6

14 McClay, W. J. (1995). Surviving the AI Winter. https://doi.org/10.7551/mitpress/4301.003.0009

15 Neuer, M.J. (2025). Supervised Learning. In: Machine Learning for Engineers. Springer, Berlin, Heidelberg. https://doi.org/10.1007/978-3-662-69995-9_4

16 Japkowicz N, Boukouvalas Z. Unsupervised Learning. In: Machine Learning Evaluation: Towards Reliable and Responsible AI. Cambridge University Press; 2024:252-286.

17 Blubaugh, D.A., Harbour, S.D., Sears, B., Findler, M.J. (2022). Reinforced Learning. In: Intelligent Autonomous Drones with Cognitive Deep Learning. Apress, Berkeley, CA. https://doi.org/10.1007/978-1-4842-6803-2_9

18 Chapelle, O., Schölkopf, B., & Zien, A. (2006). Introduction to semi-supervised learning. In Semi-Supervised Learning. The MIT Press. DOI: https://doi.org/10.7551/mitpress/9780262033589.001.0001

19 Miller, D. J., Xiang, Z., & Kesidis, G. (2023). Deep Learning Background. In Adversarial Learning and Secure AI (pp. 19–55). chapter, Cambridge: Cambridge University Press.

20 Munro, P. (2006). Backpropagation. In Encyclopedia of Cognitive Science, L. Nadel (Ed.). https://doi.org/10.1002/0470018860.s00041

21 Arellano, K. C. (2024). In Special Collection: CogNet (M. Lane & A. Sethumadhavan, Eds.). The MIT Press. https://doi.org/10.7551/mitpress/14962.001.0001

22 Baker, S. (2012). Final Jeopardy: The Story of Watson, the Computer That Will Transform Our World. Mariner Books.

23 Bretonnel Cohen, K. & Demner-Fushman, D. (2014). Introduction to natural language processing. In Biomedical Natural Language Processing (pp. 1-6). John Benjamins Publishing Company. https://doi.org/10.1075/nlp.11.01ch1

24 K. Dowding (Ed.) (2011). Nash equilibrium. In Encyclopedia of Power (pp. 435-436). SAGE Publications, Inc. https://doi.org/10.4135/9781412994088

25 PBS. (n.d.). $64,000 question. American Experience. Retrieved Feb 2025, from https://www.pbs.org/wgbh/americanexperience/features/quizshow-64000-question/

26 Guerraoui, R., Gupta, N., & Pinot, R. (2024). Basics of Machine Learning. Robust Machine Learning, 15–31. https://doi.org/10.1007/978-981-97-0688-4_2

27 Capuano, N., & Caballé, S. (2020). Adaptive Learning Technologies. AI Magazine, 41(2), 96–98. Portico. https://doi.org/10.1609/aimag.v41i2.5317

28 Nathaniel Green (2022). Bobby Fischer Wins Match Of The Century. Chess.com. https://www.chess.com/article/view/50-year-anniversary-fischer-spassky-game-21

29 Powles, J., & Hodson, H. (2017). Google DeepMind and healthcare in an age of algorithms. Health and Technology, 7(4), 351–367. https://doi.org/10.1007/s12553-017-0179-1

30 Cade Metz (2016). In Two Moves, AlphaGo and Lee Sedol Redefined the Future. Wired.com. https://www.wired.com/2016/03/two-moves-alphago-lee-sedol-redefined-future/

31 David Luther. What Is a Minimum Viable Product (MVP)? An Expert Guide. Netsuite.com. https://www.netsuite.com/portal/resource/articles/erp/minimum-viable-product-mvp.shtml

32 Blackman, R., & Euchner, J. (2024). Ethics in the Age of AI. Research-Technology Management, 67(1), 15–21. https://doi.org/10.1080/08956308.2024.2280481

33 Busulwa, R. (2022). Virtual Reality (VR), Augmented Reality (AR), and Mixed Reality (MR) Primer. Navigating Digital Transformation in Management, 381–392. https://doi.org/10.4324/9781003254614-28

www.ingramcontent.com/pod-product-compliance
Lightning Source LLC
LaVergne TN
LVHW052312200926
848481LV00002B/535
* 9 7 9 8 2 1 8 9 4 6 2 3 4 *